CULTURAL GEOGRAPHIES

THE BASICS

Andrew Lapworth and Tom Roberts

Routledge
Taylor & Francis Group
LONDON AND NEW YORK

Cover image: Photograph by Tom Roberts

First published 2027
by Routledge
4 Park Square, Milton Park, Abingdon, Oxon OX14 4RN

and by Routledge
605 Third Avenue, New York, NY 10158

Routledge is an imprint of the Taylor & Francis Group, an informa business

British Library Cataloguing-in-Publication Data
A catalogue record for this book is available from the British Library

ISBN: 978-1-032-89081-4 (hbk)
ISBN: 978-1-032-89077-7 (pbk)
ISBN: 978-1-003-54266-7 (ebk)

DOI: 10.4324/9781003542667

Typeset in Times New Roman
by Apex CoVantage, LLC

CULTURAL GEOGRAPHIES
THE BASICS

Cultural Geographies: The Basics offers an accessible introduction to one of the most exciting and eclectic fields of academic study available to students today. It unpacks key conceptual and methodological innovations in cultural geography and outlines the new perspectives these offer for making sense of our world.

Showcasing the dynamic transformations that cultural geography brings to contemporary understandings of cultural life, this book guides its readers through an exhilarating exploration of six key problematics at the cutting-edge of geographical thought: Representation, Nature, Technology, Bodies, Politics, and Methods. Through this original approach, the book outlines a selection of the most important debates and perspectives in the field, providing readers with user-friendly introductions to key concepts like 'affect,' 'micropolitics,' 'assemblage,' 'post-phenomenology,' and the 'more-than-human' along the way. The book incorporates a range of engaging empirical examples to illustrate how the conceptual, methodological, and ethico-political innovations developed by cultural geographers can be used to shed new light on the most urgent challenges of our times: from the destruction of the natural world, to the emergence of new spaces and forms of political activism, to the ethical and existential implications of advanced technologies like artificial intelligence.

This book will be essential reading for undergraduate students making their first forays into cultural geography, as well as readers and researchers from other humanities and social science disciplines (like Sociology, Media and Film Studies, Anthropology, Cultural Studies, and Philosophy) interested in what a geographical approach to culture has to offer.

Andrew Lapworth is a senior lecturer in Cultural Geography at UNSW Canberra, Australia. His research interests lie in contemporary cultural geography, with specific expertise in continental philosophy and its implications for geographical thought and practice; human-technology relations; art and aesthetics; and cinema and popular visual culture. His research has been published in a range of leading geographical and social science journals, including *Social & Cultural Geography, Cultural Geographies, Transactions of the Institute of British Geographers, Area, Theory, Culture & Society,* and *Body & Society*.

Tom Roberts is a senior lecturer in Cultural Geography at UNSW Canberra, Australia. Tom's research explores matter and materiality across a range of cultural contexts, from science and technology to artistic practice and experimentation. His work contributes to conceptual debates in cultural geography, including more-than-human geography, relational thinking, non-anthropocentric theories of subjectivity, and non-representational research methodologies. His work is published in *Progress in Human Geography, Dialogues in Human Geography, Cultural Geographies, Area, Geohumanities,* and *Transactions of the Institute of British Geographers.*

THE BASICS

The Basics is a highly successful series of accessible guidebooks which provide an overview of the fundamental principles of a subject area in a jargon-free and undaunting format.

Intended for students approaching a subject for the first time, the books both introduce the essentials of a subject and provide an ideal springboard for further study. With over 50 titles spanning subjects from artificial intelligence (AI) to women's studies, *The Basics* are an ideal starting point for students seeking to understand a subject area.

Each text comes with recommendations for further study and gradually introduces the complexities and nuances within a subject.

For more information about this series, please visit: www.routledge.com/The-Basics/book-series/B

SENECA
CHRISTOPHER V. TRINACTY

GLOBAL COMICS
FREDERICK LUIS ALDAMA

CONTEMPORARY INDIA
REKHA DATTA

POLYGAMY
BRUCE WHITEHOUSE AND WILLIAM JANKOWIAK

SUICIDE
MATIAS GAY

ROMANTICISM
ELIZABETH A. FAY

LEADERSHIP
MORGEN WITZEL

HUMAN-COMPUTER INTERACTION
ALAN DIX

ECOLOGY
PHILIP JAMES

TRANSGENDER PHILOSOPHY
MATTHEW J. CULL

CULTURAL GEOGRAPHIES
ANDREW LAPWORTH AND TOM ROBERTS

AMERICAN FREEDOM
GEOFF HAMILTON

CONTENTS

FIGURES

BOXES

ACKNOWLEDGEMENTS

This book was devised and written on Ngunnawal land. We acknowledge the Ngunnawal people as the traditional custodians of the lands on which we live and work, and we recognise that their sovereignty was never ceded. We would also like to pay our respects to Elders past, present, and emerging.

This book would not have been possible without the support and inspiration of a great many people. We owe special thanks to JD Dewsbury. From Bristol to the Bush Capital, JD has been our principal guide to the world of cultural geography for nearly two decades. The example set by his passionate commitment to concepts and ideas, and the generativity of his thinking and writing, continues to be the kind of cultural geography that we both aspire to.

Thanks to our geography colleagues at UNSW Canberra – Nina Williams, George Burdon, Tara Jeyasingh, Thomas Oliver, and Alissa Flatley – whose support, intellectual passion, and good humour have made those early field school wake-ups (and much more besides!) worth it.

We count ourselves very lucky to have been able to work with an extraordinarily talented group of PhD students at UNSW Canberra: Joyce Deng, Nat Miles, Deepak Tiwari, Christian Sirois, Eliza Arias, Yi Lan, Sabrina Shanto, Carlota de La Herrán Iriarte, Kushani Liyanage, Nazanin Hosseinpour, Raj Kaithwar, Ziyang Zhou, and Zhe Li. Their creativity and passion have been a constant source of inspiration, and we are incredibly proud of all they continue to achieve.

Our moves 'Down Under' were made that much easier by the incredible support we have received from colleagues in Australia.

Here, we would like to extend special thanks to Richard Carter-White, David Bissell, Lesley Head, Michele Lobo, Candice Boyd, Cameron Duff, and Ian Buchanan.

We have also been profoundly affected by the mentorship and friendship of geography colleagues back in the United Kingdom. The list of these individuals could run for pages and pages! But we would especially like to extend our appreciation to Joe Gerlach, Thomas Keating, James Ash, Maria Fannin, Thomas Jellis, Merle Patchett, Mark Jackson, Keith Bassett, Paul Harrison, Andrew Barry, and Derek McCormack.

We'd also like to sincerely thank our editors at Routledge. Thanks to Andrew Mould for the initial invitation to write this introduction to cultural geography. It has been an absolute privilege. And to Niamh Hitchmough, for her kindness and patience in guiding us through the process of writing our first book. Thanks also to the reviewers of both the original proposal and the full draft manuscript for their excellent suggestions on how to sharpen the contribution and coverage of the text.

Finally, the book owes a tremendous amount to the love and support of both our families and friends.

Andrew would like to give his heartfelt thanks to: my co-author, Tom, for being a great friend over the years, and for helping me elevate my thinking and writing every time we work together; my family (Mum, Dad, Nan, Amy, Nadine, Roman, Mark, Auntie Patricia, Elliot, Oliver); my wife, Saori; and my babies, Wilson and Lillian.

Tom would like to say a big thank you to: family, both in the United Kingdom (Mum, Jess, Harry, Charlie, and Ruby) and in Australia (Helen, Viv, Jally, Oscar, and Leo); friends (Roland, Joe, Jack, Jake, Charlie, and Nicholas); and my awesome (and extremely patient) partner, Ella. Finally, thanks to Andy for making this such an enjoyable and rewarding writing experience from start to finish – we made it through, and, thanks to your enthusiasm, it was a blast.

1

INTRODUCING CULTURAL GEOGRAPHIES

WHAT IS CULTURAL GEOGRAPHY?

Being a cultural geographer can sometimes feel like you are a member of an exclusive club or secret society. For those, like us, who are on the inside, the question of what cultural geography is all about (and why it matters) might seem obvious. However, for those who are not familiar with it, cultural geography can appear somewhat vague and even, at times, downright mysterious! This book is intended to introduce cultural geography to new audiences by providing an overview of the key debates that continue to animate the field and by exploring their relevance for making sense of a changing world. Yet it is often the case that the breadth of topics that cultural geographers are interested in only adds to the sense of mystery when it comes to the question of *what* cultural geography is. The aim of this opening section is to pull back the curtain on cultural geography and to give readers a clearer sense of what this exciting subdiscipline is all about.

Flick back a few pages to the book's content page, and you will quickly get a sense of the dizzying variety, which has become something of a hallmark of research in cultural geography. Perhaps you are interested in understanding how the interface between human beings and the environment is shaped by texts, photographs, movies, or songs. If so, cultural geography's innovations in non-representational theory will be especially relevant, having inspired generations of researchers across the humanities and social sciences to think differently about the force of representations (see ***Chapter 2***). Alternatively, you might be interested in the way

DOI: 10.4324/9781003542667-1

different bodies, embodied experiences, and bodily practices show up (or, alternatively, are rendered invisible) in specific places and environments – for example, at the airport security checkpoint, in the 24-hour gym, or on your social media feed. Cultural geographers have spent a good deal of time thinking about the body as a site where questions of identity, subjectivity, agency, and spatial politics play themselves out and are viscerally felt (see ***Chapter 5***). Or perhaps you are about to embark on a research project of some kind, and you find yourself feeling uninspired by the more conventional suite of research methods traditionally employed in the social sciences. In which case, look no further: cultural geography is widely recognised for its rich tradition of challenging the methodological conventions by which we capture, interpret, and re-present cultural life as social scientists (see ***Chapter 7***).

As exciting as these topics might sound, you're probably still wondering what it is that unites such a hodgepodge of interests under the disciplinary umbrella of cultural geography. Representations, nature, technology, bodies, politics, and methods: these chapter titles certainly provide a sense of the *content* of cultural geography research. What is not so clear, however, is what it means to practise cultural geography or to think like a cultural geographer. What aspects of our contemporary world does a cultural geography perspective bring into clearer focus? Which problems become interesting? And which problems become vital? By the end of this section, we hope to have provided you with the means of answering these questions.

One of the reasons why cultural geography can seem mysterious is that, for many people, the sheer variety of topics of interest to cultural geographers can appear at odds with more commonplace definitions of its constituent terms, namely, 'geography' and 'culture.' Let's begin by taking each in turn. The concept of geography tends to be associated with the study of spatial phenomena. Geographers are interested in understanding where things are and why they are there – at least, this is how geography is often understood by non-geographers. Culture, on the other hand, is a much more nebulous term, and perhaps for this reason, it tends to be associated with things like nationality, ethnicity, and other expressions of shared identity among human beings. This sense of culture is what is implied by the term 'Australian culture,' for instance, but also by the phrase 'cultural experience,' which is commonly used to signify an immersion in the shared identity of an unfamiliar nationality or ethnicity. Starting from these everyday understandings of geography and culture, it would seem reasonable to assume that cultural geographers are primarily concerned with understanding how experiences of shared identity and the various practices and traditions that support them differ according to the 'where' of spatial context; or, in other words, the geography of culture.

By now, you have likely begun to suspect that, given the kinds of topics that we will be exploring in the pages to come, there must be more to cultural geography than this everyday definition suggests (and, indeed, you would be correct in trusting this suspicion!). Of course, questions relating to shared identity and its spatial variation *are* topics of long-standing interest to cultural geographers. For this reason, our assertion that cultural geographers are interested in understanding the geography of culture still holds true. What we want to emphasise from the outset, however, is that, for most cultural geographers, the terms geography and culture have much more expansive definitions when compared to their usage in everyday contexts. One of the key arguments that we make in this book is that cultural geography provides a unique approach to *culture* and that this distinguishes what cultural geographers do from researchers in related fields like sociology or cultural studies, to take two obvious examples (see **Box 1.1**). To get closer to a definition of what cultural geography is and why it matters, we need to have a clearer sense of what it means to think geographically. In the sections that follow, we identify three broad features of geographical thought that shape how cultural geographers approach culture in and through their research, beginning with geography's affinity for relations.

BOX 1.1 Culture

Culture . . . where on earth to begin? The question of what culture is has a long, complicated, and contested trajectory within cultural geography (Lapworth, 2023). We tend to speak of culture as if it were a concrete reality, but, in practice, it is an abstract category. Cultural geographers study all sorts of objects, representations, and practices – from artworks, institutions, and knowledge practices to emotions, animals, and artificial intelligence – and it is through these myriad engagements with the world around them that something resembling culture comes into focus. A more interesting question to consider is whether this indirect approach to culture is cause for concern. Mitch Rose (2026: 127) makes the case for a renewed attention to culture, arguing that an unwillingness to theorise culture head-on "has taken away something from the field." Others might contest this narrative by emphasising what cultural geography has gained in the process of exploring emerging articulations of culture through new questions, concepts, and methods. For what it's worth, we think culture has a lot to do with the way individuals and collectives capture, make sense of, and express life's excessive forces. Like all living organisms, human beings find themselves traversed by intensities that make them constantly overstep their biological individuality. Think, for instance, of a creative project that keeps you awake at night, a political injustice that inspires you to pick up a placard and occupy the streets, a movie scene that breaks you open in a new way, or even just the knowledge that there are black holes out there in the cold depths of the universe where time . . . simply . . . stops. Culture, we believe, has something to do with this productive excess or 'too-muchness' of life that impels us beyond our organic needs – and, crucially, with how we make sense of the world's vital push by inventing new forms of collective expression. To the extent that these practices are embedded in the materiality of objects, representations, institutions, habits, and even fleeting atmospheres, culture is a repository of techniques geared towards the *cultivation* of life and, therefore, the creation of the new.

RELATIONAL THINKING

The first important thing to know about geographical thinking is that it represents a fundamentally *relational* approach to understanding our world. This includes, of course, the mapping of spatial relations through cartographic (i.e. map-making) practices. But geography is relational in a much more fundamental sense. For those readers who studied geography at high school or college, it is highly likely that your course syllabus included both human and physical geography components. For human geography, you may have studied things like population growth, sustainable cities, and economics; in physical geography, you might have been introduced to the science of climate change, the development of geological landforms, or natural hazards. Geography's long-standing interest in bringing the human and physical sciences into relation is a big part of what makes it such a unique area of study, despite overlapping with other more specialised disciplines (e.g. sociology, geology). Immanuel Kant (1724–1804), one of the most influential philosophers in European intellectual history, famously referred to geography as a synthetic science (May, 1970). For this reason, we would argue that a defining feature of geographical thought lies in its underlying commitment to relationality – and, most importantly, to understanding those relations that complicate and/or undermine the conventional split between society and nature.

This rosy picture of geography as a community of polymaths is, however, not entirely accurate. Sooner or later in their careers, there comes a time when most geographers will specialise. This usually happens over the course of a university geography programme, where electives in specific subfields encourage students to concentrate their studies on either human or physical geography (often during the second and third years of a typical undergraduate geography programme, following a more holistic introduction in the first year). Specialising as a human geographer (as we both did) could involve taking electives across a broad range of human geography topics or subfields, including social geography, economic geography, political geography, historical geography, and this book's central focus, cultural geography. Undertaking research degrees at masters or PhD level further solidifies these tendencies towards specialisation because completion of these programmes requires students to submerse themselves in – and ultimately contribute to – a highly targeted area of research. By identifying as cultural geographers, then, we are doubly specialised: first, as human geographers within the overarching discipline of geography; second, as cultural geographers within the smaller sub-field of human geography.

This tension between geography's desire to be seen as a synthetic science, bridging the gap between the physical and human sciences, and the reality of specialisation within the field, is something that geographers have discussed, written about, and debated over the years (see Livingstone, 1992; Johnston and Sidaway, 2016). At its most extreme, scepticism regarding the coherence of the discipline has resulted in the dissolution of dedicated geography libraries – and, in the most extreme cases, entire university departments – with the impact being that the uniqueness of geography's relational approach is lost (Wainwright et al., 2014). This is a particular risk for academic geography in the twenty-first century, when universities across the world are facing funding cuts while also battling rising anti-intellectualism associated with far-right populism around the globe. As cultural geographers, we have both had the good fortune to gain valuable experience working at universities with dedicated geography departments or research groups (we realise that we are privileged in this regard and that this is very much not a given in today's academic landscape). These institutional contexts are vitally important for the future of the discipline because they provide environments where the underlying geographical concern for the interrelation of society and nature can be explored. This includes day-to-day activities like programme design, assisting with field schools, and even chatting about research activities in shared spaces like libraries and tea rooms.

The point we want to make here is that, despite an unavoidable tendency towards sub-disciplinary specialisation, most geographers do maintain an underlying affinity with geography's relational aspirations. Within the context of cultural geography, one way that this plays out is through its theorisation of culture as something fundamentally continuous with the messy ***materiality*** of our world (see **Box 1.2**). Cultural geography approaches are sensitive to the idea that the convenient categories we refer to as culture (i.e. the human) and nature (i.e. the non-human) are abstractions from a much more complicated, relational world. Instead of being seen as mutually exclusive categories, culture and nature are compositions of relations that are neither cultural nor natural in and of themselves. And while more recent theoretical work in cultural geography has taken an interest in the concept of 'non-relation' (Harrison, 2007; Dekeyser et al., 2022), we would argue that these approaches nonetheless retain an underlying concern with relation; to the extent that they are geographical (which we believe they are), they remain fundamentally interested in understanding how humans exist in the world – not humans (or culture) in isolation or abstraction from the world.

BOX 1.2 Materiality

The term materiality is often used by cultural geographers to refer to (and sometimes emphasise) a thing's material or physical qualities. In the case of an everyday object like a smartphone, for example, we might be interested in exploring not only the information that it makes available to the user but also the materiality of the object itself: the smoothness of the touchscreen, the feel of the different materials it is composed of, etc. Materiality could also refer to the material qualities of an event: from the oppressive physicality of boredom to the visceral pulse of a synthesised bass tone played at high volume. While materiality has been a long-standing interest for cultural geographers, there has been a renewed excitement around the term since the early 2010s. During this time, an interdisciplinary movement known as new materialism caught the imagination of many cultural geographers, who saw it as an opportunity to re-examine our shared materiality with the world of non-human things. If you are interested in reading more about materiality from a new materialist perspective, Jane Bennett's (2010) book *Vibrant Matter* is an excellent place to start.

What does this focus on relationality mean for cultural geography? One interesting implication is that culture can no longer be thought of as an interpretive lens detached from the world itself. Studying culture, from a cultural geography perspective, is *not* simply a matter of understanding how human beings collectively ascribe meaning to the world; it is also about delving into the materiality of that world to see how this thing we habitually refer to as culture takes shape. To continue the metaphor: the lens itself (and the images it brings into focus) is made of the same material stuff as the world. A quick example here would be photographic images. At first glance, it seems obvious that photographic images (whether still or moving) are cultural objects and so would be of interest for cultural geographers. We might assume that photographs are interesting because they tell us something about the cultural context in which they were created. But if you look more closely at a photograph – and think more relationally – you will see that these objects are in fact continuous with nature and the world they claim to represent (see ***Chapter 2***). The 'culture' embedded in the photograph *is* the 'nature' of the photons hitting the camera's sensor, the behaviour of the silicon semiconductors, or the organic compounds embedded in your OLED display.

EMPIRICAL FIELDWORK

A second key aspect of geographical thinking that shapes how cultural geographers approach culture lies in the discipline's commitment to *empirical research* (see **Box 1.3**). By empirical, we are referring to geography's association with fieldwork – that is, the practice of going out into the world to do your thinking. Some readers may well have experienced fieldwork while studying geography at high school or college: perhaps taking measurements on an exposed scree slope, soaked through to the skin, or handing out surveys in your local shopping centre. Whatever the activity, carrying out fieldwork is a key characteristic of what it means to think geographically, and this includes thinking geographically about culture. This dimension of geographical thinking does have an unsavoury history, however, the reason being that it is linked to the imperialistic origins of early academic geography and its implication in the violent conquest of exotic lands (Livingstone, 1992). Indeed, the association of fieldwork with the image of a heroic scientist (usually white and male) bringing the civilising force of modern science to bear on an uncharted wilderness before retreating with his intellectual spoils has proven to be a difficult one for the discipline to shake off.

Cultural geographers are, by virtue of their academic training, acutely aware of their implication in these troubling, often bloody histories of violence, conquest, and dispossession. It is perhaps for this reason that the practice of doing fieldwork in cultural geography strives to be far less appropriative in its approach to knowledge. For most cultural geographers, embarking on fieldwork is not motivated by a desire to objectively know the world through the collection of data; nor is it a straightforward process of testing theories or disproving hypotheses. Instead, conducting fieldwork in cultural geography is a much more complex, non-linear process of thinking *with* the world. What is produced in the process of fieldwork is never a definitive statement about how the world is or what the world is like; rather, what we end up with (if things go to plan) is a different perspective on an idea, problem, or situation that we can then use to unlock new areas of interest, out there in the world, that perhaps we would not have thought about (or even noticed) before.

BOX 1.3 Empiricism

Empiricism is an approach to knowledge that begins with experience. As a philosophical standpoint, empiricism is based on the idea that all human knowledge is acquired from experience – that is, through our five senses. Empiricism is often opposed to rationalism, which locates the basis of knowledge in human reasoning rather than experience. There are, of course, different ways of thinking about empiricism. One approach that has caught the attention of some cultural geographers in recent years is the concept of 'radical empiricism,' first developed by the philosopher and psychologist William James (1842–1910) in the late nineteenth century. James believed that experience is more capacious than we ordinarily assume and includes perceptions of things that we cannot easily point to or measure: relations between things, transitions between states, and flows, being key examples. For more on why James' radical empiricism matters for cultural geography, see Derek McCormack (2010).

Another interesting (and unusual) aspect of cultural geography's empiricism is that it includes encounters with ideas, concepts, and theories within its definition of fieldwork. For Derek McCormack (2010), this makes cultural geography *radically empirical* in the expanded range of what it includes under the umbrella of experience (and, therefore, of what constitutes fieldwork). For many cultural geographers, then, going out into the field provides a means of experiencing new ideas, concepts, and theories relating to culture. What makes this exciting is the sheer variety of potential fieldwork encounters that are available to cultural geographers – encounters with movies, buildings, institutions, archives, bodily practices, objects, atmospheres, etc. – but also the way these encounters can then be used to breathe new life into the really big questions that arise when reflecting on the human condition. In our own research, this includes hanging out in an IKEA superstore as a way of thinking about objects, agency, and the materiality of our own bodies (Roberts, 2012); exploring how bio-artists and biohacking communities are rewriting the boundaries between the living and material through their experiments (Lapworth, 2016); or questioning what it means to trust intelligent technologies by asking people about their experiences using Google Maps (Roberts et al., 2025). Through these and many other examples of fieldwork, cultural geographers are uniquely positioned to grapple with the complex interweaving of the conceptual and the empirical that is itself a key aspect of culture.

SPECIFICITY AND THE SINGULAR

To recap, then, a geographical approach to culture is both relational and empirical: relational, in the sense that culture is continuous with the world in all its materiality (not a field of meaning floating detached above it); and empirical, in its commitment to thinking *with* the constellations of materials, spaces, practices, and ideas that give consistency to our lives. Building on these, the third and final characteristic of geographical thinking that we want to emphasise is its sensitivity towards the specific and the singular. These two terms require definition, but before we get to this, and to give readers a broader sense of why we have chosen these terms, it might be useful to consider some of the conventional associations attached to the word culture. Thinking about culture can be tricky, in part because it is quite an abstract term. For this reason, it is tempting to imagine that culture is like a system of traditions, rules, or practices that sits above (or 'transcends') the material world and determines how spaces and events are experienced by the human beings that inhabit it. The problem with this approach, however, is that it can lead to situations where what is most interesting about a space or an event is glossed over or ignored in the rush to conceptualise culture as a coherent system.

This is where geography's attention to the specific and singular dimensions of culture comes into play. By using the word 'specific,' we are referring to the way that space *makes* culture and is not merely a reflection or expression of culture as an abstract system of rules or norms (see Massey, 2005). This is a challenging idea to grasp, but it is one that will reappear in various forms throughout this book. To help make sense of it, let's return to an example of our own research that we introduced in the previous section: IKEA as a site of cultural geography research. A cultural analysis of IKEA could encompass many things. We could, for instance, explore how aesthetic ideals and values associated with Swedish nationality are expressed in the kinds of products available to buy. Alternatively, we might be interested in the way IKEA has shaped how people see their relationship with furniture in a world where job security is becoming a thing of the past for many. While both approaches represent interesting (and important) lines of enquiry, our inner cultural geographer cries out: "What about the agency of the space itself as a force that shapes culture?" Posing this question brings new dimensions of culture to the fore, dimensions that are enacted in/through a space's materiality: embodiment, architecture, habit, feeling, desire, and atmosphere. To be sure, it is possible (and in many cases legitimate) to interpret or read a space as an expression *of* culture; for cultural geographers, however, it is important to remember that the most seemingly abstract dimensions of culture remain thoroughly entangled with the specificity of places, sites, environments, and contexts.

If cultural geography's commitment to the specific redirects our attention towards the spatial 'here' of culture, its interest in the singular is all about the temporal agency of the 'now.' This now can be many things: it could be an event, a performance, a declaration, or an act of witnessing, but it could also be a sudden flush of serotonin, passing your driving test, or a consequential change in the weather. Perhaps even more confusingly, the kinds of singular 'nowness' that cultural geographers are interested in are not necessarily fleeting instances. Some of them might be. Yet there are other kinds of now that have a longer duration. The acclaimed American writer John Steinbeck (2000: 129) captures this sense of an extended now in the following passage, taken from his well-known play *Of Mice and Men*:

> As happens sometimes, a moment settled and hovered and remained for much more than a moment. And sound stopped and movement stopped for much, much more than a moment.

What matters, then, for cultural geographers, is not instantaneousness but rather the 'liveness' of culture: the here *and* the now, the specific *and* the singular, the stage *and* the performance. Between each of these dyads, there are all sorts of interesting relays at play.

It is difficult – indeed, perhaps impossible – to do justice to the material specificity of a space without also grappling with the sense of its nowness: the happening of a space. Similarly, honing-in on the nowness of an event tends to amplify our sensitivity towards the specificity of context: the spatiality of an event. Borrowing from the title of Anderson and Harrison's (2010) influential cultural geography collection, we could describe this productive relaying of the specific and the singular as the "taking place" of culture.

To summarise, in this section, we have explored what it means to adopt a geographical approach to culture and why this might be important today (we will elaborate more on this second point regarding cultural geography's relevance in the chapters to come). Cultural geographers think geographically about culture, but geographical thought is about much more than spatial distribution. Here, we highlighted three key characteristics that we believe are central to geographical thinking and thus what the study of culture looks like from a geographical perspective. These include (1) a long-standing affinity for *relational* understandings of the world and our place within it; (2) a commitment to empirical fieldwork as an activity of thinking *with* this world; and (3) a cultivated sensitivity towards the specificity and singularity of culture – that is, its *liveness* in the here and now.

TURNS AND RETURNS: A BRIEF HISTORY OF CULTURAL GEOGRAPHY

Engaging with a new academic discipline for the first time can be an overwhelming experience. There is often a new and complicated vernacular to learn and a never-ending litany of key thinkers and texts to memorise. Now that we've got more of a grip on what it means to think geographically about culture, another way that we can start to get our bearings is to ask questions about its origins: *Why* and *where* did cultural geography emerge? *What* have been some of the key phases or changes in its history? And *how* have these left their imprint on the way the discipline is understood and practised today?

Accounts of disciplinary history are often presented in a fairly dramatic fashion, making them appear well-suited to a blockbuster cinematic dramatisation! We hear of clashes and skirmishes (often in the question-and-answer sections of geography conferences), backstabbing and betrayal (of the new generation turning their backs on the old ways), the waning of powerful (theoretical) dynasties, and even full-blown 'revolutions' that give rise to a new (disciplinary) order. The conventional or 'official' history of cultural geography that we ourselves encountered in our undergraduate studies very much follows this kind of narrative (although we'll leave it up to our readers to decide whether it deserves a Christopher Nolan adaptation!). This history often traces a succession of disciplinary *turns* that are seen to have produced a reinvention in both the ambit and remit of cultural geography. While the discourse of turns can be reductive and problematic (something we'll return to at the end of this section), we nevertheless believe that it can be a useful heuristic for helping to identify those moments where we see a coalescing of intellectual energies around a distinct set of concerns and problems. For us, a disciplinary turn is something that does at least two (but ideally all three) of the following: (1) it introduces a new set of thinkers, concepts, and conceptual frameworks into the discipline; (2) it opens a different range of empirical spaces for study (for instance, in cultural geography, expanding our sense of what sites, objects, or practices make up the domain of 'the cultural'); and (3) it introduces a new suite of methodologies or techniques through which cultural geographers research the world. Put more succinctly, a disciplinary turn is something that has important implications for how we *think*, how we *perceive* the world, and how we *do* research in it.

In this section, then, we provide an overview of four of the key turns that are often discussed in official histories of cultural geography. We also highlight a few exciting recent strands of cultural geography emerging in the last decade and unpack how they've sought to expand the theoretical, methodological, and ethical scope of the subdiscipline. Our account in this section is quite selective and brief, and we'll be returning to these (and many other) strands at various points throughout the book. We end this section by emphasising the limitations and dangers of such linear and paradigmatic stories of historical development (especially in terms of the voices and perspectives they sometimes exclude) and introduce the different approach that we want to take in presenting cultural geography's past, present, and future.

CARL SAUER AND THE BERKELEY SCHOOL

Most accounts of cultural geography's origins begin in the 1920s, with what would come to be known as the 'Berkeley School' of cultural geography. Its name comes from its emergence in the work of geographical scholars based at the University of California, Berkeley, although its influence would spread much further than the leafy campus of Berkeley. The head of this influential school of cultural geography was the American geographer Carl Otwin Sauer (1889–1975). The main area of interest for Sauer and his colleagues was the way in which people left their imprint on the natural world through different cultural activities and practices (such as the cultivation of plants, the production of material objects, and the building of settlements). Sauer's work can be understood as a critique of another very influential approach in geography at the start of the twentieth century: *environmental determinism*. Environmental determinism was a set of theories, popularised by geographers like Friedrich Ratzel (1844–1902) and Ellsworth Huntington (1876–1947), that tried to develop causal arguments for the role that the physical environment (topography, resources, climate, etc.) plays in human culture and development. Environmental determinist arguments often intended to provide scientific justification for racist and prejudicial theories about other cultures and places. In *The Character of Races,* for example, Huntington (1924) linked data on 'climactic energy' (which he claimed was highest in North America and Western Europe and lowest in the tropics and Africa) with indices of human civilisation (again believed to be highest in America and Europe). Sauer attempted to challenge these prevailing theories by arguing that while environments do influence cultures, cultures also shape their environments in very significant ways. Like environmental determinism, Sauer was also developing a causal argument, but one that gave primacy to the cultural over the natural (see ***Chapter 3***, where we discuss how contemporary cultural geography has sought to challenge the traditional dichotomy between nature and culture).

The most famous expression of Sauer's theories appeared in his paper 'The Morphology of Landscape' (Sauer, 1925). Sauer's paper begins by positioning the cultural landscape as the "unit concept of geography" (Sauer, 1925: 25). He distinguishes the 'cultural landscape' from the 'natural landscape,' with the former having been "fashioned out of a natural landscape by a culture group" (Sauer,

1925: 46). Sauer (1925: 46) famously expressed the causal logic of his central argument as follows: "culture is the agent, the natural area is the medium, the cultural landscape is the result." An example of this that Sauer (1966: v) gives in a later work is the boundary between the Southern United States and Mexico, which he argued was a cultural rather than physical divide:

> The same mountains and deserts, pine forests, oak woodlands, scrub, and grasslands extend north and south: the difference is the people and their ways. On this side [the USA], change has been accelerating and innovation has become the dominant order of living. On the other side [Mexico], ways of past experience and acceptance have been retained in gradual modifications.

At the heart of Sauer's approach was what can be termed a 'super-organic' conception of culture. As Peter Jackson (1989: 18) notes in his critical review of Sauer, "a super-organic approach adopts the view that culture is an entity at a higher level than the individual, that is governed by a logic of its own, and that it actively constrains human behaviour." Culture was thus conceived by Sauer and his colleagues as a static and essentialised 'whole,' following its own mysterious, causal laws. However, as can be seen in the quotation about the United States and Mexico above, Sauer's essentialist arguments of different cultural landscapes (the idea that the landscapes produced by different cultural groups are clearly demarcated and internally uniform) meant that his early brand of cultural geography was just as liable as the environmental determinists he disagreed with to reductive and stereotyped arguments. While the ideas of Sauer and his colleagues have been subject to strong critiques by subsequent generations of cultural geographers, his legacy continues to be felt, not least in his elevation of the concept of landscape in cultural-geographical enquiry, which remains one of the central organising concepts in our discipline.

HUMANISTIC GEOGRAPHIES

A resurgence of interest in the themes and approaches of cultural geography emerged in the 1970s with the rise of 'humanistic geography.' Humanistic geography developed as a critique of the so-called quantitative revolution of the 1960s that sought to rebrand geography as a spatial science, one focused on producing generalisable, causal models of social and spatial organisation. Humanistic geographers, like Yi Fu Tuan, Anne Buttimer, and David Seamon, were concerned about the denial of human agency in much quantitative geographical work and, instead, wanted to shift geography's focus to the qualitative richness of people's experiences and the events of everyday life. To do so required a reorientation of the discipline away from the physical and social sciences and more towards philosophy and the humanities. In what is now regarded as its foundational treatise, Tuan (1976: 266) argued that humanistic geography seeks to achieve "an understanding of the human world by studying people's relations with nature, their geographical behaviour as well as their feelings and ideas about space and place." Crucially, in humanistic geography, the focus shifted from *space* (defined as an abstract container for human action, like in spatial science approaches) to *place* (understood as sites imbued with meaning through culture, memory, and emotion).

Humanistic geographers, as Jackson (1989: 20) notes, continued the Berkeley School's "obsessive interest" in the concept of landscape. However, instead of a cultural object, attention in humanistic geography fell on landscape as an environment that is lived in, perceived, and interpreted by human subjects. The emphasis here was on descriptive analysis of the individual's perception and experience of landscape, often turning to literature and art to help understand or capture the subjective qualities of place (Tuan, 1976). Many of humanistic geography's concepts (such as lifeworld, experience, subjectivity, and the everyday) and methods (ethnography and creative writing) strongly informed some of the subsequent turns in cultural geography that we'll discuss below, including 'new cultural geography' in the 1990s and 'non-representational theory' in the 2000s (Simpson, 2020). But it also became subject to quite sustained and vigorous critique from the 1980s onwards. The humanistic geographer, David Ley (1981: 252), sums these major lines of critique up nicely when he writes:

> In retrieving man [sic] from virtual oblivion in positivist science, humanists have tended to celebrate this restoration per-

> haps too much. As a result, values, meanings, consciousness, creativity, and reflection may well be overstated, while context, constraint, and social stratification have been under-developed.

A new generation of cultural geographers thus increasingly challenged humanistic geography for its universal homogeneous understanding of experience and subjectivity, which tended to privilege predominantly white, masculine, bourgeois, and heterosexual subjects as the norm for cultural geographic knowledge (Rose, 1993). As a result, this gave rise to growing calls for a new kind of cultural geography, one that would place questions of identity, difference, and power at the core of its theorising.

'NEW CULTURAL GEOGRAPHY'

Dissatisfaction with humanistic geography's shallow treatment of social and political context in thinking about cultural landscapes was a key motivator for the next major phase of cultural geography's history: *new cultural geography*. As Jackson (1989) notes in *Maps of Meaning* – one of the landmark texts of this period of cultural geography – the 'New' in new cultural geography was also an attempt to signal the distance of this emerging body of work from the 'Old' style of cultural geography, associated with the work of Carl Sauer and the Berkeley School. Unlike Sauer's homogeneous sense of the cultural domain, new cultural geographers instead sought to recognise the plurality of cultures and the complex power relations shaping the ways in which people ascribe meaning to the world. In what is considered as one of the early manifestos of this new cultural geography, Denis Cosgrove and Peter Jackson (1987: 95) note that what distinguishes it from previous styles of cultural geography is that:

> It would be contemporary as well as historical (but always contextual and theoretically informed); social as well as spatial (but not confined to narrowly-defined landscape issues); urban as well as rural; and interested in the contingent nature of culture, in dominant ideologies and in forms of resistance to them.

Cosgrove and Jackson (1987) noted that new cultural geography offered an opportunity for convergence between two emerging emphases in British geography: a 'critical' *social geography* developing new approaches to social identity and difference (Jackson, 1989); and a theoretically reinvigorated *cultural geography* focused on new understandings of landscape, text, metaphor, and iconography (Cosgrove, 1984). Interest in the overlap between social and cultural geography can be seen in the renaming in 1987 of the Institute of British Geography's Social Geography Study Group to the Social *and Cultural* Geography Study Group. This remains the name of the research group to this day (Philo and Zhang, 2024).

However, in a recent review of this period, Chris Philo (a cultural geographer and one of the members of the IBG committee involved in the name change) suggests that the new cultural geography of this period was riven by two main poles. The first – which he calls "Jacksonian" after Peter Jackson – sought to bring new and innovative theorisations of race, sexuality, and class from the burgeoning field of cultural studies (especially from the writings of the British cultural theorist, Stuart Hall) into social geographic research (Philo and Zhang, 2024: 2). Its guiding principle was to address how "[the social] at all scales from the domestic to the geopolitical was always indelibly shaping and shaped by" the medium of culture (Philo and Zhang, 2024: 3). The second pole is what Philo terms "Cosgrovian," after Denis Cosgrove. This pole retained focus on the concept of landscape in cultural geographic enquiry but sought to rethink it not as a material 'thing' but rather as (and here drawing on the ideas of art theorists like John Berger) a 'way of seeing' that is always shot through with power relations and political identities. Summarising, Philo notes how the Cosgrovian strand of new cultural geography sought "to address how the 'earth' (the ecumene as earthy landscapes, ecologies, habitats) becomes the locus of contested imaginations, representations, interventions, constructions, and destructions" (Philo and Zhang, 2024: 3).

Despite initial attempts at rapprochement, the 1990s saw these two poles of new cultural geography grow steadily apart. We see, for instance, the formation in 1994 of the academic journal *Ecumene* (renamed *cultural geographies* in 2002), which became a home for the more humanities-inclined work published by cultural geographers. In fact, Denis Cosgrove was one of the founding editors of this journal. And then, in 2000, we see the formation of the journal *Social and Cultural Geography*, which sought to publish more social science-inflected, empirically grounded research exploring the cultural dimensions of a range of social issues, such as consumption, identity and community, activism and resistance, and poverty and homelessness. While not an editor, Peter Jackson wrote the first substantive article in the first issue of this journal on the topic of 'Rematerialising social and cultural geography' (Jackson, 2000), which argued that cultural geography's focus on texts and meaning had come at the expense of engagements with the material world of 'real' objects and questions of social difference.

Both journals remain the principal fora for the publication of new research in cultural geography and are essential resources for new students. So, do get them added to your website bookmarks! But in the last decades, these journals have been accompanied by a range of other new outlets for cultural geographic work (including *Gender, Place & Culture*, *Emotion, Space & Society*, *Geohumanities*, and *Literary Geography*) that further reflect the ongoing evolution and diversification of contemporary cultural geographies.

NON-REPRESENTATIONAL GEOGRAPHIES

It wasn't long after new cultural geography's emergence onto the scene that the first murmurs of change could be heard. There was a growing sense of dissatisfaction, first in the seminar rooms of geography conferences and workshops (such as the New Words/New Worlds conference in Lampeter, Wales, in 1991, published as Philo (1991)), and then in the pages of the major human geography journals, of the absences and exclusions within new cultural geography, especially around issues of gender and sexuality (Rose, 1993) and post-colonial identity (Nash, 2002). But there were also growing concerns, expressed by cultural geographers like Nigel Thrift (1991: 144), of the "over-wordy worlds" written by new cultural geography and its tendency to reduce reality to a series of 'texts' to be critically analysed and interpreted. In a series of writings starting from the early 1990s, Thrift began to sketch the contours of a radically new style of geographical research which he later came to name *non-representational theory* (Thrift, 1996). Non-representational theory attempted to "re-orientate geographic analyses beyond what was, at the time, perceived as an over-emphasis on representations (images, texts, and so on) and instead emphasise practice, embodiment, materiality, and process" (Simpson, 2020: 4). However, and despite what the use of the singular 'theory' might suggest, non-representational theory was never intended to be a unified or coherent theoretical approach. It is instead better imagined as a set of *non-representational theories*, drawing on a diverse range of philosophical and conceptual influences, that collectively seek to enliven the kinds of worlds that geographers write about (Anderson and Harrison, 2010). What gathers these somewhat disparate styles of thinking together, as Hayden Lorimer (2005: 84) puts it, is a shared focus:

> On how life takes shape and gains expression in shared experiences, everyday routines, fleeting encounters, embodied movements, precognitive triggers, practical skills, affective intensities, enduring urges, unexceptional interactions and sensuous dispositions. Attention to these offers an escape from the academic habit of striving to uncover meanings and values that apparently await our discovery, interpretations, judgement, and ultimate representation.

Following its emergence in the mid-to-late 1990s and its subsequent development by PhD students at the University of Bristol (including, most notably, JD Dewsbury, John Wylie, Paul Harrison, and Derek McCormack) in the early 2000s, non-representational theories have since become a mainstream force across multiple areas of contemporary human geography. We will be returning to its transformative impact on cultural geography (and beyond) in multiple chapters of this book (especially in ***Chapter 2***, where we tackle how it has reshaped geographical engagements with the problematic of representation). But for the purposes of introducing its unique style and ambit, we want to briefly turn to how non-representational theorists sought to refigure a key concept that has threaded our discussion so far: that of landscape.

For non-representational geographers, landscape is no longer understood as a text to be interpreted for its symbolic meaning but is instead approached as something that is lived and sensed through the body. This entails a shift towards questions of embodied *practice* (how bodies move through landscapes), *experience* (how bodies feel as they encounter different elements of the environment), and *materiality* (the very physicality of our environments and how it impinges on our bodies, often in unconscious ways). One of the most notable examples of a non-representational approach to landscape comes in the work of John Wylie (2005, 2007). In one of his most influential articles, Wylie explores the experience of encountering landscape through an account of a summer spent walking the South West Coast Path in the United Kingdom. This is the longest footpath in the United Kingdom at 630 miles, much of it following the coastlines of Cornwall and Devon in the southwest of England. Wylie notes that one of the hallmarks of traditional thinking on landscape in cultural geography is a sense of distancing, separating out the observing subject ('here') and the landscape as object ('over there'). Instead, Wylie (2005: 240) argues that a non-representational approach, through its emphasis on bodily experience, seeks to unsettle the strict dividing line that we typically erect between the self and the world:

> To be in the landscape, but also up against it. To be dogged, put-upon, petulant, breathless. Partly, of course, this emerges via the tension of self-preservation. A tactile and tactical focus: when else are your feet, the ground, so visible? The rising mercury of involvement pushes towards a meniscus of subjectivity.

Wylie's wonderfully evocative language in the quote above really captures this sense of complete material immersion in the landscape he is walking through. What Wylie is getting at here is the idea that the walking 'self' is not something that pre-exists its encounters with the landscape. It is instead best grasped as an *emergence* and thus something that is constantly changing through encounters with the various materialities and sensory elements composing the landscape (hard stone and thick mud, the calls of birds, driving rain, and scorching sunlight). Wylie speaks, for instance, of a 'sublime self' at the start of the walk, optimistic about the journey ahead; a 'fearful self' that emerges as the body enters thick, dark woodland with strange animal noises in the distance; and a 'pained self,' at the conclusion of the walk, nursing painful foot blisters at a pub in Cornwall.

In contrast to both Sauerian and new cultural geography approaches, Wylie (2005: 243) argues that "landscape is neither something seen, nor a way of seeing, but rather the materialities and sensibilities *with which* we see." Here, then, what we have is a sense of landscape as a kind of material force that shapes how we think, feel, and perceive. Landscape is, therefore, not a passive or abstract backdrop to human thought and action but rather takes on the status of an active performative agent in the ongoing production of the human (Dewsbury, 2015). One of the most significant contributions of non-representational theories for cultural geography has been its innovative engagements with a panoply of novel concepts for grasping the material and performative force of landscape, including terms like 'affect' and 'assemblage,' which we'll be elaborating in more detail in ***Chapter 2*** and ***Chapter 5***.

CONTEMPORARY DEVELOPMENTS: MORE-THAN-HUMAN GEOGRAPHIES, GEOHUMANITIES, AND THE NEGATIVE

To end our foray into cultural geography's history, we want to briefly highlight three key directions of the last decade or so that have energised cultural geographers. All three can be understood to emerge in the wake of non-representational theory, like aftershocks, each elaborating specific facets of the non-representational shock to cultural geographic thought but also supplementing it with other genealogies of thinking and practice drawn from across the contemporary humanities and social sciences. The first of these directions is *more-than-human geographies*, which addresses the concern that life had been "drained out" of earlier versions of human cultural geography through an exclusive focus on the practices and discourses of human subjects (Whatmore, 2006: 559). More-than-human geographies, as the geographer Sarah Whatmore (2006: 602) puts it, seek to "return to the livingness of the world [and] shift the register of materiality from the indifferent stuff of a world 'out there,' articulated through notions of land,' 'nature' or 'environment,' to the intimate fabric of corporeality that includes and redistributes the 'in here' of human being." Drawing on post-humanist strands of philosophy that decentre the primacy of the human in accounts of the world, more-than-human geographies seek to foreground the active role that non-human actors and agencies (including, but not limited to, animals, microorganisms, plants, technological objects, inorganic matter, and geological forces) play in the ongoing production of the social and cultural world. We engage more with this exciting strand of cultural geographic research in ***Chapter 3***.

The second direction is that of the *geohumanities* (see **Box 1.4**). The geohumanities build on cultural geography's rich tradition of engagement with artistic fields (like literature, painting, and film) in exploring cultural geographic concepts like landscape and place, bringing this into dialogue with recent developments in humanities disciplines – like the 'environmental humanities' – that bring concerns with space and the environment to the fore of artistic research. The geohumanities has helped coalesce and showcase a wealth of creative and experimental interdisciplinary collaborations that have (as we'll highlight in ***Chapter 7***) had transformative impacts on how cultural geographic research is conducted and disseminated to different publics.

BOX 1.4 Geohumanities

The 'geohumanities' refers to an interdisciplinary field of research that seeks to bridge the expressive modalities and conceptual approaches of geography with the arts and humanities. Much of the focus of geohumanities work by cultural geographers has been in exploring the potential of artistic experiences and practices to transform the relationships between people, place, and environment. The year 2015 saw the formalisation of the field with the establishment of the academic journal *GeoHumanities*, which has become an important destination for cultural geographic work since.

The final, and most recent, direction of cultural geographic scholarship relates to interest in what has come to be termed *negative geographies*. This area of research seeks to challenge what its proponents argue has been an overemphasis on 'affirmative' theories of "the possible, the potential, and the infinite nature of human (and nonhuman) capacity" in non-representational and more-than-human geographies, at the expense of enquiries into questions of impossibility, impotentiality, and finitude (Bissell et al., 2021: 2). Some geographers, seduced by this call of the negative, have thus sought to explore concerns around limits and incapacities in relation to a range of purportedly 'negative' embodied states, such as exhaustion (Dawney and Jellis, 2024), distraction (Bissell, 2025), and immobility (Mutter, 2025). The torsion between affirmative and negative approaches has become a passionate terrain for articulating the ethical and political stakes of contemporary cultural geographic thinking (see Roberts and Dewsbury (2021) for a defence of the 'vital aspirations' of geographical thought) and is something we'll return to in the book's epilogue (***Chapter 8***) in discussing cultural geography's possible futures.

THE DANGERS OF OFFICIAL HISTORIES

In bringing this section to a close, we feel it is important to highlight a few limitations of the linear and paradigmatic 'official history' that has just been set out. The first is that this account doesn't appear especially diverse in terms of *who* does cultural geography. You have probably already noticed that most of the people appearing in the above history are white men. For several decades, a wide array of cultural geographic scholarship has emphasised the exclusions and absences that result from disciplinary approaches centred on the universalist norms of white, male, and cis-heterosexual lives. Since the 1980s, feminist cultural geographers have sought not only to enhance the visibility of women's lives in academic research but also to unpick how geography itself is a "masculinist discipline" founded on a series of gendered philosophical dualisms, including nature/culture, mind/body, and active/passive (Rose, 1993: 18). This, Rose (1993: 10) argues, has historically had "serious consequences both for what counts as legitimate geographical knowledge and who can produce such knowledge." Furthermore, in the last few decades, we have seen the rise of a diversity of LGBT+ geographies that highlight how queer and trans lives complicate and unsettle dominant cultural geographic understandings of a range of concepts, including "space, time, place, belonging, embodiment, ecologies, and mobilities" (Kinkaid and Sharp, 2026: 247). And most recently, we see a burgeoning interest in the field of *Black Geographies* that, as Allen et al. (2019: 1002) highlight, is a body of work "that emphasises black experiences, as well as alternative visions and articulations of space drawn from these experiences." A renewed attention to Black lives in cultural geographic work has been vital in uncovering the markedly different lived experiences of structural inequalities (e.g. the differential exposure of Black populations to urban and environmental pollution), as well as "identifying new opportunities for resistance, activism, and social justice" (Nayak and Berwick, 2026: 151). Taken together, these different bodies of work seek to dramatically expand the range of identities, perspectives, and worlds that appear in cultural geographic writing (Queering Feminist Geography Collective, 2025).

The official history outlined earlier is also not especially diverse in terms of the question of *where* cultural geography happens. The geographical centre of gravity for this narrative – moving through the geography departments of Berkeley (Sauerian), Lampeter (New Cultural Geography), Bristol (Non-Representational), Oxford (More-than-Human), Royal Holloway (Geohumanities), and Durham (Negative Geographies) – is profoundly Anglo-American. In part, this is symptomatic of a much longer history of the geography discipline's entanglements with the project of, specifically British, imperialism (Clayton, 2011). Today, cultural geography can be studied and researched in universities across the world. However, the fact that most of the journals and publishing houses for cultural geographic work are concentrated in the United Kingdom, North America, and Australia, are edited by Anglo-American scholars, and mainly publish work in the English language, means that students and researchers rarely encounter cultural geographic research produced in other parts of the world. Some journals – such as *Social and Cultural Geography* – have sought to address this through initiatives like 'Country Reports' that invite geographers to reflect (in English) on the trends in how cultural geography is taught and researched in different countries, with pieces on Australia (Dowling, 2005), Japan (Mori, 2009), Greece (Vaiou, 2005), South Africa (Battersby, 2004), and Taiwan (Hsin-Ling et al., 2006). What these reports highlight is one of cultural geography's core intuitions: that place matters in shaping how cultural geography is produced and understood (Longhurst, 2007). The stories we tell are always circumscribed by the places in which we live and work, and our book is no different. While we acknowledge the value and importance of disrupting the dominance of Anglo-American perspectives, the work discussed in our book emerges mainly from English-language scholars working in the United Kingdom, North America, and Australasia.

The third limitation relates to the fact that such linear stories of 'progress' can give rise to the *false sense of cultural geography as a homogenous intellectual terrain*. Splitting cultural geography into different, paradigmatic phases might have given you the impression that, whereas everyone was doing new cultural geography in the late 1980s and 1990s, by the turn of the millennium, everyone became non-representational. This is not the case. Instead, cultural geography has always been, and will always be, a "pluralistic endeavour" (Price and Lewis, 1993: 3). In fact, cultural geography is arguably one of the most eclectic fields you could study, given its long-held ambition to bridge concepts and methods from across the social sciences, the humanities, and the arts (Lapworth, 2023). This eclecticism is what attracts many people (ourselves included) to study cultural geography. Its reputation for cutting-edge conceptual thinking and methodological experimentalism is something that has been forged, especially in the last few decades, with the rise of non-representational approaches. In recent years, cultural geography has also been the landing site for a whole range of innovative concepts before they are taken up in other subdisciplines of human geography and beyond (the concept of affect, which we discuss at several points in the book, being a clear example of this). The paradigmatic or epochal narrative of cultural geography also tends to emphasise transformation and novelty and can occlude much of what remains the same. The history of cultural geography, as Wylie (2010: 215) notes, might be best understood as a process of "evolution rather than revolution." This is the ethos we wish to capture in this book, where we will address both long-standing and enduring themes in cultural geography, along with an array of new concerns that have emerged as the discipline turns to face many of the urgent challenges facing our world today.

PROBLEMATICS

So far in this chapter, we have explored some of the key characteristics that help distinguish cultural geography from other disciplines, and we have provided a whistle-stop overview of the historical and geographical contexts in which it has evolved. In this final section, we want to spend some time setting out the book's structure, as well as introducing the topics that form the basis of each chapter. But before we get to this, we want to say something about the *problematic* nature of cultural geography and explain how an attention to the problems that animate our thinking has informed our approach to writing this book. We already noted, earlier on in this chapter, that cultural geographers are interested in understanding a seemingly endless array of phenomena, including processes, events, representations, and things. This, we argue, is one of its key strengths, but it leaves us with a difficult question: What kinds of problems become interesting or important when looking at the world through the eyes of a cultural geographer?

In this book, we argue that cultural geography might best be understood not as a fixed domain of inquiry focused on a specific disciplinary object (like 'culture,' for instance, which is an extremely vague term), but rather as a dynamic field for posing, organising, and responding to specific problems that recur, change, and evolve over time. In considering how cultural geography is oriented by and around different problematics, we draw on the innovative approach to understanding problems that appears in the work of the French philosopher, *Gilles Deleuze* (see **Box 1.5**). We turn to Deleuze because his work challenges conventional habits of thinking when it comes to problems, which we tend to imagine as phenomena that are secondary (i.e. as obstacles blocking the path towards correct solutions) and subjective (i.e. as things arising from a person's lack of knowledge). For Deleuze, problems are instead *primary* in the sense that they are generative of a field of possible solutions rather than derivative of them. They are also *objective* in that they are produced by the world rather than by human minds. As Deleuze (2004: 176) puts it, "something in the world forces us to think." That 'something' could be an intense and unexpected encounter with a new technology, an art-house film, a temple on a trip abroad, or another person. While the object encountered is different in each case, the problematic effect is the same in disrupting our habitual patterns of thought and demanding a creative response in how we think and act.

By inscribing problems at the heart of what it means to think, Deleuze is also saying that we risk overlooking the most interesting – indeed, the most vital – dimensions of a problem when we focus too much on the endgame of finding a solution. This might seem a little strange given the long list of real-world problems that are crying out for solutions today. Perhaps the choices that led you to studying cultural geography (and picking up this book) involve a desire to look for solutions to some of the wicked problems of our time, whether that be climate change, profound (and increasing) inequality, discrimination, or creeping technofascism. As cultural geographers, we are motivated by these same desires, and we firmly believe that cultural geography (and hopefully this book) can provide some of the tools to help transform our world for the better. What Deleuze's approach helps us to understand, however, is that it is sometimes necessary to invent new ways of articulating established problems by shifting how we relate to specific ideas and concepts. This is especially the case if we want a future that differs from the present. If there is an underlying ethics to cultural geography, we believe that it is an ethics characterised by a willingness to question the terms by which problems are conventionally framed and to reinvent the concepts we use to think about them. The solution we arrive at matters, but, as Deleuze (1991: 16) suggests, "the problem always has the solution it deserves, in terms of the way in which it is stated." Thus, the ethics of cultural geography lie in the creative pursuit of *new* solutions – which, if you think about it, really are the only solutions worthy of the name!

The titles of the six following chapters (representation, nature, technology, bodies, politics, and methods) are what we perceive to be six of the most important problematics for cultural geography in the way we just described. Think of each as a kind of problem space where the concepts we conventionally think with need shaking up. While many of these constitute important problematics for a range of different social science and humanities disciplines, each of our chapters will highlight how they matter for cultural geography in quite specific and unique ways. As we noted earlier in the introduction, the remit of what counts as an important problem for cultural geography is very broad because of what studying culture from the perspective of geography brings. Nonetheless, we hope that our use of examples throughout the book gives a sense of how cultural geography's reinvention of conceptual problematics provides new perspectives on many of the difficult problems that societies are faced with today.

BOX 1.5 Gilles Deleuze

A French philosopher, born in 1925 and died in 1995. He wrote and taught on an eclectic range of topics, including art (especially literature, cinema, and painting), politics, psychoanalysis (with his collaborator Felix Guattari), ethics, as well as studies of other (often maligned) thinkers in the history of philosophy. Deleuze's philosophy resists a simple and clean summary. But a defining quality was his ongoing attempt to construct a metaphysics that prioritises difference, becoming, and process over categories of the same, identity, and stasis. His work has been enormously influential in contemporary human and cultural geography (as well as the wider social sciences), especially since the 2000s with the rise of non-representational and more-than-human geographies, which draw succour from his detailed critique of the representationalist 'image of thought,' as well as his conceptualisation of the human subject as an emergent, relational assemblage comprising cultural, technological, inorganic, and unconscious components. In the context of cultural geography, Dewsbury's (2000) article remains the best introduction to many of the central concepts of Deleuze's 'philosophy of difference' and their implications for geographical thinking. Outside of geography, John Marks (1998) book *Gilles Deleuze: Vitalism and Multiplicity* is an incredibly lucid account of many of Deleuze's major works. For those looking to start with Deleuze himself, we'd recommend starting with the more interview and discussion format of *Negotiations* (Deleuze, 1995) or *Dialogues II* (Deleuze and Parnet, 2006), which provide helpful introductions to several facets of his thought that can help direct new readers towards which aspects of his philosophy they might like to read next.

We begin in ***Chapter 2*** with the problematic of *Representation*. The chapter explores the changing status of representations in cultural geography, tracing how the various intellectual turns discussed in the opening chapter have differently conceived what they are and what they can do in our worlds. One of the main arguments in this chapter is that there has been an important shift from thinking about representations as epistemological constructs to approaches that conceive them as ontological forces. The chapter highlights non-representational theory as one of the emblems of this more ontological apprehension of representations and challenges the mistaken assumption that the implications of such interventions are that cultural geography has moved away from a concern with images, words, and other practices of (re-)presenting the world. On the contrary, the last decades in cultural geography have brought a new energy to engagement with the practices and materialities of representations, conceiving them not as static objects, but rather as modes of encounter that materially and performatively reshape ways of thinking and living. Through discussions of recent cultural geographic work on cartography, film, and literature, we explore how the emphasis in non-representational geographies falls on what representations *do*: the affective *forces* they express, the transformative *encounters* with thought they produce, and the relational *assemblages* they enter us into.

Chapter 3 focuses on *Nature* as a long-standing problematic in cultural geography. We begin by showing how cultural geography addresses the ontological, epistemological, ethical, and political dimensions of nature – dimensions which cannot be addressed through physical science alone. We then explore how nature as an idea is shaped by the aesthetic preferences, meanings, and values associated with cultural context. To illustrate this, we ask ChatGPT to visualise nature, and we critically analyse its output from a cultural geography perspective. The next section examines how cultural geographers have sought to enlarge their engagement with nature beyond the limits of social constructionist approaches by attending to the natures within culture itself. Here, we turn to Singapore's biophilic architecture to illustrate the contemporary significance of these more recent innovations in cultural geography. The final part of the chapter explores how cultural geography approaches have been applied to the topic of human nature. We show how, for many cultural geographers, the category of 'the human' is not the rigid, unchanging thing we often take it to be, and we explain the significance of this for understanding life in the Anthropocene.

Chapter 4 explores how insights from cultural geography can help us to understand our relationship with *Technology* and to critically evaluate the increasingly pervasive role played by technical machines and devices in shaping our everyday lives. We begin by reflecting on the astounding pace of technological change that has transformed life over the course of the twentieth and twenty-first centuries. Next, we show how the ambiguity of these transformations has led to reactionary conceptualisations, where technology is seen as something that distances human beings from their 'true' nature or destiny. The philosophy of Martin Heidegger provides a key example of such a reactionary approach, and we spend some time unpacking his key ideas and their limitations. Following this, we examine how cultural geographers have developed approaches to technology that are less reactionary by emphasising the co-constitutive relationship between humans and machines, and we unpack this idea through an analysis of intergenerational differences associated with technological change. Finally, we show how researchers in cultural geography are engaging with artificial intelligence (AI) as an emerging technology that is reshaping assumptions about what it means to think, trust, and create today.

Chapter 5 traces the visceral force of *Bodies* across different aspects of cultural geographic thought. Cultural geographers have had much to say about the body and its problematic exclusion from knowledge-making practices. To begin this chapter, we show how cultural geographers have adopted insights from feminist theory to challenge this exclusion and its patriarchal lineage. We then move on to discuss the ideas of Judith Butler, a philosopher whose theory of gender as performative discourse has profoundly shaped cultural geography's engagements with the body since the early 1990s. Butler's work remains an essential tool for grappling with the cultural geographies of the body, and we explain why this is the case through a critical analysis of the Trump Administration's *Executive Order 14168*, which seeks to deny gender by returning to biological essentialism. The final section discusses approaches in cultural geography that push beyond Butler's focus on discourse by emphasising the excessive materiality of bodies. These include insights from critical phenomenology, which focuses on the lived experience of marginalised bodies, and theories of affect and assemblage, which approach the body as an integration of intensive forces and unconscious desires.

Chapter 6 focuses on the rich vein of cultural geographic scholarship exploring the relation between *Politics* and cultural life. It begins with a discussion of cultural geography's understanding of power, which continues to owe a debt to the philosophy of Foucault and, in particular, his *productive* conception of power. A history of modes of power, we argue, is therefore also a history of the kinds of subjects produced by power: from the obedient subjects of sovereign power to the docile and regulated subjects of discipline to the normalised and self-regulating subjectivities of contemporary biopolitics. The chapter also introduces recent scholarship on the concept of 'micropolitics,' and how such work contributes to cultural geography's ongoing efforts to expand the envelope of what counts as the political. We highlight how this concept shifts focus from the already-individuated, sovereign subjects of traditional political theorising to instead engage with the more pre-individual and unconscious forces of affect and desire that give political thought and action so much of its inventive potential.

Chapter 7 addresses the problematic of how to practise cultural geography in the context of empirical research *Methods*. It traces cultural geography's long history of engagement with and innovation in qualitative methodologies, especially 'talk' (interviews, focus groups, and ethnography) and 'text' (discourse analysis and hermeneutics)-based methods. It then addresses the intensification of methodological experimentation in the subdiscipline in the last few decades, as cultural geographers increasingly recognise that addressing the non-human, affective, and non-representational dimensions of cultural life that we set out in earlier chapters of the book demands a move beyond the standard suite of research methods and modes of presentation and dissemination. The chapter highlights two main directions of methodological innovation in contemporary cultural geography. The first relates to ongoing attempts to extend cultural geography's sensory palette beyond its traditional focus on the textual and visual domains through a range of multi-sensory and post-humanist methodologies that emphasise a fuller range of the human body's sensory engagement with the world. The second area of experimentation relates to the growing interest in creative and arts-based methodologies in which we see cultural geographers engaging with the arts and other practices (including film, comic books, creative writing, and drawing) to explore new pathways or the production and dissemination of geographic research.

Chapter 8 ends the book with a brief *Epilogue* on what we call the *ethos* or ethical project of cultural geography. Here, we emphasise how thinking geographically about culture is much more than a matter of generating knowledge about the world: it is also about the way cultural geography perspectives embed new possibilities for valuing the world at the level of our experiences, thoughts, and actions. Our short epilogue offers a speculative sketch of what we believe are the two main facets of this ethos of cultural geography. The first facet is how cultural geography folds a politics of *critique* with an ethics of *creativity*. Rather than just negating or disqualifying the already-existing, cultural geographic thought is also often oriented towards creative experiments with new and different modes of thinking and practising. The second facet is cultural geography's critique of anthropocentric habits of thought and its creative commitment to think both the question of 'culture' and 'the human' anew in relation to a more-than-human world.

HOW TO READ THIS BOOK

We have written this book with the intention that it can be read in different ways, depending on the reader's interests, the constraints placed on their time, and the level of familiarity that they may (or may not) have with cultural geography and related disciplines. How you approach this book will depend on these and other variables; however, to help readers navigate their way through the book, we want to briefly discuss some of its key features.

Perhaps most importantly, we have deliberately structured the book to enable the individual chapters to be read independently and even out of order. Our reason for doing this is that we realise undergraduate students are increasingly time-poor (especially if they are working part-time jobs to fund their university studies). Each of the book's chapters stands on its own, which means you can skip topics that aren't of interest or choose your own adventure by jumping between chapters. Reading the book from cover to cover will provide a deeper sense of the way concepts, debates, and key figures recur and relate to one another across the full range of cultural geography's research problematics, but we realise that this mode of reading is not available to everyone.

Text Boxes are another key feature of this book; you will find a selection of these in each chapter. Each Box has been designed to provide a concise discussion of a key idea, intellectual movement, or influential thinker that has had a significant impact on cultural geography. We appreciate that cultural geography's diversity, while being one of its main strengths, can also be disorienting for those who are encountering it for the first time, and so we hope that the inclusion of these Boxes will serve as waypoints for these readers. We have also provided prompts for readers to return to earlier Boxes for more concise overviews where appropriate.

Finally, a Further Reading section can be found at the end of each chapter. Here you will find a short selection of key resources for those readers wishing to explore the topics encountered in each chapter in greater detail. A full list of all the sources cited can be found in the Reference list.

FURTHER READING

Dewsbury, J.-D. "Performativity and the event: Enacting a philosophy of difference." *Environment and Planning D: Society and Space* 18, no. 4 (2000): 473–496. https://doi.org/10.1068/d200t

Johnston, R. and J. D. Sidaway (eds.). *Geography and Geographers: Anglo-American Human Geography since 1945* (7th ed.). London: Routledge, 2016.

Livingstone, D. *The Geographical Tradition: Episodes in the History of a Contested Enterprise*. Oxford: Blackwell, 1992.

Whatmore, S. "Materialist returns: Practising cultural geography in and for a more-than-human world." *Cultural Geographies* 13, no. 4 (2006): 600–609. https://www.jstor.org/stable/44251128

Wylie, J. *Landscape*. London: Routledge, 2007.

REFERENCES

Allen, D., M. Lawhon and J. Pierce. "Placing race: On the resonance of place with black geographies." *Progress in Human Geography* 43, no. 6 (2019): 1001–1019. https://doi.org/10.1177/0309132518803775

Anderson, B. and P. Harrison (eds.). *Taking Place: Non-Representational Theories and Geography*. Farnham: Ashgate, 2010.

Battersby, J. "Country reports: Seeking African solutions: The new social and cultural geographies of South Africa." *Social & Cultural Geography* 5, no. 1 (2004): 151–157. https://doi.org/10.1080/1464936042000181371

Bennett, J. *Vibrant Matter: A Political Ecology of Things*. Durham, NC: Duke University Press, 2010.

Bissell, D. "Feeling out of it: Displacement, disengagement and dispossession in experiences of brain fog." *Dialogues in Human Geography* (2025). https://doi.org/10.1177/20438206251321091

Bissell, D., M. Rose and P. Harrison (eds.). *Negative Geographies: Exploring the Politics of Limits*. Lincoln, NE: University of Nebraska Press, 2021.

Clayton, J. "Colonising, settling and the origins of academic geography." In J. A. Agnew and J. S. Duncan (eds.) *The Wiley-Blackwell Companion to Human Geography* (pp. 50–70). New Jersey: Wiley Blackwell, 2011.

Cosgrove, D. *Social Formation and Symbolic Landscape*. Madison, WN: University of Wisconsin Press, 1984.

Cosgrove, D. and P. Jackson. "New directions in cultural geography." *Area* 19, no. 2 (1987): 95–101. https://www.jstor.org/stable/20002425

Dawney, L. and T. Jellis. "Endurance, exhaustion and the lure of redemption." *Cultural Geographies* 31, no. 2 (2024): 153–166. https://doi.org/10.1177/14744740231191535

Dekeyser, T., A. Secor, M. Rose, D. Bissell, V. Zhang and J. L. Romanillos. "Negativity: Space, politics and affects." *Cultural Geographies* 29, no. 1 (2022): 5–21. https://doi.org/10.1177/14744740211058080

Deleuze, G. *Bergsonism*. New York: Zone, 1991.

Deleuze, G. *Negotiations 1972–1990*. New York: Columbia University Press, 1995.

Deleuze, G. *Difference and Repetition*. London: Continuum, 2004.

Deleuze, G. and C. Parnet. *Dialogues II*. London: Continuum, 2006.

Dowling, R. "Social and cultural geographies of Australia." *Social & Cultural Geography* 6, no. 5 (2005): 767–775. https://www.tandfonline.com/doi/abs/10.1080/14649360500258427

Harrison, P. "How shall I say it . . .? Relating the nonrelational." *Environment and Planning A: Economy and Space* 39, no. 3 (2007): 590–608. https://doi.org/10.1068/a3825

Hsin-Ling, W., J. Sue-Ching and L. Kong. "The development of social and cultural geographies in Taiwan: Knowledge production and social relevance." *Social & Cultural Geography* 7, no. 5 (2006): 827–845. https://doi.org/10.1080/14649360600974790

Huntington, E. *The Character of Races as Influenced by Physical Environment, Natural Selection, and Historical Development*. New York: Charles Scribner's Sons, 1924.

Jackson, P. *Maps of Meaning: An Introduction to Cultural Geography*. London: Routledge, 1989.

Jackson, P. "Rematerialising social and cultural geography." *Social & Cultural Geography* 1, no. 1 (2000): 9–14. https://doi.org/10.1080/14649369950133449

Kinkaid, E. and W. Sharp. "Queer and trans lives." In P. Merriman, S. Sumartojo and A. Secod (eds.) *The Routledge Handbook of Cultural Geographies* (pp. 247–259). London: Routledge, 2026.

Lapworth, A. "Theorizing bioart encounters after Gilbert Simondon." *Theory, Culture & Society* 33 no. 3 (2016): 123–150. https://doi.org/10.1177/0263276415580173

Lapworth, A. "Cultural geographies." In L. Lees and D. Demeritt (eds.) *Concise Encyclopedia of Human Geography* (pp. 84–88). Cheltenham: Edward Elgar Publishing, 2023.

Ley, D. "Cultural/humanistic geography." *Progress in Human Geography* 5, no. 2 (1981): 249–257.

Longhurst, R. "Cultural geography: Different encounters, encountering difference." *Documents d'Anàlisi Geogràfica* 50 (2007): 105–120. https://doi.org/10.5565/rev/dag.1037

Lorimer, H. "Cultural geography: The busyness of being more-than-representational." *Progress in Human Geography* 29, no. 1 (2005): 83–94. https://doi.org/10.1191/0309132505ph531pr

Marks, J. *Gilles Deleuze: Vitalism and Multiplicity*. London: Pluto Press, 1998.

Massey, D. *For Space*. London: Sage, 2005.

May, J. A. *Kant's Concept of Geography and its Relation to Recent Geographical Thought*. Toronto: University of Toronto Press, 1970.

McCormack, D. "Thinking in transition: The affirmative refrain of experience/experiment." In B. Anderson and P. Harrison (eds.) *Taking Place: Non-Representational Theories and Geography* (pp. 201–220). London: Ashgate, 2010.

Mori, M. "Translation and transformation: Transactions in Japanese social and cultural geography." *Social & Cultural Geography* 10, no. 3 (2009): 369–397. https://doi.org/10.1080/14649360902759956

Mutter, S. " 'The encounter may not take place': Negative geographies, negative mobilities." *Cultural Geographies* 32, no. 4 (2025): 485–500. https://doi.org/10.1177/14744740251343601

Nash, C. "Cultural geography: Postcolonial cultural geographies." *Progress in Human Geography* 26, no. 2 (2002): 219–230. https://doi.org/10.1191/0309132502ph365pr

Nayak, A. and D. Berwick. "Black lives." In P. Merriman, S. Sumartojo and A. Secod (eds.) *The Routledge Handbook of Cultural Geographies* (pp. 141–153). London: Routledge, 2026.

Philo, C. *New Words, New Worlds: Reconceptualising Social and Cultural Geography*. Lampeter: Social and Cultural Geography Research Group, 1991.

Philo, C. and V. Zhang. *Revisiting 'New Words, New Worlds': A Correspondence*. Bristol: Social and Cultural Geography Research Group, 2024.

Price, M. and M. Lewis. "The reinvention of cultural geography." *Annals of the American Association of Geographers* 83, no. 1 (1993): 1–17. https://doi.org/10.1111/j.1467-8306.1993.tb01920.x

Queering Feminist Geography Collective, E. Kinkaid, W. Sharp, S. Fogel, A. Bandagi Kandlakunta, G. Kirk and K. Emard. "Queering feminist geography II: Working through and working against trans-exclusionary feminisms." *Gender, Place & Culture* 32, no. 9 (2025): 1445–1455. https://doi.org/10.1080/0966369X.2025.2516848

Roberts, T. "From 'new materialism' to 'machinic assemblage': Agency and affect in IKEA." *Environment and Planning A: Economy and Space* 44, no. 10 (2012): 2512–2529. https://doi.org/10.1068/a44692

Roberts, T. and J-D. Dewsbury. "Vital aspirations for geography in an era of negativity: Valuing life differently with Deleuze." *Progress in Human Geography* 45, no. 6 (2021): 1512–1530. https://doi.org/10.1177/0309132521996462

Roberts, T., A. Lapworth, L. Koh and M. Ghasri. "Negotiating trust in AI-enabled technologies: Imaginaries, ecologies, habits." *Social & Cultural Geography* 26, no. 2 (2025): 160–178. https://doi.org/10.1080/14649365.2024.2399239

Rose, G. *Feminism and Geography: The Limits of Geographical Knowledge*. Minneapolis, MN: University of Minnesota Press, 1993.

Rose, M. "Defining culture." In P. Merriman, A. Secor and S. Sumartojo (eds.) *The Routledge Handbook of Cultural Geographies* (pp. 127–137). Abingdon: Routledge, 2026.

Sauer, C. O. "The morphology of landscape." *University of California Publications in Geography* 2, no. 2 (1925): 19–54.

Sauer, C. O. *The Early Spanish Main*. Berkeley, CA: University of California Press, 1966.

Simpson, P. *Non-Representational Theory*. London: Routledge, 2020.

Steinbeck, J. *Of Mice and Men*. Harlow: Pearson Education Ltd, 2000.

Thrift, N. "Over-wordy worlds: Thoughts and worries." In C. Philo (ed.) *New Words, New Worlds: Reconceptualising Social and Cultural Geography* (pp. 144–148). Lampeter: Social and Cultural Geography Study Group, 1991.

Thrift, N. *Spatial Formations*. London: Sage, 1996.

Tuan, Y-F. "Humanistic geography." *Annals of the American Association of Geographers* 66, no. 2 (1976): 266–276.

Vaiou, D. "Country report: The ambiguities of social and cultural geography in Greece." *Social & Cultural Geography* 6, no. 3 (2005): 455–469. https://doi.org/10.1080/14649360500111469

Wainwright, E., J. Barker, N. Ansell, S. Buckingham, P. Hemming and F. Smith. "Geographers out of place: Institutions, (inter)disciplinarity and identity." *Area* 46, no. 4 (2014): 410–417. https://doi.org/10.1111/area.12126

Wylie, J. "A single day's walking: Narrating self and landscape on the South West Coast Path." *Transactions of the Institute of British Geographers* 30, no. 2 (2005): 234–247. https://doi.org/10.1111/j.1475-5661.2005.00163.x

Wylie, J. "Cultural geographies of the future, or looking rosy and feeling blue." *Cultural Geographies* 17, no. 2 (2010): 211–217. https://doi.org/10.1177/1474474010363852

2

(NON-)REPRESENTATION

INTRODUCTION: CULTURAL GEOGRAPHY AND REPRESENTATION

Geographers have been interested in the problematic of representation for a very long time. In fact, representation is part of geography's ancient origin story. The Greek origins of the word geography (γεωγραφία) are *geo*-(meaning 'earth') and *graphia*-(meaning 'to write'). Geography, as 'earth-writing,' thus literally means taking the world as we experience it and translating this into words and images that re-present this experience. Another way of thinking about this is that geography, as a mode of thinking and practice, is something that emerges at the interface between *word* and *world.* Whenever we do geography, we are therefore always involved in the practice (and, as we'll see, the *politics*) of re-presenting the things that matter to us.

While representation is an important concern across multiple subdisciplines of human geography (including social, economic, and political geographies), it is in cultural geography that we witness the deepest and most passionate engagement with the concept of representation. We decided to begin our book with this theme because some of the most significant transformations in cultural geography over the last few decades have been concerned with the status of representations: how we should conceptualise them; what exactly they 'do' in our worlds; and even how much importance should be placed on them in cultural geographic thought and practice. These transformations, which have also had

DOI: 10.4324/9781003542667-2

an impact beyond cultural geography on how representation is imagined across the broader social sciences, are the focus of this chapter.

In brief, one of the main arguments we want to make in this chapter is that there has been an important shift from thinking about representations as *epistemological* constructs to approaches that conceive them as *ontological* forces (see **Box 2.1** and **2.2**). The epistemological approach to representation has a long history in Western philosophy. For the French philosopher, René Descartes, representation was seen as synonymous with thought and reason. The capacity to represent the world in complex perceptions and abstract concepts was seen by Descartes as precisely that which separated humans from animals (we will return to Descartes' philosophy in greater detail in subsequent chapters). The vital role of representation in human cognition was famously developed even further in the transcendental idealism of Immanuel Kant. Kant's philosophy sought to uncover the inherent (or *a priori*) rules of human thought that allow representations to take place. Moral judgement, common sense, and the *a priori* Forms of the understanding (e.g. 'Space' and 'Time') are examples of such transcendental rules that enable humans to organise the otherwise chaotic sensory data of the world into recognisable and spatially situated objects. While the universalising impulses of Kantian idealism have been the subject of serious challenges in geography, his fundamental understanding of representation as an epistemological process that mediates our access to the world, and through which knowledge and meaning of objects and places are constituted, has been a pervasive influence on geographical and social science thinking.

BOX 2.1 Epistemology

Epistemology is a branch of philosophy concerned with the theory of knowledge. It is interested in asking the question of what we are capable of knowing and the procedures and methods through which we come to know the world.

BOX 2.2 Ontology

Ontology is a branch of philosophy concerned with the nature of being. It probes the question of what exactly constitutes reality, or 'what exists'?

However, since the late 1990s, we have seen the emergence within cultural geography of alternative perspectives that think of representations differently: as *ontological* 'forces' (Anderson, 2019) or 'events' (Dewsbury et al., 2002) that are constantly in flux and that more immediately and materially intervene in our worlds. Often referred to as non-representational theories, such works shift attention "from the *posited meaning* towards the *material composition and conduct* of representations" (Dewsbury et al., 2002: 438). The focus here is thus not what a representation means or signifies, but rather the material and inventive transformations that representations enact in our modes of thinking and living. In other words, what non-representational theorists are interested in is not just what representations mean but what representations *do*. This might be the sudden tears that well up while watching a scene of a film that brings back memories of a departed loved one. Or the random and seemingly insignificant line of a novel that brings a dramatically new perspective of the sense and significance of the events currently happening in your life. Most of us have a painting, a film, a song, or a performance that has done something like this. Of course, these non-representational transformations don't need to be quite so dramatic. The American author, Raymond Carver (2009: 748), nicely captures the more modest interventions that representations can play in stretching the expression of the world when he writes:

> If we're lucky, writer and reader alike, we'll finish the last line of a story and then just sit there for a minute. Ideally, we'll ponder what we've just written or read; maybe our hearts or our intellects will have been moved off the peg just a little from where they were before. Our body temperature will have gone up, or down, by a degree. Then, breathing evenly and steadily once more, we'll collect ourselves . . . and go on to the next thing: Life. Always life.

But we've got some ground to cover before we get to this! The next few sections of the chapter will explore the changing status and understanding of representation in geography, moving through key phases of conceptual and methodological innovation in how cultural geographers engage with the representational domain. The emphasis of this discussion will often fall on the differences between how the important subdisciplinary 'turns' that we discussed in the introduction – like humanistic geography of the 1980s, the 'new cultural geographies' of the 1990s, and non-representational theories of the 2000s – differently conceive of representations and their significance in cultural life. However, we feel it is also important to note a couple of first principles that we believe most contemporary cultural geographers, of whatever theoretical stripe, are likely to (probably!) agree on.

The first of these is that *representations matter*. Representations can and do arouse passionate feelings and emotions in people. As a result, they also become the site of intense disagreement and contestation over who and what are represented (and conversely, who and what aren't). For example, we might think of the protests related to Black Lives Matter in Bristol in the United Kingdom in July 2020 that saw the toppling of the bronze statue of the transatlantic slave trader, Edward Colston, and its dumping at the bottom of Bristol harbour. Such an event is the latest in a long history of popular struggles regarding which identities get represented and which histories get told in the iconic spaces of our cities. Second, *representations are never neutral*. They are not transparent and unbiased windows on reality 'as-it-is.' They are instead always selective presentations of the world that foreground certain aspects (e.g. identities, objects, thoughts, perceptions, and affects) and background or silence others. Representations are thus always the product of diverse and ever-shifting contexts and are profoundly shaped by, for example, the institutional interests, social desires, and technological processes that define the times and places of their emergence. Third, *representations do things*. They are, in the words of Anderson (2019: 1120), "activities that enable, sustain, interrupt, consolidate, or otherwise (re)make forms or ways of life." It is on this final point that non-representational theories really prove their salt by highlighting how representations do not simply reinforce or subvert already-existing meanings and identities but instead performatively re-make the world, inventing entirely new ways of thinking, feeling, and living.

However, despite these overlaps, the differences between the approaches to representation discussed in this chapter matter. These differences are much more than just a subtle change in emphasis or a slightly different set of conceptual terminologies. There are important ethical and political stakes in the philosophies and theoretical frameworks we choose to engage with in our work. Theory transforms the kinds of questions it is possible to ask, redirecting attention to aspects of our world long underexplored or underappreciated. Deleuze (2001: 66) succinctly captures this sense of the transformative entanglement of thought and life when he writes, “modes of life inspire ways of thinking; modes of thinking create ways of living.” By the end of this chapter, we hope you will have a sense of the different implications of these theoretical approaches to representation in cultural geography and the new ways of thinking and inhabiting the world they make possible.

THE 'CRISIS OF REPRESENTATION'

For a long time, representations were often taken at face value in geography. As Barron and Blakey (2023: 343) note, the rise of quantitative approaches in human geography from the 1950s “shifted the discipline away from providing detailed accounts of places towards abstracted representations based on seemingly objective and transparent mathematical modelling.” The geographical models, maps, and graphs produced by this new spatial science were viewed as objective and transparent windows to the world, supposedly unimpeded by the experience and identity of the researcher. From the 1970s onwards, a whole series of challenges emerged against the quantitative representations of this spatial science in geography. The first of these relates to the rise of humanistic geographies which sought to challenge the “emaciated version of the human that existed within spatial science” (Simpson, 2020: 26). Instead, these approaches introduced more qualitative and phenomenological accounts of embodiment and dwelling (drawing primarily on the work of philosophers like Martin Heidegger and Maurice Merleau-Ponty) that sharpened attention to the role of subjective experience, beliefs, memories, attachments, and aesthetic judgements in the creation of geographical knowledge. The second challenge arose from Marxist-informed *radical geographies* of the 1970s and 1980s (see **Box 2.3**). Across a series of works, critical human geographer David Harvey developed a neo-Marxist political economy of the city, one which took forward the ideas of philosopher Henri Lefebvre to emphasise the crucial role that representational practices (e.g. the idealistic visions of the city in the master plans of architects and urban elites) play in the reproduction of social injustice.

BOX 2.3 Radical geographies

A movement that emerged in human geography from the 1970s out of a dissatisfaction with the apolitical character of quantitative geography and in response to social issues of the late 1960s, including inequality, racism, environmental destruction, and the Vietnam War. One of its notable figureheads was (and remains) David Harvey, who saw in radical geography the attempt to create a "radical science which seeks not only to explain what is happening but also to prescribe revolutionary change" (Peet, 1998: 109). The theoretical basis for Harvey (and other radical geographers) was the philosophy of Karl Marx and his analysis of capitalist economic development and class struggle.

But it is in the 1980s, and through the rapid spread of *post-structuralism* across geography and the wider social sciences, that we witness some of the most profound transformations in how representations were conceived in the discipline. Post-structuralism, as the name suggests, challenged *structuralist* accounts that asserted the primacy of human language in the making of meaning and viewed this language as a structured system of 'signs' and 'significations.' Perhaps the most influential structuralist thinker of the twentieth century was the Swiss linguist, Ferdinand de Saussure, who viewed humans as *semiotic creatures* that generate meaning through the interpretation of various 'signs' that compose our social worlds. Saussure argued that each sign is composed of the relation of two elements: the *signified* (the idea or concept of something in our minds) and the *signifier* (the material referent, such as a sound, a written inscription, or a material object). For example, we can think of the word 'OPEN' hanging on a board in a shop window (*signifier*) and our understanding that the shop is open for business (*signified*). Human communication and sense-making, Saussure argues, depend on these semiotic chains of signifier-signified that we come to learn through cultural convention and habit. However, one of Saussure's central arguments is that these semiotic relations are arbitrary social constructions, shaped by culture. There is no natural or necessary reason why any given word or image should correspond to a specific object or idea. Saussure argues that if semiotic chains are arbitrary, then there must be a set of rules and principles (much like the rules of a board game) to which we must abide if communication is to work. The task of a structuralist linguistics is to uncover the structures and rules that govern communication and which shape how meaning is created and interpreted.

Post-structuralist thinkers were influenced by this constructivist understanding of meaning and sense. But they were also deeply suspicious of the idea of there being some universal and unconscious structures or foundations to human knowledge and the supposed capacity of the theorist to step back and unveil its hidden structure. Challenging the supposed uniformity and stability of meaning in human communication, the rise of post-structuralism incited what many termed a 'crisis of representation' in the social sciences, giving rise to "doubts about the existence of a world filled with naturally given and enduring meanings that could be unlocked, as well as of new understandings of knowledge as inescapably partial and power-laden" (Scott, 2009: 351). Several key theorists served as sources of inspiration for this post-structuralist reimagining of representation, including philosophers like Jacques Derrida, Roland Barthes, Jean Baudrillard, and Michel de Certeau. However, here we want to spotlight two post-structuralist thinkers who were arguably of the greatest importance in driving this renewed engagement with representation in cultural geography.

BOX 2.4 Michel Foucault

A French philosopher and historian who was born in 1926 and died in 1984. He is one of the most highly cited thinkers in the social sciences and humanities, and his influence on cultural geography has been immense. Foucault is best known for his writings on the genealogy of institutions (especially asylums and prisons), the relation of power and knowledge (which will be discussed in more detail in ***Chapter 6***), and theories and practices of the self. His work has had a transformative impact on cultural geography since at least the 1980s, especially in relation to debates around subjectivity, the body, and social power. For an early and clear exposition of the import of Foucault's philosophy for geographical theories of space, see the paper 'Foucault's Geography' by Chris Philo in the journal *Environment and Planning D: Society and Space* (Philo, 1992).

The first of these is the French philosopher *Michel Foucault* (see **Box 2.4**). While Foucault's writings comprised a vast terrain of concerns and ideas, early geographical engagements tended to primarily focus on his concept of discourse (we will return to this concept in more detail when we explore cultural geography's engagement with the body in ***Chapter 5***). Foucault's understanding of discourse, however, is something quite different from our colloquial understandings of the term, where it is often used to mean written or spoken communication. Discourse signifies much more than just text and speech for Foucault. It instead refers to sets of material acts and bodily practices that affect the knowledge we produce about ourselves and others and the stories we tell about the things around us. Foucault's 'genealogical method' – developed in books like *Discipline and Punish* and *The Order of Things* – involved the historical tracing of discursive formations and how they differently constitute what it was possible to see and say – the visible and sayable – within different social and spatial contexts. In other words, what can and can't be represented in specific places and times. Foucault argues that discursive formations are never neutral but are rather shot through with relations of power, including, as Kobayashi (2020: 423) notes, "the power of the body to represent itself . . . as well as the power of historical institutions to regulate the body." One of the aspects of Foucault's work that most attracted geographers was the explicit attention he drew to how the spatial and material design of a society's institutions (like prisons, asylums, hospitals, and other spaces of confinement) impose limits on what can be seen and said about bodies and what bodies can think and do.

Geographical engagements with Foucault's work have also sought to develop modes of discourse analysis as a distinct approach for interpreting various types of representational objects and texts. J. B. Harley (1988: 278), for example, applies discourse analysis to the study of colonial-era maps, uncovering how subliminal geometries (e.g. the centring of Europe in the famous Mercator projection), deliberate distortions (misrepresentations of the relative size of countries), and cartographic absences and silences (of original inhabitants and place names in colonial maps) contribute to how maps come to shape "ways of conceiving, articulating, and structuring the human world which is biased towards . . . particular sets of social relations." An example studied by Harley in his landmark text, *The New Nature of Maps: Essays in the History of Cartography* are cartographic representations of the British Empire produced in the 1800s. Such maps often overemphasised the size of the United Kingdom, which appears bigger than countries in Africa, including the island of Madagascar, which in reality is more than twice the size of the United Kingdom! Imperial maps also often depicted Britain's colonial possession using the colour pink, showing the global reach of its empire. The purpose of such colonial maps was not simply to describe, but to express and legitimise sovereign ownership over particular places. They were made to persuade the map's readers on both sides of the Atlantic of British ownership rights over parts of the North American continent and in other territories across the globe. Far from innocent representations, Harley (1988: 282) argues that maps must be understood as much a "weapon of imperialism" as guns and warships.

The second perspective comes from a range of critical theoretical approaches in cultural geography in the 1980s, including feminist, anti-racist, and, especially, *post-colonial* geographies (see **Box 2.5**). Geographical engagements with post-colonial theories, as Anderson (2019: 1124) notes, brought a critical focus on the question of "who speaks," attempting to understand "how the content (and occasionally the form) of representations expressed and reproduced social structures." A major influence on this kind of geographical engagement with representation is the theorist Gayatri Chakravorty Spivak. In her iconic essay 'Can the Subaltern Speak?' Spivak (1988) distinguishes between two main types of representation. The first is what Spivak refers to as 'speaking *of* others.' The focus here is on how representations often work to construct others according to "historically specific norms of race, class, and gender"

(Kobayashi, 2020: 424). For example, Edward Said's (1978) famous discussion of 'Orientialism' has been particularly influential for geographers in thinking about the role of cultural texts and practices (like novels, travel diaries, and films) in producing a certain exoticised imaginary of colonial peoples and spaces and as a means to perpetuate and justify forms of colonial power and domination (Clayton, 2011).

BOX 2.5 Post-colonial theory

A field of study concerned with the impact of colonialism (usually understood as the period between the sixteenth and eighteenth centuries) on both colonised and colonising populations and the way in which these impacts continue to be felt in the practices, representations, identities, and relations of the present. Post-colonial theories have their origins in literary and cultural studies, especially the ideas of Edward Said and Gayatri Chakravorty Spivak, whom we briefly discuss in this chapter. Key areas of debate that have shaped post-colonialist work in cultural geography include histories of colonial mapping of 'Other' peoples and places; the transgression of dominant identities through forms and processes of hybridity; the reproduction of colonial dominance through various 'neo-colonial' institutions at national and transnational scales; and emerging forms of resistance to the past and present violences of colonialism through projects of decolonisation.

The second type of representation is what Spivak calls 'Speaking *for* others.' Here, representations aren't always only about domination and subjugation but can also form the basis through which "social groups can mobilise in order to create the discursive space for social change" (Kobayashi, 2020: 424). This may involve forms of strategic disruption or inversion of dominant representational logics and imaginaries of (gendered, raced, and classed) bodies. A cultural geographic example of this is Catherine Nash's analysis of the gendered representation of landscape in the photography series *Abroad* created by the Irish artist Diane Bayliss. Analysing one of the images from this collection, Nash shows how what appears at first glance to be a pastoral scene of undulating hills and patchy shrubs is, on closer inspection, really an image of a man's naked torso. Here, the naked male form in Bayliss' photographs becomes an allegory for the gendered symbolism and meaning of traditional landscape art, which commonly portrays women's bodies as 'passive' objects to be interpreted by the 'active' male gaze. Nash (1996: 166) thus shows how Bayliss disrupts "the dominant representational systems and gendered and sexual subject positions and offers pleasures which are not limited to male heterosexual appraisal of women."

'NEW CULTURAL GEOGRAPHY' AND THE POLITICS OF REPRESENTATION

Common to post-structuralist, post-colonial, and feminist analyses of representation is an explicit attention to the (more or less obvious) *political* dimensions of cultural representations. These approaches coalesced in the mid-to-late 1980s with the emergence of what is often referred to as 'new cultural geography.' A key aspect of new cultural geography was to conceive of representational objects and practices (like maps, films, paintings, and so on) as forms of *text* that could be subject to critical interpretation by the geographical researcher. To analyse such representational texts, cultural geographers developed a series of interpretative methodologies drawn from art history and the humanities, especially the iconographic method popularised by the art historian Erwin Panofsky (Daniels and Cosgrove, 1988). Seen from an iconographic perspective, and rather than providing transparent windows on a purported 'real' world, "images and language are now regarded as a sort of sign that presents a deceptive appearance of naturalness and transparency concealing an opaque, distorting, arbitrary mechanism of representation, a process of ideological mystification" (Cosgrove and Jackson, 1987: 98). For new cultural geographers, analysing representations in this way also invariably meant an analysis of power relations and how specific cultural texts expressed or reproduced existing social hierarchies. As Anderson (2019: 1121) puts it, the principal concern of cultural geographers in this period was to try to uncover the "symbolic and material violence of representations" and to demonstrate how they "(re)produced unequal classed, gendered, and racialized power relations" in the very world that they claimed to represent.

As well as emphasising the social and political dimension of representations, another key contribution of new cultural geography was to shift the subdiscipline away from what authors like Cosgrove and Jackson (1987: 98) perceived as its "elitist and antiquarian predilections" for certain kinds of high art (e.g. poetry, literature, classical painting). In this regard, new cultural geographers took inspiration from the exciting work emerging from the Birmingham Centre for Cultural Studies in the 1970s and 1980s, and especially that of one of its figureheads, Stuart Hall (Hall, 1997). Unlike traditional cultural studies work, the research of Hall and his colleagues was focused on the diversity of cultural practices adopted by various subcultural groups (such as Black British art and culture in Britain in the 1980s) and their expression within various forms of 'popular' culture. Starting from the late 1980s, we thus see cultural geographers exploring issues of cultural identity and power in relation to an expanded range of spaces of cultural representation, including Hollywood films, country music, TV comedy shows, newspapers and magazines, and even popular comic books.

This broadening of the kinds of representations that were deemed deserving of critical analysis continues to shape work within cultural geography to this day. Jason Dittmer (2005, 2012), for example, has published work analysing the popular Marvel series *Captain America* from 1940 to the present, exploring how comic book representations can reinforce notions of American national identity as well as construct geopolitical frames that shape how readers interpret historical and world events. Dittmer (2005) explores how, for much of the post-war period, *Captain America* comics often represented a dichotomous geopolitical landscape comprising the 'Self' (Captain America as the personification of US national identity) in constant struggle with the 'Other' (America's geopolitical 'enemies' – Imperial Japan, Nazi Germany, and the USSR), but also how this narrative changes in the wake of the events of 9/11 towards a more nuanced and self-critical reflection on American imperialism and hegemony and its potential role in creating a more unsafe world. By analysing these different forms of 'textual' representation, the work of Dittmer and other cultural geographers was interested in how popular cultural representations can come to inform practices of domination or resistance, as well as infuse the assertion or subversion of specific identities and subjectivities.

NON-REPRESENTATIONAL THEORIES AND GEOGRAPHY

As we noted in the introduction, by the mid-1990s, a growing number of geographers began to express dissatisfaction about the tendency of new cultural geography to fix the vibrancy and multiplicity of the world into "dead geographies" of text, discourse, and meaning (Thrift and Dewsbury, 2000: 411). One of the leading figures of this charge against the 'deadening' impact of new cultural geography's representationalism was the British geographer Nigel Thrift. Thrift (1996: 5) rallied against a dominant tendency in cultural geography in which "a hardly problematised sphere of representation [was] allowed to take precedence over lived experience and materiality, usually as a series of images or texts which a theorist contemplatively deconstructs thus implicitly degrading practice." In his book *Spatial Formations*, Thrift (1996) levelled three main charges at the representationalism that had come to dominate 'new' cultural geography. The first concerns *distance*, and the scholarly disposition of representational geographies to divorce the 'observing subject' from the 'observed object' of research. New cultural geography, for Thrift, was thus based on a kind of "discursive idealism," one which presumed that people's access to and knowledge of the world was principally an interpretive one mediated by the signifying systems of language and textuality (Anderson, 2019: 1121). The second charge levelled at representationalism was its emphasis on a kind of *codification* that seeks to capture and fix the represented according to an already-existing grid of stable identities and meanings (Castree and MacMillan, 2004). What is missed by such an approach, Thrift argues, is the ongoing creative *process* of our lives (those transformative events, chance encounters, and unexpected detours that make up the everyday), which cannot be fully and neatly understood according to the frameworks and logics of the already-known. Third, Thrift was concerned with the overemphasis in cultural geography on cognition, speech, and vision "as if they were the only or privileged way of knowing things and, thus, of doing things" (Castree and MacMillan, 2004: 472). Instead, Thrift's ambition was to get in touch with a much broader range of the sensory processes and practical intelligences through which bodies come to think and act in the world, including precognitive reflexes, embodied habits, and unconscious feelings, or 'affects' (we will have more to say on these embodied dimensions of culture in ***Chapter 5***).

There has been a misplaced assumption in critical engagements with non-representational theory that it is associated with a turn away from representational objects and practices (see Nash, 2000). It is perhaps more accurate to say that the issue is not representations per se but *representationalism*, understood as a particular, interpretative mode of engaging with things like texts and images (Dewsbury et al., 2002). Instead, non-representational geographers have brought a renewed energy and vitality to the study of texts and images and offered a much more empirically expansive sense of what representations can do in the world. In one of the most influential manifestos of early non-representational geographies, Dewsbury et al. (2002: 438) set out non-representational theorising in the following terms:

> We want to work on presenting the world, not on representing it, or explaining it. Our understanding of non-representational theory is that it is characterised by a firm belief in the actuality of representations. It does not approach representations as masks, gazes, reflections, veils, dreams, ideologies, as anything, in short, that is a covering which is laid over the ontic. NRT takes representation seriously; not as a code to be broken or as an illusion to be dispelled, rather representations are apprehended as performative in themselves; as doings. The point here is to redirect attention from the posited meanings to the material composition and conduct of representations.

Another way of grasping this is to say that non-representational geographies re-engage representations as live 'problems' in the sense we described in the introduction. Here, the interest falls on how representations perpetually exceed the known categories and frameworks of thought, to instead enact novel transformations in how we think, feel, and relate. In developing this more transformative apprehension of representations, Dewsbury et al. (2002) take special inspiration from the philosophy of Gilles Deleuze. In the work often regarded as his magnum opus – *Difference and Repetition* (Deleuze, 2004) – Deleuze mounts a sustained attack on what he terms the 'representational image of thought' that deadens our thinking and experience of the world, reducing our encounters to logics of resemblance, identity, and the repetition of the same. What is lost here, Deleuze argues, is precisely our capacity to grasp hold of and to think about what is different, new, and surprising in the world around us. Dewsbury et al. (2002) argue that what Deleuzian philosophy offers is a way of theorising things like art, images, and texts outside of the representationalist set-up: in other words, as ontological events generative of difference rather than merely as reproductions of the same. And here they turn to the ontological account of the art encounter outlined by Deleuze and Guattari (1994) in *What is Philosophy*, where they define the artwork as a "being of sensation." If the sensations produced by art 'refer to' or 'represent' anything, then it is only to the materialities of art itself and not the objects or persons that their depictions happen to resemble (Roberts et al., 2022). As Deleuze and Guattari (1994: 166) themselves put it:

> If resemblance haunts the work of art it is because sensation refers only to its material: it is the percept or affect of the material itself, the smile of oil, the gesture of fired clay, the thrust of metal, the crouch of Romanesque stone, and the ascent of Gothic stone.

A non-representational approach to artistic representations thus pays explicit attention to these pre-conscious and material sensations (the 'affects' and 'percepts' mentioned by Deleuze and Guattari in the quote above) that bypass the habitual and conditioned responses that we presume to be the unchanging and universal features of human experience and instead give rise to creative potentials of thinking and acting.

This emphasis on the pre-individual and non-conscious dynamics of affect and sensation has been one of the aspects of non-representational theory that some human geographers have found the most difficult to digest. Early critics of non-representational theory in geography expressed anxieties around what they perceived to be a kind of universalist sense of the human that is unable to attend to the lived realities and specificities of embodied and social difference, especially as it pertains to questions of gender (Thien, 2005) and race (Tolia-Kelly, 2006). Responding to these critiques, several geographers have developed quite innovative understandings of embodiment and identity (e.g. Saldanha (2005) and Lim (2010)) that use non-representational theories to develop new understandings of the material and affective processes through which racial difference emerges in relation to specific spaces, like at a rave in

Goa, India (see further discussion of Saldanha's research on Goa in ***Chapter 5***).

In another frustrated critique, the cultural geographer Tim Creswell (2012) took issue with the manner in which non-representational theories speak about representational practices. Cresswell gives as an example Thrift's early discussions of dance. As Creswell (2012: 99) puts it, "it was not the focus on dance that annoyed me. . . . I was more disturbed by what he wrote about dance – as about dance being beyond representation and power." Creswell's critique, however, is something of a misunderstanding of the point that non-representational geographers were making. The point for non-representational theories is not that dance is completely beyond power and representation. This would obviously be a silly argument to make, given the intimate links between dance and expressions of cultural and political identity and the ways in which dance has frequently become the target of political control through bans and forms of censorship. Here, for example, we might think of the banning of the Sardana dance by Spain's Franco dictatorship (1939–1975) due to its links to Catalan identity and democracy, or, more recently, the criminalisation of public dancing in Iran. Instead, what non-representational theorisations draw attention to is that there is *something* in the material event of dance that perpetually exceeds the known identities and actual contexts of the present. Dewsbury (2012: 52), drawing here on the language of Deleuze, captures a sense of this performative excess, expressing it in terms of dance's disclosure of tendencies and potentials (of bodies, spaces, and their relations) that intensify and transform physical actuality:

> Dance thus presents the vital presencing of the flesh's heartbeat and what we 'see' in our neural vibrations, blockages, nerve snaps and internal image screens, when confronted by dance is also scaled at the level of the quick without code. Dance is that which becomes coded but is not itself code in its point of incessant emergence. Dancers are coded, genres are coded, dance choreography is coded, but the dance itself, like all art forms when considered in their pure state, manifests the power of the present to disrupt, disclose, and expose these codifications. Herein, whilst the body may be the marker and the container of these codes of representation with all their politics the

> body is not itself representational. It is because of the body's presentational status that dance is so difficult, perhaps precisely impossible, to textually represent and interpret.

Other critics have focused on the naming of non-representational theory, suggesting the need for less antagonistic and inclusive language, like the post-representational (Castree and MacMillan, 2004) and the *more-than-representational* (Lorimer, 2005). As non-representational geographers ourselves, our preference is to stick with the name 'non-representational' in our own work. We argue that these alternate terms dilute the full shock of the non-representational for contemporary geographical thinking, working according to an additive logic that turns non-representational concepts into a series of additional extras that can exist alongside business-as-usual representationalism (Lapworth, 2021). We hope that it is clear from the discussion above that the 'non' in non-representational is not to be read in the spirit of the negative (i.e. as anti-representation), but is instead a positive and generative prefix that radically transforms our understanding of what representations do in the context of thought and life.

In the final sections of this chapter, we want to give a more explicit account of the implications of non-representational styles of thinking for how cultural geographers address the problematising capacity of representations. Here, we outline three significant conceptual frames that have become important in shaping how cultural geographers have sought to reimagine the pragmatics and politics of representations: as *force*, as *encounter*, and as *assemblage*. While these concepts differ in some of their emphases, what they share is the attempt to think more ontologically about representations as things implicated in the ongoing production and transformation of the world (rather than the re-production of the already-existing). To give some empirical meat to these conceptual bones, we also want to end by highlighting some of the exciting research currently being done by cultural geographers in this space, research that uses these different conceptual frames to generate new and transformative understandings of the representational domains that have dominated thinking, not just in geography, but across humanities and social science disciplines. In what follows, we focus on three particularly significant domains for cultural geography, both historically and today: the cartographic, the cinematic, and the literary.

FORCE (CARTOGRAPHY)

> Maps . . . are first and foremost expressions of force rather than meaning. Maps are action, not re-presentation; intervention, not reflection.
>
> (Doel, 2006: 343)

It is hard to believe that a film as fun as *Barbie* – the 2023 blockbuster directed by Greta Gerwig and starring Margot Robbie as Barbie and Ryan Gosling as Ken – would be the trigger for a serious geopolitical spat. But that's exactly what happened when, just before its release in July of 2023, the Head of the Department of Culture in Vietnam announced that the film would be banned for its depiction of an 'offending image.' The image in question was a crude, childlike drawing of a map that appears momentarily in the background of a few scenes in the film. The map aroused such strong passions from the Vietnamese government because it contained what is referred to in the cartographic community as the 'nine-dash line.' This line depicts a series of hotly contested islands

Figure 2.1 The 'offending' cartographic image in *Barbie* (Gerwig, 2023).

in the South China Sea (including the Paracel Islands and the Spratly Islands) as part of the territorial claim of the People's Republic of China. Following the Vietnamese ban, the Philippines government (which also has territorial disputes in this region with China) only allowed the film to be screened after Warner Bros Pictures agreed to blur this controversial cartographic line.

What the furore over *Barbie's* cartographic representations reveals is something that cultural geographers (like Doel in the quote above) have known for some time: maps are always *expressions of force* that "incite, move, anger, transform, delight, enchant, or otherwise affect" (Anderson, 2019: 1120). Despite their appeals to scientific objectivity, maps don't simply represent reality as a kind of faithful mirror image. They instead "perform realities," intervening in the material processes through which the world comes to be imagined and known (Gerlach, 2017: 94). Maps, in the words of Thrift (2011: 9), "have always been engines rather than cameras." Maps do *work* in and with our worlds, producing effects that bring identities and events into being.

The force of maps to make a difference in the world has been a central theme of cultural geographic engagements with cartography since at least the 1980s. In particular, the work of J. B. Harley (1988: 279) forged a new kind of critical engagement with cartography in geography, highlighting "the mechanisms by which maps . . . became a political force in society" through the close imbrications of cartography and imperial and state power. Far from holding up a transparent mirror to the world, Harley (2002: 35) claimed that "maps redescribe the world . . . in terms of relations of power and the cultural practices preferences, and priorities." The work of other new cultural geographers, like Cosgrove (2008: 162), emphasised how maps should not be grasped as "tangible, finished objects," but rather as "provisional and ephemeral processes" whose meaning is transformed through their encounters with different users and in relation to different spatial and temporal contexts. Common to both Harley and Cosgrove is a representationalist tendency to approach the map as a kind of 'textual' system of signs and significations. As a result, the force of maps becomes circumscribed by an epistemological terrain of meaning and knowledge in a way that often misses the more material and affective transformations that maps can produce.

More recently, geographers have sought to extend this thinking of the force of maps in more ontological and non-representational terms. Kitchin and Dodge (2007), for example, argue that previous representational approaches to mapping in geography tend to conceive maps as stable, coherent, and secure objects. They instead argue that:

> Maps have no ontological security . . . they are transitory and fleeting, being contingent, relational, and context-dependent . . . maps are practices, they are always mappings; spatial practices enacted to solve relational problems (e.g., how best to create a spatial representation, how to understand a spatial distribution, how to get between A and B, and so on).
>
> (Kitchin and Dodge, 2007: 335)

Drawing on the philosophy of Gilbert Simondon, and specifically his concept of 'ontogenesis' that rethinks objects and images as emergent processes, Kitchin and Dodge (2007) contend that maps are always coming into being at the confluence of a multitude of embodied, discursive, social, and technical processes. Developing this ontogenetic line, some of the most innovative work outlining a non-representational account of the ethical and political potentials of cartography can be found in the work of Joe Gerlach. Turning to the conceptual vocabulary of Deleuze and Guattari (1987), Gerlach (2015: 275) argues that cartographies of any kind always involve the expression of both "major" categories (those known identities, dominant representations, and familiar meanings that often compose the content of maps) as well as a vast array of "minor" forces (the material, non-human, and technical processes involved in the practice of mapping) that expose the map to creative variations and unforeseen connections. Attending to the minor forces of maps, he argues, entails a conceptual and analytical shift "away from a concern for the cartographic politics of representation and toward a political apprehension of the affective and virtual vectors of cartography" (Gerlach, 2015: 274).

A focus on the minor thus entails attention to the non-representational aspects of maps and how they serve to cultivate "affects, attitudes, collectives, sensibilities, spaces and events that are transformative of the world, but often in a register largely ignored" (Gerlach, 2015: 274). To explore where these minor forces of cartography might take us, Gerlach turns to the example of OpenStreetMap: an online and open-source geographical database that allows its community of millions of users worldwide to create and edit maps of real-world locations. Focusing on the 'mapping parties' of amateur and hacktivist cartographers in Peru, Gerlach (2015: 282) highlights how OpenStreetMap opens mapping to a "cartography of affects" at the level of the sensorium of the body and its *encounters* with the world.

ENCOUNTER (CINEMA)

> Something in the world forces us to think. That something is an object not of recognition, but of encounter.
>
> (Deleuze, 2004: 178)

A second concept that has emerged in the past decade as particularly important for thinking cultural objects and texts beyond the framework of representationalism is the concept of the *encounter* (Lapworth, 2015). Such discussions often draw on a Deleuzian understanding of encounters as intense moments or instances that cannot be reduced to a logic of recognition that would bind the encountered thing to the terrain of the already known. Instead, encounters are generative events that transform bodies at the level of their capacities to affect and be affected. This non-representational concept of the encounter has become a particularly dominant motif in recent cultural geography engagements with cinema (Doel and Clarke, 2007; Doel, 2022). Here, attention falls on the ethical capacity of the filmic encounter to stage a "shock to thought" that disrupts habitual coordinates of thinking (Massumi, 2002: xii). Cinema, from this non-representational perspective, is an event that can – and often does – transform how you make sense of yourself and the world. Since its invention in the 1890s, cinema has delivered a series of profound shocks of thought to audiences throughout its history: whether this is the affective clash of images in the montages of Soviet cinema (e.g. Sergei Eisenstein); the intensive, non-human perceptions of matter (Dziga Vertov) and the body (Carl Dreyer) generated by new shot types and techniques of framing; or the alternate experiences of time and space produced by non-linear styles of narrative and editing (Akira Kurosawa and Michelangelo Antonioni).

At work, non-representational scholarship on cinema is also a very different concept of the 'filmic image' from what we might be accustomed to in geography and the wider social sciences. As Clarke and Doel (2016: 5) explain, the image in non-representational theory is no longer understood as a kind of "secondary representation of an underlying reality," nor as a kind of mental or psychic content of a human subject. Instead, images are understood in terms of intensity and non-human forces. While there are several sources of inspiration for such a reimagined concept of the image, cultural geographers have drawn special influence from the French philosopher, Henri Bergson (1859–1941), and specifically his notion of the image as a peculiar type of existence "which is more than that which the idealist calls a representation, but less than that which the realist calls a thing" (1988: 9). Bergson places the image at the heart of his metaphysical system, arguing that the universe itself is composed of a multiplicity of moving images (including the human subject, which he argues is a special kind of image), and these images are constantly acting and reacting upon each other in constant variation. Following Bergson, and as the geographers Latham and McCormack (2009: 253) put it:

> [I]mages can be understood as resonant blocks of space-time: they have duration, even if they appear still. Furthermore, the force of images is not just representational. Images are also blocks of sensation with an affective intensity: they make sense not just because we take time to figure out what they signify, but also because their pre-signifying affective materiality is felt in bodies.

As expressions of material and affective intensities, our encounter with moving images bypasses conscious reflection to instead impinge directly on our nervous systems and bodies. In two philosophical volumes on cinema, Deleuze (2005a, 2005b) develops Bergson's philosophy of the image to argue that it is at the level of thought and the materiality of the brain that we should understand cinema's transformative potentials. Great filmmakers, for Deleuze, are thus those who invent new kinds of images, expressing forces and intensities that profoundly reshape our sense of what it is possible to think. Cinema, when it's at its most cinematic, is a machine that generates new images of thought, a machine that we become a part of when we take our seat in the theatre or press play on our streaming platform at home.

Engagements with Bergson's and Deleuze's ideas in the subfield of *film geography* have generated novel insights into the capacity of cinema to transform the way we think about one of the fundamental concepts of geography: *space*. For us, some of the most powerful expressions of the capacity of cinema to think space differently can be found in the classic films of the Japanese director Yasujiro Ozu (1903–1963) (see Jones, 2013; Lapworth, 2016). Almost all of Ozu's films take place in the city of Tokyo. But the Tokyo expressed in his films is not the famous image of the sweeping cityscape of neon-lit *Zakkyo* buildings, but rather the interior spaces of suburban developments and the cramped alleyways of old entertainment districts. In filming these fragmented, everyday spaces of the city, Ozu wanted to disrupt the way in which cinema traditionally frames

Figure 2.2 'Empty spaces' of the city in Yasujiro Ozu's *Tokyo Story* (Ozu, 1953).

space as nothing more than a passive backdrop to the requirements of dramatic narrative. In *Tokyo Story* [1953], for example, Ozu subverts traditional techniques for orienting the audience to the space of action – such as the 180-degree rule and establishing shots – to instead punctuate scenes with images of empty spaces that are detached from the actual perspectives or movements of the film's characters. Adopting a non-representational approach, Ozu's empty spaces (also referred to as 'pillow shots' in the film studies literature) are not simply aesthetic motifs but rather ontological techniques that shift the intensive axis of the image "from action to sensation and thought" (Lapworth, 2016: 23). What Ozu demonstrates, then, is how cinema can offer a very different thinking and experience of space. Divorced from already-given determinations and functions, cinematic spaces become sites of undecidability and encounter, offering unforeseen possibilities of thinking, perceiving, and acting.

ASSEMBLAGE (LITERATURE)

Cultural geographers have long looked to literary texts as an important site through which the relationship between people and place can be understood, negotiated, and challenged (Anderson, 2015). Such work, often situated at the interface of geography and literary studies, has coalesced in the past few decades with the emergence of the "interdiscipline" of 'Literary Geographies' (Hones, 2022: 154), which now boasts several monograph-length expositions and even a dedicated journal (*Literary Geographies,* which started in 2015). A distinctive feature of literary geography work, as Sheila Hones (2008) notes, was its attempt to challenge traditional framings of the event of reading, which tend to understand it as a simple encounter between an object (the literary text) and a subject (the reader), both conceived as already constituted and discrete terms. Such a subject-object framing flattens the complex and multifaceted dynamics of meaning-making in encounters with literature, leading to a kind of wrenching duality between approaches that either put emphasis on the "reader-response" that obscures "the significance of the text and the creative agency of the author," while approaches that focus on the structuring of the literary text "tend in contrast to efface the agency of the reader" (Hones, 2008: 1310). In addition, literary geographies also sought to foreground that the meaning and experience of a text isn't generated in a vacuum but is instead profoundly shaped by the spatial context in which both the reading and writing of a text 'happens.'

Human geography's broader relational turn (Massey, 2005), and its foregrounding of the primacy of relations over constituted terms, has been of particular significance for literary geographers interested in rethinking the cultural significance of literature beyond the dualism of subject-object frameworks. Relational thinking, as Jon Anderson (2015: 122) puts it, "does not consider concepts/things/objects/representations as *a priori* in the world, but rather considers them to be continually ephemeral, (re)composing, and emergent." From a relational perspective, the character and meaning of representational objects like literary texts are thus constantly undergoing metamorphosis depending on their changing position in a field of relations. We can point to two key examples of what such a relational approach to the literary text might entail. The first of these relates to what Hones (2008, 2022) refers to as the 'text-as-it-happens' approach in literary geographies. Drawing on Colum McCann's (2009) novel, *Let the Great World Spin*, Hones (2008: 1302) notes that such an approach encourages us to think of literary texts (like novels) not as isolated or discrete things, but rather as "spatial events . . . which is to say, something which happens at the intersection of agents and situations scattered across time and space, both human and non-human, absent and present." Examples here include the dynamic and unfolding processes of things like writing, editing, translating, proofing, typefacing, designing, marketing, purchasing, reading, and reflection, all of which have explicitly spatial and temporal dimensions.

A second kind of relational approach to literature relates to engagement with the concept of *assemblage*, which has become a key idea across multiple areas of the discipline over the last decade (Roberts, 2021; see also further discussion of assemblages in the context of theories of 'the body' in ***Chapter 5***). Like Hones' text-it-happens approach, the concept of assemblage enables literary geographers to identify the diverse components that have agency and influence on fiction, including authors, translators, publishers, readers, places, and so on (Anderson, 2015). But unlike Hones,' the assemblage approach tends to imagine these elements and components in much less individuated terms. As Robbins and Marks (2010: 179) put it:

> There is no longer a tripartite division between a field of reality (the world) and the field of representation (the book) and the field of subjectivity (the author). Rather, an assemblage establishes connections between certain multiplicities drawn from each of these orders.

The literary assemblage thus comprises a diverse array of components that are themselves composed of a multiplicity of contingent elements and processes (Lapworth, 2023). Thinking of literature as an assemblage thus helps literary geographers identify the "meaningful processes that have produced a text, diagnose where the individual components come from, where they are going to, and how they have come together" (Anderson, 2015: 127).

A second key difference is that the concept of assemblage (especially in its more Deleuzian iterations) enables a sharper attention to the *valency* (or 'power') of specific sets of literary relations. An assemblage, as Dewsbury (2011: 150) emphasises, is "less about what it *is* . . . and more about what it can *do*, what it can affect and bring about." The concept of assemblage has therefore enabled geographers to deepen the critique of a long-held ontological separation between 'textual' and 'extra-textual' (i.e. real-world) spaces, foregrounding how things like novels can enact real, material transformations in the world. This might entail a consideration of how a reader's motivations, desires, and impulses co-compose with those of the author in ways that (re-)assemble worlds of meaning and experience. Anderson (2015) explores this process of reassembling worlds through a discussion of his encounter with Tessa Hadley's 2012 novel *The London Train*, showing how the imaginative geographies of the novel (i.e. the situations and settings of the characters' interactions) came to coincide and reshape his own experience of personally meaningful sites in the city of Cardiff.

However, through a more rigorous reading of its genealogy across the *Capitalism and Schizophrenia* books, where Deleuze and Guattari (1987, 2004) first introduce the term, we can see how the concept of assemblage can help direct us to those much less subjectivist and personological registers of transformation generated by encounters with the world. Roberts (2021), for example, emphasises the need to experiment with "new processes of assemblage that no longer assumes the figure of a universal human subject as their transcendental horizon." In a rich analysis of the novels of the Chinese author Mo Yan, Zhe Li (2022) dramatises the force of literature to unravel (or "deterritorialise," to use Deleuze and Guattari's parlance) the stratified forms and identities that comprise the assemblage of the individualised human subject. Turning to Mo Yan's 1994 book *Big Breasts and Wide Hips*, Li (2022) demonstrates how the description of a character's process of 'becoming-bird' should not be read as simply a representational matter of a character imitating an animal, but rather as an intensive, non-representational process of experimenting with non-human intensities and affects that open new possibilities of life. Becoming, then, can be understood as an encounter between two or more kinds of intensive assemblages (in Mo Yan's novel, between a woman and a bird) that offer lines of escape from the intolerable experiences or unliveable modes of life associated with the Chinese political context from which he writes. Through this encounter with Mo Yan, Li (2022) thus highlights the ethical power of literary assemblages to produce modes of thought and perception beyond the human, ones which may "offer potentials to rethink the human-animal relationship in a non-anthropocentric way" (p. 74).

CONCLUSION

In this chapter, we have surveyed the different ways in which representations have been conceptualised in cultural geography over the last few decades. We hope you now have an appreciation of how representational objects and practices are an essential part of cultural life, which explains why scholars across the Humanities and Social Sciences have spent so much time thinking about them and the role they play in society. Of all disciplines, cultural geographers have arguably led the way in developing innovative accounts of representations, especially since the 2000s, with work falling under the banner of 'non-representational theory.' As we've seen in the final three sections of this chapter, the emphasis with non-representational geographies is on the question of what representations do: the affective *forces* they express; the transformative *encounters* they produce; and the relational *assemblages* they enter us into. What connects this heterogeneous body of work is thus an *ontological* understanding of the environment where things like texts, images, maps, films, and so on are just as real (i.e. have the same ontological status) as the physical dimensions of our environments. They are not, therefore, of a purely symbolic or imaginary order. As a result, the crucial point for non-representational geographers is not to get too tied down with the question of what a representation means or signifies. Instead, the more interesting question is what representations like novels, films, or photographs *do* as problematising interventions in how we think, relate, and live. In studying representations, we are thus returned to where we began: "Life. Always Life" (Carver, 2009: 748).

FURTHER READING

Anderson, B. and Harrison, P. *Non-Representational Theories and Geography*. London: Routledge [especially Introduction, and chapters by Doel and Dewsbury], 2010.

Dewsbury, J. D., P. Harrison, M. Rose and J. Wylie. "Enacting geographies." *Geoforum* 33, no. 4 (2002): 436–440. https://doi.org/10.1016/s0016-7185%2802%2900029-5

Gerlach, J. "Editing worlds: Participatory mapping and a minor geopolitics." *Transactions of the Institute of British Geographers* 40, no. 2 (2015): 273–286. https://doi.org/10.1111/tran.12075

Latham, A. and McCormack, D. "Thinking with images in non-representational cities: Vignettes from Berlin." *Area* 41, no. 3 (2009): 252–262. https://doi.org/10.1111/j.1475-4762.2008.00868.x

Simpson, P. *Non-Representational Theory*. London: Routledge, 2020.

REFERENCES

Anderson, B. "Cultural Geography II: The force of representations." *Progress in Human Geography* 43, no. 6 (2019): 1120–1232. https://doi.org/10.1177/0309132518761431

Anderson, J. "Towards an assemblage approach to literary geography." *Literary Geographies* 1, no. 2 (2015): 120–137.

Barron, A. and J. Blakey. "Representation/al." In L. Lees and D. Demeritt (eds.) *Concise Encyclopedia of Human Geography* (pp. 343–347). Cheltenham: Edward Elgar Press, 2023.

Bergson, H. *Matter and Memory*. New York: Zone Books, 1988.

Carver, R. *Raymond Carver: Collected Stories*. London: Random House, 2009.

Castree, N. and T. MacMillan. "Old news: Representation and academic novelty." *Environment and Planning A: Economy and Space* 36, no. 3 (2004): 469–480. https://doi.org/10.1068/a3656

Clarke, D. and M. Doel. "Cinematicity: Cinema and city after Deleuze." *Journal of Urban Cultural Studies* 3, no. 1 (2016): 3–11. https://doi.org/10.1386/jucs.3.1.3_1

Clayton, J. "Colonising, settling and the origins of academic geography." In J. A. Agnew and J. S. Duncan (eds.) *The Wiley-Blackwell Companion to Human Geography* (pp. 50–70). New Jersey: Wiley Blackwell, 2011.

Cosgrove, D. "Cultural cartography: Maps and mapping in cultural geography." *Annals de Geographie* 660–661 (2008): 159–178. https://doi.org/10.3917/ag.660.0159

Cosgrove, D. and P. Jackson. "New directions in cultural geography." *Area* 19, no. 2 (1987): 95–101. https://www.jstor.org/stable/20002425

Creswell, T. "Nonrepresentational theory and me: Notes of an interested sceptic." *Environment and Planning D: Society and Space* 30, no. 1 (2012): 96–105. https://doi.org/10.1068/d494

Daniels, S. and D. Cosgrove. *The Iconography of Landscape: Essays on the Symbolic Representation, Design, and Use of Past Environments*. Cambridge: Cambridge University Press, 1988.

Deleuze, G. *Cinema I: The Movement-Image*. London: Continuum, 2005a.

Deleuze, G. *Cinema II: The Time-Image*. London: Continuum, 2005b.

Deleuze, G. *Difference and Repetition*. London: Continuum, 2004.

Deleuze, G. *Pure Immanence: Essays on A Life*. New York: Zone Books, 2001.

Deleuze, G. and F. Guattari. *Anti-Oedipus: Capitalism and Schizophrenia*. London: Continuum, 2004.

Deleuze, G. and F. Guattari. *A Thousand Plateaus: Capitalism and Schizophrenia*. Minneapolis: University of Minnesota Press, 1987.

Deleuze, G. and F. Guattari. *What is Philosophy?* London: Verso, 1994.

Dewsbury, J. D. "Dancing: The secret slowness of the fast." In T. Cresswell and P. Merriman (eds.) *Geographies of Mobilities: Practices, Spaces, Subjects* (pp. 51–68). Farnham: Ashgate, 2012.

Dewsbury, J. D. "The Deleuze-Guattarian assemblage: Plastic habits." *Area* 43, no. 2 (2011): 148–153. https://doi.org/10.1111/j.1475-4762.2011.01006.x

Dittmer, J. "Captain America's Empire: Reflections on identity, popular culture, and post-9/11 geopolitics." *Annals of the American Association of Geographers* 95, no. 3 (2005): 626–643. https://doi.org/10.1111/j.1467-8306.2005.00478.x

Dittmer, J. *Captain America and the Nationalist Superhero: Metaphors, Narratives, and Geopolitics*. Philadelphia: Temple University Press, 2012.

Doel, M. "Film. Geography: Stirring still remains." *GeoJournal* 87, no. 1 (2022): 11–21. https://doi.org/10.1007/s10708-022-10648-x

Doel, M. "The obscenity of mapping." *Area* 38, no. 3 (2006): 343–345. https://doi.org/10.1111/j.1475-4762.2006.688_2.x

Doel, M. and D. Clarke. "Afterimages." *Environment and Planning D: Society and Space* 25, no. 5 (2007): 890–910. https://doi.org/10.1068/d436t

Gerlach, J. "Mapping as performance." In A. Kent and P. Vujakovic (eds.) *The Routledge Handbook of Mapping and Performance* (pp. 90–100). London: Routledge, 2017.

Gerwig, G. *Barbie*. Warner Bros., 2023.

Hall, S. E. *Representation: Cultural Representation and Signifying Practices*. London: Sage, 1997.

Harley, J. B. "Maps, knowledge, and power." In S. Daniels and D. Cosgrove (eds.) *The Iconography of Landscape: Essays on the Symbolic Representation, Design, and Use of Past Environments* (pp. 277–312). Cambridge: Cambridge University Press, 1988.

Harley, J. B. *The New Nature of Maps: Essays in the History of Cartography*. Baltimore: Johns Hopkins University Press, 2002.

Hones, S. "Text as it happens: Literary geography." *Geography Compass* 2, no. 5 (2008): 1301–1317. https://doi.org/10.1111/j.1749-8198.2008.00143.x

Hones, S. *Literary Geography*. London: Routledge, 2022.

Jones, O. ""I was born but . . .": Children as other/nonrepresentational subjects in emotional and affective registers as depicted in film." *Emotion, Space and Society* 9, no. 1 (2013): 4–12. https://doi.org/10.1016/j.emospa.2013.02.001

Kitchin, R. and M. Dodge. "Rethinking maps." *Progress in Human Geography* 31, no. 3 (2007): 331–334. https://doi.org/10.1177/0309132507077082

Kobayashi, A. "Representation and re-presentation." In A. Kobayashi (ed.) *International Encyclopedia of Human Geography* (pp. 423–425). Amsterdam: Elsevier, 2020.

Lapworth, A. "Cinema, thought, immanence: Contemplating signs and empty spaces in the films of Ozu." *Journal of Urban Cultural Studies* 3, no. 1 (2016): 13–31. http://dx.doi.org/10.1386/jucs.3.1.13_1

Lapworth, A. "Habit, art, and the plasticity of the subject: The ontogenetic shock of the bioart encounter." *Cultural Geographies* 22, no. 1 (2015): 85–102. http://dx.doi.org/10.1177/1474474013491926

Lapworth, A. "Responsibility before the world: Cinema, perspectivism and a nonhuman ethics of individuation." *Deleuze and Guattari Studies* 15, no. 3 (2021): 386–401. https://doi.org/10.3366/dlgs.2021.0447

Lapworth, A. "Thinking the unconscious beyond the psychoanalytic subject: Simondon, Murakami, and the transductive forces of the transindividual." *Social and Cultural Geography* 24, no. 9 (2023): 1501–1518. https://doi.org/10.1080/14649365.2022.2073469

Li, Z. *Deleuze and Mo Yan: A Cartography of Becomings*. Unpublished PhD Thesis, 2022. https://doi.org/10.26190/unsworks/24262

Lim, J. "Immanent politics: Thinking race and ethnicity through affect and machinism." *Environment and Planning A: Economy and Space* 42, no. 10 (2010): 2392–2409. https://doi.org/10.1068/a42234

Lorimer, H. "Cultural geography: The busyness of being more-than-representational." *Progress in Human Geography* 29, no. 1 (2005): 83–94. https://doi.org/10.1191/0309132505ph531pr

Massey, D. *For Space*. London: Sage, 2005.

Massumi, B. *A Shock to Thought: Expression after Deleuze and Guattari*. London: Routledge, 2002.

McCann, C. 2009. *Let the Great World Spin*. London: Bloomsbury.

Nash, C. "Performativity in practice: Some recent work in cultural geography." *Progess in Human Geography* 24, no. 4 (2000): 653–664. https://doi.org/10.1191/030913200701540654

Nash, C. "Reclaiming vision: Looking at landscape and the body." *Gender, Place and Culture* 3, no. 2 (1996): 149–170. https://doi.org/10.1080/09663699650021864

Ozu, Y. *Tokyo Story [Tokyo Monogotari]*. Shochiku, 1953.

Peet, R. *Modern Geographical Thought*. New Jersey: Wiley-Blackwell, 1998.

Philo, C. "Foucault's geography." *Environment and Planning D: Society and Space* 10, no. 2 (1992): 137–161. https://doi.org/10.1068/d100137

Robbins, P. and B. Marks. "Assemblage geographies." In S. Smith, R. Pain, S. Marston and J-P. Jones (eds.) *Sage Handbook of Social Geographies* (pp. 176–194). London: Sage, 2010.

Roberts, T. "A constructivism of desire: Conceptualising the politics of assemblage with Deleuze and Guattari." *Area* 53, no. 4 (2021): 691–698. https://doi.org/10.1111/area.12735

Roberts, T., A. Lapworth and J. D. Dewsbury. "From 'world' to 'earth': Non-phenomenological subjectivity in Deleuze and Guattari's geophilosophy." *Subjectivity* 15 (2022): 135–151. https://doi.org/10.1057/s41286-022-00135-6

Said, E. *Orientalism*. New York: Pantheon, 1978.

Saldanha, A. "Trance and visibility at dawn: Racial dynamics in Goa's rave scene." *Social and Cultural Geography* 6, no. 5 (2005): 707–721. https://doi.org/10.1080/14649360500258328

Scott, H. V. "Representation, politics of." In A. Kobayashi (ed.) *International Encyclopedia of Human Geography* (pp. 351–356). Amsterdam: Elsevier, 2009.

Spivak, G. C. "Can the subaltern speak?" In C. Nelson and L. Grossberg (eds.) *Marxism and the Interpretation of Culture* (pp. 271–316). Basingstoke: Macmillan Publishing, 1988.

Thien, D. "After or beyond feeling? A consideration of affect and emotion in geography." *Area* 37, no. 4 (2005): 450–454. https://www.jstor.org/stable/20004485

Thrift, N. "Lifeworld inc – and what to do about it." *Environment and Planning D: Society and Space* 29, no. 1 (2011): 5–26. https://doi.org/10.1068/d0310

Thrift, N. *Spatial Formations*. London: Sage, 1996.

Thrift, N. and J. D. Dewsbury. "Dead geographies – and how to make them live." *Environment and Planning D: Society and Space* 18, no. 4 (2000): 411–432. https://doi.org/10.1068/d1804e

Tolia-Kelly, D. "Affect: An ethnocentric encounter? Exploring the 'universalist' imperative of emotional/affectual geographies." *Area* 38, no. 2 (2006): 213–217. https://www.jstor.org/stable/20004528

3

NATURE

INTRODUCTION

For those readers who are new to cultural geography, it may well come as a surprise to see an entire chapter of this book devoted to nature. You might be wondering, for instance, what the geographical study of culture could possibly contribute to humanity's understanding of nature and the natural world, particularly given the stunning achievements of physicists, chemists, and biologists in deepening our understanding of nature's laws and processes. In everyday conversation, nature and culture tend to be presented in dualistic terms and are often understood as mutually exclusive categories – at least, this tends to be the case within the context of those Western philosophical traditions that have dominated such intellectual discussions through the suppression of non-Western and Indigenous worldviews (Braun, 2005). Indeed, this dualistic account of the relationship between nature and human society underpins what most people understand to be the two fundamentally distinct branches of academic inquiry through which human beings come to know the world: the physical sciences, which generate knowledge about nature, and the social sciences, which generate knowledge about human beings – including knowledge about culture.

And yet, cultural geographers have had much to say about nature, which remains one of the most significant topics of interest within this dynamic field of social science research (Ginn and Demeritt, 2010). In this chapter, we will introduce you to some of the most influential and exciting research agendas relating to the theme of nature in cultural geography, both past and present, while also

DOI: 10.4324/9781003542667-3

outlining some important real-world applications of these ideas for future societies across the world. But first, a proviso: so much has been written on the cultural geographies of nature that we will not be able to cover it all in a single chapter. Indeed, there are already many books out there, written by cultural geographers, that focus solely on this question of nature – and in much more detail than we can realistically achieve in a single chapter of an introductory textbook (see Whatmore, 2002; Castree, 2005, 2013; Hinchliffe, 2007; Clark, 2011). What we aim to provide instead is a summary of what we believe are three key agendas that characterise cultural geographic research on the topic of nature, with the hope that this will both enable and inspire you to delve more deeply into these extensive literatures while also providing a better sense of *why* they matter when it comes to understanding our contemporary world.

In terms of the chapter's structure, each section corresponds to one of these three key agendas. In the following section (*Cultures of nature*), we explore how cultural geographers have developed the idea that people's understanding and experience of nature are shaped by culture in ways that are often taken for granted. This is the first agenda. The next section (*Natures in culture*) unpacks the second agenda, where we examine how cultural geographers have sought to broaden conventional understandings of culture and its production by turning to forms of non-human agency (of animals, plants, and even non-living materials) that have traditionally been confined to the category of nature. And in the final section (*Human nature?*), we discuss how cultural geography's tendency to blur the boundaries between the social and the natural changes how we frame the philosophical question of what it means to be human, as well as the more speculative question of what this human might become.

Before turning to these three agendas, however, and to further set the scene, we want to carve out some space in what remains of this introduction to reflect on cultural geography's unique position relative to the traditional distinction made between the physical and social sciences. While cultural geography is clearly focused on understanding phenomena associated with human culture, the way it approaches this task is shaped by the broader philosophy of geographical thought that strives to understand the relationship *between* human beings and their physical environments (for more on this, see our introduction to geographical thinking in ***Chapter 1***). This is an important point to bear in mind because it is something that distinguishes cultural geography from disciplines like sociology or cultural studies, which are also clearly motivated by a desire to understand culture in their own ways. For cultural geographers, then, the study of culture remains thoroughly situated within this broader geographical interest in the entanglements between human society and non-human nature (Kirsch, 2014), and this is one of the reasons why discussions about nature continue to play such an important role in shaping research agendas in cultural geography.

An important implication of this is that research in cultural geography fundamentally challenges the everyday assumption that it is only through physical science (e.g. physics, chemistry, biology, etc.) that human beings can hope to know and understand nature. Indeed, thinking about nature from geography's unique vantage point *in-between* humans and their environments also requires an understanding of scientific knowledge production as itself a thoroughly human set of practices, one that is indelibly shaped by culture in significant ways (Demeritt, 1998). In other words, there is no science of nature that exists 'outside' of the messy relationships between human beings and their environments that together make up what cultural geographers call culture. This is not to question the veracity of the knowledge that science generates about nature; rather, what cultural geographers are interested in are the often-unspoken assumptions and ideas about nature that inevitably shape practices of scientific knowledge production and that give them meaning (Instone, 2004).

More specifically, what cultural geography helps us to better understand are the ontological, epistemological, ethical, and political dimensions that necessarily accompany all forms of scientific inquiry and the knowledge of nature that they produce. As some of these terms might be unfamiliar to our readers, let's take some time to unpack them in turn, beginning with the ontological. We provided a brief definition of the term ontology in our discussion of the cultural geographies of representation in ***Chapter 2*** (see **Box 2.2**). To recap, ontology refers to the foundational assumptions people make regarding the kinds of things, categories, and relationships that make up reality. The most obvious example of an ontological assumption that arises in relation to the production of scientific knowledge about nature is the notion that human beings differ fundamentally from the rest of nature by virtue of their capacity to act as willing subjects rather than mere objects. As we will see later in this chapter, this is an ontological assumption about the nature of nature – and, by extension, the nature of *human* nature – that cultural geographers have sought to challenge, most notably by engaging with innovative accounts of non-human agency associated with theoretical movements including new materialism (Kirsch, 2012; Roberts, 2012) and actor-network theory (Bosco, 2006; Allen, 2011), as well as, more recently, through long overdue engagements with non-Western and Indigenous ontologies (Cameron et al., 2014; Ganambarr et al., 2024). For now, though, the point we wish to make is that the empirically verifiable knowledge about nature produced by physical science is always shaped by philosophical assumptions about what reality or existence is ultimately like: assumptions that cultural geographers would encourage us to critically interrogate.

Whereas ontology directs our attention towards questions of what exists, epistemology poses questions about knowledge and how we come to know things about the world – and, therefore, how we can know things about nature (for a concise definition of epistemology, see **Box 2.1**). All science is underpinned by an epistemology or 'theory of knowledge,' even if it is not explicitly acknowledged. When it comes to our understanding of nature, then, the physical sciences are characterised by an epistemology that aspires to complete objectivity through a fundamental detachment of the knower (i.e. the human) from the known (i.e. nature). Thus, for most physical scientists, a key epistemological assumption is that it is only possible to produce valid knowledge about natural phenomena by detaching ourselves from nature and by minimising those subjective dimensions of experience associated with meaning, imagination, feelings, desires, etc. Here, again, cultural geographers have played an important role questioning these epistemological assumptions, particularly through their contributions to feminist theories of situated knowledge (Rose, 1997) as well as engaging with interdisciplinary debates in science and technology studies (Whatmore, 2009; Braun and Whatmore, 2010). But before we get too theoretical, we encourage readers to reflect upon the multitude of ways – beyond the physical sciences – that people come to know things about nature and the natural world, for instance, through the feelings of awe, majesty, or dread captured by visual artists and creative writers, or the more mundane experiences of connection and embodied know-how generated through everyday practices such as gardening. The take-home point here is that these non-scientific practices and procedures produce knowledge about nature that has its own validity, without aspiring to the kind of objectivity associated with physical science.

The desire for detachment associated with objective science also implies that our knowledge about nature can (and should) be separated from ethical questions regarding the different ways human beings ascribe value to their non-human environments. The assumption here is that the rigour and validity of our knowledge about nature rests upon a firm distinction between 'facts' and 'values.' Cultural geography has a number of things to say on this front (see Williams and Keating, 2022), but here we will stick to two key points. First, to the extent that it remains a fundamentally human endeavour, scientific knowledge production about nature is inevitably shaped by the value systems associated with a particular culture, whether this be the micro-cultures associated with a particular laboratory or the broader cultural proclivities towards particular research problems that determine the allocation of research funding. Contrary to what we might ordinarily assume, then, cultural geography contends that scientific knowledge about nature is never value-neutral and that, for this reason, we should critically consider how what we know is coloured by the ethical question of what we value.

Second, the ethical question of how we value nature takes on a far greater sense of urgency in an age characterised by environmental destruction, biodiversity loss, and the shocking realities of global heating that are now being felt across the globe (including in Australia, where we live and work). While scientific understanding is certainly necessary, it is safe to say that the knowledge that it produces will not suffice to save the Amazon rainforest from destruction, nor will it prevent the imminent extinction of endangered species like Australia's koala. Instead, what these environmental problems illustrate is the need to foreground ethical questions of value, responsibility, and care as a crucial and often neglected dimension of what it means to know or understand nature

(Head, 2025). Cultural geography, as we will show, is well placed to explore these questions.

Finally, then, comes politics. Here, a cultural geography perspective encourages us to pay attention to the ways that ideas about nature – and, especially, appeals to 'the natural' – can be weaponised as a means of maintaining power, often marginalising and/or excluding specific groups of people in the process. So, in a similar sense to our previous point about ethics, cultural geography emphasises that knowledge about nature is inherently tied up with political questions concerning the distribution of power in society. A key example here is the way the adjective 'natural' is sometimes used by those in positions of power to maintain the status quo by quashing dissent. To describe something as natural implies that it is as it *should* be, thus dissuading others from asking more critical questions about *why* something is the way it is (and, by extension, why it couldn't be otherwise). Thus, when addressing the nation in the wake of the bushfires that ravaged Australia during the so-called Black Summer of 2019–2020, Prime Minister Scott Morrison went to great lengths to emphasise how bushfires constitute a natural part of the Australian landscape. By using this language, he was attempting to dodge questions about Australia's woeful track record on climate change inaction and the political responsibility of those in positions of power (Peace, 2020).

What is more, to describe something as natural inevitably implies the existence of things deemed to be *unnatural* or out of place in the perceived natural order of things. A key example here that we will return to in more detail in ***Chapter 5*** relates to debates about gender and sexuality and the way that certain modes of existence that challenge the traditional distribution of power in patriarchal societies are often labelled as unnatural expressions of human identity or desire. What these two quite different examples show, therefore, is the need to understand how knowledge about nature intersects with broader political questions about power, in terms of both how power is unevenly distributed throughout society and how it might be questioned or resisted.

We hope that this somewhat lengthy introduction has gone some way to explaining why cultural geographers have had so much to say on the topic of nature, given the ontological, epistemological, ethical, and political issues tied up with this complex term.

Crucially, these are issues that require forms of expertise that are not typically found within the physical sciences, and this is where cultural geography perspectives on nature really come into their own. In the following three sections, we unpack what these perspectives look like in more detail, beginning with cultural-geographical arguments about the social construction of nature.

CULTURES OF NATURE

A curious characteristic of the word nature is that, while it is often used to refer to something universal that exists independently of human beings (i.e. the 'natural world'), what we mean by nature is in fact shaped by historically and geographically situated assumptions, values, and beliefs about ourselves and the world around us. These assumptions are what we might call cultural, to the extent that they provide an unspoken backdrop for the kinds of collective experience, understanding, and meaning that underpin human social interactions in specific times and places. In this section, we will be exploring the somewhat counterintuitive idea that nature is, to a certain extent, a profoundly cultural phenomenon. More specifically, we show how, for some cultural geographers, the experience of nature as something outside or beyond culture is itself a product of a specific cultural context, rather than something that we can simply take for granted as an essential feature of reality. This is what we mean by the phrase *cultures of nature*, which forms the title of this section.

One way of grasping this cultural-geographic idea that our experiences of nature are shaped by culture is to reflect on what immediately comes to mind when thinking about nature or when we imagine a natural landscape. So, before you read any further, we encourage you to take a moment to undertake the following simple thought experiment: What imagery does the concept of nature conjure in your mind's eye? Are there particular feelings or emotions associated with these images that you can identify? Or perhaps there are certain cultural objects – movies, artworks, or books, for example – that spring to mind when thinking about natural landscapes? You can extend this simple exercise by posing the same questions to friends and family. What similarities and differences are you able to observe?

The purpose of this thought experiment is to prompt you to critically reflect on the kinds of assumptions that shape not only your understanding but also your perception and experience of this thing we habitually refer to as nature. In doing so, our intention is to give you a better sense of why cultural geographers have sought to critically interrogate the origins of these assumptions that we are referring to as cultures of nature. If you were able to talk to others, you would likely have found many subtle differences in the way individuals talk about, experience, and imagine nature. However, it is also likely that you will have discovered some striking commonalities. Perhaps you were even able to identify a specific culture of nature composed of shared assumptions and beliefs shaping how you and others see the so-called natural world in a shared framework of perception and understanding.

IMAGINING NATURE WITH AI

To help further illustrate this point, we asked the generative AI software ChatGPT to participate in this thought experiment. As we will explore in greater detail in ***Chapter 4***, generative AI technologies build a picture of what the world is like by extracting patterns from the vast repositories of data that make up humanity's digital culture. This data includes accumulated information that reflects how people tend to think about, imagine, and represent nature. So, by asking ChatGPT to imagine nature, the result that we are given will reflect the dominant tropes and assumptions embedded within the digital footprint of human culture (acknowledging, of course, that not everyone has the same ability to participate in this digitally mediated form of culture). This is how ChatGPT responded to our prompt:

> Picture a serene forest scene: tall, lush trees with sunlight filtering through the leaves, a gentle stream winding its way over smooth stones, and vibrant wildflowers blooming along the banks. In the background, you might hear birds chirping and a soft breeze rustling in the foliage. Does that help paint a picture in your mind?

What do you notice about this description? On first inspection, this might appear to be a perfectly reasonable attempt at evoking an image of nature. However, when we start to think like cultural geographers, the culturally situated aspects of this image quickly become apparent. First and foremost, the association of nature with the imagery of lush trees, green leaves, and vibrant wildflowers tells us something of the *geographies* that tend to shape the dominant imaginaries of nature. Wouldn't it be just as valid to imagine nature through the red dust and rocky landscape of an arid desert? Or perhaps the crushing pressures and intense blackness of a deep ocean trench? The fact that the description of nature generated by ChatGPT appeals more clearly to certain forms of European and North American environments tells us that our experiences of nature are geographically contingent and historically situated rather than universal and ahistorical as is often assumed.

A second characteristic of this image of nature that we might pay critical attention to, as cultural geographers, is the use of the word 'serene.' Today, in many parts of the world, but particularly in Europe and North America, we have grown accustomed to the idea that spending time in nature can provide respite from the stress, noise, and speed of modern urban living. Similarly, we might think about the ways nature-based experiences, such as holidays or expeditions, are commonly marketed as opportunities to slow down and reconnect with your authentic self. And yet this association of natural landscapes with serene environments amenable to humanity's quest for authenticity and self-discovery is itself a relatively recent way of representing and relating to nature, one that was closely associated with the establishment of the first national parks in North America during the end of the nineteenth century (Cronon, 1996). Prior to this, however, people were much more likely to associate nature with more negative experiences of fear, exile from human culture, and even madness. Even today, the experience of nature as a space of serenity is clearly a somewhat privileged experience that is not equally available to all. And as the impacts of a changing climate begin to make themselves felt, a growing proportion of people are beginning to experience nature not so much as space of serenity but through the emotional registers of anxiety, grief, and loss (Head, 2016).

The final characteristic of this image that we would like to draw your attention to is arguably the most significant from a cultural-geographical perspective: the complete absence of human beings from this seemingly natural scene. Indeed, this idea that nature is where human beings *are not* is an assumption that has, in many ways, come to define the globally dominant culture of nature associated with Western philosophy and modernity. It is important to emphasise that this modern desire to separate nature from the human is as much a conceptual or philosophical project as it is a spatial one. In other words, to define nature according to the absence of human beings is also to make an *ontological* claim that humans are uniquely different from the rest of nature. Geographer Noel Castree makes this point when he notes that it has become common to associate nature almost exclusively with "the nonhuman world" (2005: 8). What we end up with, in this familiar account, is a binary vision of reality that is split into two mutually exclusive categories: on one side of the binary lie nature and the non-human; on the other side, society and human culture.

This way of thinking about nature as something fundamentally opposed to humanity is clearly at odds with what the biological sciences tell us about evolution and the ecological interrelations upon which our own existence as a species depends. Human beings are undoubtedly a part of nature: they are no less natural than anything else that exists and remain subject to the same processes that shape the physical universe. And yet, as an idea that remains deeply embedded within the prevailing cultures of nature in the West, the nature-society dualism continues to shape the way people perceive and experience their environments in significant ways. The description generated by ChatGPT reflects this pervasive culture of nature, embodied most vividly in forms of popular media such as nature documentaries, which have traditionally relied upon an aesthetic of human absence in their portrayal of seemingly natural landscapes and environments. And while more recent examples within this genre have attempted to question this aesthetic by exploring nature in contexts such as cities and post-industrial environments, the idea that nature is most natural in the absence of human activity and culture remains a powerful assumption.

There are, however, a number of problems associated with this way of thinking about nature. First and foremost, understanding that the nature-society dualism is a feature of a specific culture of nature, rather than something universally given, is important to the extent that it reminds us of the continuing existence of non-Western

Indigenous cultures around the world that have developed dramatically different relationships to their environments. Drawing on years of in-depth ethnographic research in South America, anthropologist Eduardo Viveiros de Castro (2014) has documented how Amerindian tribes attribute culture to non-humans, to the extent that all beings – human or otherwise – experience themselves as uniquely distinct from what they perceive to be nature. Another way of putting this is that, from the perspective of Amerindian ontology, to exist is to experience oneself as a uniquely cultural being. Thus, the idea that we humans are unique or exceptional beings, distinct from the rest of nature, is, for some Amerindian peoples, how *all* beings (not just humans) experience themselves. By this account, even an animal like the jaguar experiences itself and its relationship to the environment through its own version of the nature-society dualism. Jaguars, tapirs, monkeys – indeed, all living beings – experience themselves as cultural beings, according to Amerindian ontologies.

The complex and sophisticated ontologies of Aboriginal and Torres Strait Islander peoples, living on the unceded lands referred to as Australia, offer another powerful example of how Indigenous worldviews challenge the perceived universality of Western cultures of nature. While it is important to note the diversity of Indigenous cultures across this vast continent, cultural geographers working in close collaboration with Aboriginal groups have explored how the interconnection of human and non-human – and thus of the social and natural worlds – takes precedence, both conceptually and ethically, in their interactions with the environment. This emphasis on interconnection and co-dependence is encapsulated in the Aboriginal and Torres Strait Islander concept of 'Country,' which, according to Wiradyuri, Ngemba and Paakantji woman Gemma Pol (2023: np), "is a term used by First Nations peoples to refer to the lands, waters and skies to which they are connected through ancestral ties and family origins." For Australia's First Nations peoples, then, human beings are a part of the reciprocal relations between all beings that together make up Country, in a way that fundamentally unsettles the Eurocentric categories of nature and society associated with Western ontologies. Country is comprised of relations rather than categories. This includes ecological relationships of co-dependence, but it also includes knowledge as a relationship that is embedded in and communicated through cultural practices like storytelling, painting, and dance: "Humans are part of Country along with the mullet, the tides, the moon, the songs and stories, along with the spirits, the plants and animals, the feelings and dreams" (Bawaka Country et al., 2015: 271).

WILDERNESS AND THE ALLURE OF PRISTINE NATURE

What these brief examples of Amerindian and Aboriginal and Torres Strait Islander ontologies illustrate is the need to critically interrogate the all-too-familiar idea that nature is most natural when human beings are absent from the landscape in question. The work of environmental historian William Cronon has served as a key touchstone for cultural geographers in this regard, including his influential essay 'The trouble with wilderness: or, getting back to the wrong nature.' In this essay, Cronon examines how a particular idea of wilderness came to shape the North American experience of nature from the nineteenth century onwards. Wilderness, as Cronon (1996: 7) sees it, is an everyday concept that has come to represent nature as a landscape absent of humans:

> For many Americans wilderness stands as the last remaining place where civilization, that all too human disease, has not fully infected the earth. It is an island in the polluted sea of urban industrial modernity, the one place where we can turn for escape from our own too-muchness. Seen in this way, wilderness presents itself as the best antidote to our human selves, a refuge we must somehow recover if we hope to save the planet.

Cronon's argument is multifaceted. A key aspect to grasp here is that the romanticised perception of nature as a pure or pristine wilderness that must be preserved away from humans is itself the product of a spatially and temporally situated human culture. Indeed, for Cronon (1996: 7), what we need to understand is that wilderness – and, crucially, the value we assign to it – is "the creation of very particular human cultures at very particular moments in human history."

Cronon's essay unpacks the genealogy of wilderness through the cultural transformations that took place in North America during the nineteenth century, when writers, poets, photographers, and other artists associated with the Romanticist movement turned to nature as a means of articulating the awe-inspiring and the sublime. It was within this historical and geographical context that wilderness, understood as an idealised version of pristine nature, began to take on an almost sacred dimension in the collective psyche. This was especially true for those wealthy urban elites who could afford to travel the distances necessary to experience it, far beyond the city limits. Moreover, through the process of shaping people's experiences of their environment, the culture of nature associated with this wilderness mentality also left its mark on the physical landscape. The reason for this, Cronon explains, is that the romanticisation of wilderness was a key tenet in the emerging environmental movements that were taking shape in North America at the time and which ultimately led to the establishment of the world's first national parks. Thus, America's iconic national parks, including Yellowstone and Yosemite (see Figure 3.1), were specifically designed to preserve wilderness by preventing the spatial encroachment of human society. This is what Cronon (1996: 7) means when he states that wilderness is "quite profoundly a human creation."

Perhaps the most significant dimension of Cronon's critique for cultural geographers, and a reason why it remains relevant almost 30 years after it was first published, is the way it highlights the trouble with wilderness thinking (Vannini and Vannini, 2016). One of the problems that Cronon identifies is that, by valorising the ideal of nature as a pristine landscape, wilderness thinking tends to undervalue forms of nature that exist in messy interrelation with human spaces, including those that are found in cities or agricultural regions (1996: 22). We will return to this question of messy interrelations in the next section. But Cronon also argues that wilderness thinking has been complicit in acts of colonial violence, having served as an intellectual framework for justifying the forced removal of Indigenous peoples from their traditional lands. As Cronon (1996: 15) argues, the creation of national parks across North America meant that Indigenous groups were evicted and "kept out by dint of force, their earlier uses of the land redefined as inappropriate or even illegal." The irony, however, is that the very landscapes colonisers valorised as pristine and sought to protect from human activities were, in fact, shaped by Indigenous cultures and their land management practices stretching back hundreds, if not thousands of

Figure 3.1 A photograph of 'El Capitan,' a three-thousand-foot-high sheer granite monolith located in Yosemite National Park, USA.

years (Fletcher et al., 2021). The troubling legacy of the so-called 'fortress conservation' approach to environmentalism, originally associated with the North American wilderness ideal and then later exported across the globe, continues to reproduce these patterns of dispossession today amid renewed calls to increase the proportion of the globe's surface area currently under conservation protection.

To summarise, then, this section has explored the idea that the way we perceive, experience, and value our environment is shaped by culturally mediated assumptions about nature, which we refer to here as cultures of nature. An important aspect of cultural geography's engagement with nature as a concept thus lies in its invitation to critically interrogate familiar assumptions associated with nature as an idea or concept – in particular, the modern assumption of an ontological divide between nature and society. Finally, through Cronon's work, we showed how the nature-society dualism became both conceptually and physically embedded in the idealised notion of wilderness as a pristine environment, to be protected from human beings at all costs. Underlying the wilderness ideal is a value judgement that nature is most natural when it is devoid of human activity and influence. This ideal, we argue, has fed into, and, in some cases, explicitly justified colonial violence through the devaluation of non-Western ontologies and the physical dispossession of Indigenous groups in the name of wilderness preservation. Attending to cultures of nature, as cultural geographers have done, is thus much more than a philosophically interesting exercise: it provides a critical tool for understanding how power and politics are written into the environment through contestations over nature, its meaning, and its value.

NATURES IN CULTURE

So far, we have been exploring approaches to nature that emphasise the agency of culture, understood as a shared framework of beliefs and aesthetic valuations that shape how people experience their environments in historically and geographically situated contexts. To the extent that they prioritise culture as the dominant force shaping people's experience of (and interactions with) their environments, these approaches can be categorised as examples of *social constructionism* (see **Box 3.1**). Influential amongst the new cultural geographers during the late 1980s and early 1990s (see Duncan and Ley, 1993), social constructionism refers to a philosophical movement based on the idea that our most basic knowledge of the world is mediated by ideas and concepts (i.e. representations) and thus that what we claim to know about reality actually tells us more about ourselves and our modes of representing our environments than it does about reality *per se*. Thus, when Cronon (1996: 7) states that "we too easily imagine that what we behold is Nature when in fact we see the reflection of our own unexamined longings and desires," he is engaging in a form of social constructionism: the aesthetic and moral values attached to the concept of wilderness are, for Cronon, an example of how nature is socially constructed within the specific historical and geographical contexts associated with Western modernity.

BOX 3.1 Social constructionism

Social constructionism is a critical social science framework that explores how our experience and knowledge of the world are shaped by a culture's ideas, values, norms, and desires. Social constructionists argue that there is no such thing as unmediated access to the world; as human beings, we know the world through the lens of collective meaning. For social constructionists, then, it is important to understand how concepts like 'nature' and 'gender,' which appear to refer to an objective reality untouched by culture, are in fact expressions of specific cultural contexts and their associated discourses. Within cultural geography (and particularly non-representational theory), social constructionist approaches have been criticised for placing too much emphasis on the mediating power of representation at the expense of more material and embodied modes of encounter with the world. Nonetheless, the importance of social constructionism as a tool for thinking critically about the politics of representation and the power of discourse would be difficult to deny, given the powerful role concepts like nature continue to play in contemporary society. For a nuanced discussion of social constructionism and its implications for how cultural geographers think about nature, we recommend Noel Castree's (2014) *Making Sense of Nature*.

One of the key strengths of social constructionism is that it has enabled cultural geographers and other social scientists to critically interrogate aspects of our world that are traditionally assumed to be self-evident truths, immune to critical questioning. Such phenomena are often assumed to exist independently of the power structures and value systems that characterise the social world. Social constructionism challenges this assumption by showing how even the most seemingly self-evident facts are situated within and shaped by culture. In the case of nature, then, arguments based on social constructionism are important because they remind us that nature is an idea with multiple genealogies and thus that it is not the self-evident fact that we often assume it to be. So, whereas in some cultural contexts, such as North America, nature might be socially constructed through the idealised aesthetic of a pristine wilderness, in others, nature could include more messy configurations of human and non-human elements that would otherwise be devalued or even overlooked entirely. Gender is another key example where social constructionist arguments have been used by cultural geographers to critically interrogate the self-evidence of the world around us – in this case, the assumed naturalness of heterosexual identities and relationships – and this is something that we will return to in greater detail in ***Chapter 5***.

As significant as they have been, social constructionist arguments are not without their critics. This is especially the case in cultural geography, where, during the late 1990s, there was a shift away from the representational focus of the so-called 'new' cultural geographies to make way for a radically experimental interest in the non-representational forces of affect, embodiment, and practice (see ***Chapter 2*** for an introduction to non-representational theory). A significant consequence of this shift was that it challenged the idea that the study of culture could be reduced to an interpretive analysis of representations and their meanings. Culture, according to non-representational theorists, is always much more than representation: it includes forms of encounter and relation that precede the self-conscious discernment required to represent the world through the mediation of words and concepts. Returning to the concept of wilderness as an example, we might consider how our visceral reactions to a particular environment inevitably exceed the meanings, values, and ideals that we might ascribe to it. There is, in other words, an *excessiveness* to the world that enlivens culture in its irreducibility to human systems of representation, an excessiveness that limits what social constructionist approaches can tell us about the world (Dewsbury et al., 2002).

For many cultural geographers, but particularly those working within or adjacent to non-representational theory, a significant problem with social constructionism is that it leaves little room to consider forms of agency beyond the human. The idea that nature is socially constructed paints the picture of a non-human world that is inherently passive: a blank canvas or empty stage waiting patiently to be shaped by the agency of human societies and their systems of representation. The social constructionist argument assumes that human beings are the sole actors crafting the action on the world's stage; it implies, in other words, a fundamentally *anthropocentric* worldview (see **Box 3.2**). The anthropocentrism associated with social constructionism was explicitly targeted as a cause for concern by cultural geographer Sarah Whatmore (2006) in her seminal paper 'Materialist returns: practising cultural geography for a more-than-human world.' In a bid to break away from the anthropocentrism of social constructionist approaches, Whatmore called for "a cultural

BOX 3.2 Anthropocentrism

Anthropocentrism refers to any way of thinking about reality that privileges human beings over and above all other existing things. While there are many different worldviews that could be described as anthropocentric, in cultural geography the term is typically associated with the humanistic tradition in Western philosophy, with particular emphasis on figures like René Descartes (1596–1650) and Immanuel Kant (1724–1804). Cultural geographers have critiqued Anthropocentrism from a variety of standpoints. Ethically, anthropocentrism is problematic because it grants human beings a greater intrinsic value than other living organisms, which, some would argue, has legitimised centuries of environmental destruction in Western societies. In a deeper sense, anthropocentric approaches are philosophically problematic because they base their ontological claims about the nature of reality on a limited selection of *human* experiences – notably consciousness, thought, reason, etc. Anthropocentrism also ignores how our encounters with animals, plants, and non-living materials have shaped the course of history in unpredictable ways.

geography attentive to the livingness of the world" (2006: 603) – a world which she described as fundamentally 'more-than-human.'

A more-than-human cultural geography, Whatmore (2006: 604) argued, should "neither presume that socio-material change is an exclusively human achievement nor exclude 'the human' from the stuff of fabrication." So, whereas social constructionist frameworks focus attention on the cultures of nature that shape how people experience their environments, Whatmore's more-than-human approach starts from the assumption that culture is itself shaped by the agency, force, or liveliness of non-human nature in its dizzying array of forms. We will return to the issue of the human and its fabrication in more detail in the next section of this chapter. For now, however, the key point to take away from Whatmore's intervention is the idea that culture can no longer be thought of as a purely human sphere, defined by our capacity to perceive, experience, and know the world through the lens of representation. Instead, culture is – and, as Whatmore herself argues, always has been – a thoroughly more-than-human affair, such that the familiar categories of nature and society begin to bleed into each other in interesting ways (hence the subtitle for this section, natures 'in' culture).

Cultural geography's more-than-human turn has continued to flourish since Whatmore's intervention. As a vibrant movement within cultural geography, it has been characterised by a sustained engagement with innovative philosophies and theories as a way of challenging the anthropocentric foundations of geographical thought. Of particular note here is the work of French sociologist and philosopher Bruno Latour (1947–2022), whose work on *Actor-Network Theory* has been taken up by cultural geographers seeking to question anthropocentric accounts of society and culture (see **Box 3.3**).

BOX 3.3 Actor-Network Theory

Actor-Network Theory (ANT) is a social science framework developed by in the late 1980s by key figures in Science and Technology Studies, including Michel Callon, John Law, and Bruno Latour. ANT is known for its radically expansive understanding of 'the social,' which includes not only human actors but also a multitude of non-human things – or *actants*, as Latour (2005) collectively calls them. According to ANT, 'the social' is not a separate domain of reality shaped by mysterious social forces or structures: it is composed of material networks of *actants*, many of which are non-human. As you may have guessed from the word network, ANT is a fundamentally relational theory. Things gain their agency and become *actants* through the networks they form with other things. This means that anything can play a significant role in shaping social reality. Methodologically, ANT traces the networks of associations between the multitudes of *actants* that comprise the social, however unexpected these associations might be. Ideas from ANT have been hugely influential in cultural geography, most notably in shaping Sarah Whatmore's (2006) conceptualisation of 'more-than-human' geography.

Thinking in more-than-human terms requires making space for messy interrelations between humans and non-humans by experimenting with a more capacious, less anthropocentric account of culture and its production. For animal geographers, this entails tracing the material presence and agency of various non-human animals throughout human societies, whether in relation to domestication (Anderson, 1997), consumption (Neo and Emel, 2017), companionship (Fletcher and Platt, 2018), scientific and medical research (Roe and Greenhough, 2023), or emerging forms of co-habitation (and conflict) in urban environments (Barua, 2023). Other geographers have explored similar questions in relation to the liveliness of plants. Examples here include the place-making capacities of urban trees (Phillips et al., 2024); the significance of vegetal spaces such as suburban gardens as key sites in the production of identity and memory (Ginn, 2014); and the capacity for 'weedy' plants to challenge culturally mediated preconceptions about what forms of life belong in particular spaces and times (Virens, 2023).

For these cultural geographers, the production of culture has never been a purely human affair, because human societies have become what they are in/through complex networks of constitutive entanglement with their more-than-human environments. This way of thinking challenges the commonly held assumption that culture is what distinguishes humans as exceptional beings, ontologically separated from the rest of nature. In doing so, it *also* complicates the conventional understanding of culture as a system of representations, encapsulated in language, that human beings then project upon the world. This is not to say that more-than-human geographers are no longer interested in the kinds of phenomena more traditionally associated with culture – things like experience, emotion, understanding, memory, identity, and so on. Far from it! Instead, cultural geographers who are experimenting with more-than-human approaches emphasise how these phenomena ultimately emerge through events of embodied practice and affective encounter, where the material world beyond the human makes an active difference in shaping the times and spaces of the everyday. Here, the experimental techniques and methods associated with non-representational theory (see ***Chapter 7***) have played an important role in enabling geographers to craft alternative narratives about culture, narratives that are more attuned to the non-human natures folded within the most apparently human of experiences.

SINGAPORE: A MORE-THAN-HUMAN CITY?

We want to conclude our discussion of nature 'in' culture through a brief example that, we believe, illustrates both the conceptual significance and practical applications of the more-than-human approaches developed by cultural geographers. This example is the high-tech tropical metropolis of Singapore: a densely populated city-state located off the southern tip of the Malay Peninsula. One of the things that makes Singapore so interesting for cultural geographers like ourselves is the way that it has sought to integrate non-human nature into the material fabric of the city in various ways, including the architectural design of buildings, the planning of public spaces such as walkways and paths, and the innovative use of new technologies (Wang, 2024). For these reasons, Singapore is seen by many as a shining example of what has come to be known as biophilic urbanism: a school of thought that re-imagines city spaces as opportunities for increased contact with non-human nature – a 'city in a garden' instead of a concrete jungle.

Singapore's biophilic approach to urbanism is based on the idea that a greener city is not only more environmentally sustainable but also benefits the physical and mental health of its residents. Green walls and vertical gardens are commonly deployed in indoor spaces such as shopping centres and airport terminals with the aim of dampening the usual stress responses ordinarily associated with the hustle and bustle of city life. Interestingly, many of Singapore's urban natures would not be possible without a whole range of sophisticated technologies. Changi Airport's famous green wall provides a clear example of this. Consisting of approximately 10,000 individual plants and incorporating 25 species, this monumental green wall is one of the world's largest and is maintained by a computer-controlled automated irrigation system. Similarly, the skyline of Gardens by the Bay, Singapore's iconic reinterpretation of the traditional botanic garden, is dominated by the imposing steel structures of its 18 futuristic 'Supertrees' (see Figure 3.2). These structures provide a vertical habitat for over 200 species of plants while also acting as exhaust stacks and platforms for generating solar power. In the words of Andrew Grant, founding director of the architecture consultancy that designed the gardens, the idea behind the supertrees was to create "a fusion of nature, culture and technology on a heroic scale to echo the vision for Singapore as a City in a Garden" (ECT Travel, 2025: np).

Singapore provides an intriguing example for re-imagining what urban life might be like if we no longer base the design of cities on the assumption of a fundamental distinction between society and nature. Strictly speaking, cultural geographers would argue that cities have *always* been more-than-human in some shape or form, despite the modernist desire to present (and oftentimes to physically design) these spaces as triumphs of human rationality over non-human nature (Gandy, 2022). In Singapore, however, what we see taking shape are new forms of entanglement mediated by sophisticated technologies, new instances of nature 'in' culture that are being written into the material fabric of space and place in ways that encourage a radical rethinking of what a more-than-human city is – indeed, of what such a city might become. With its sensitivity towards the liveliness of non-human nature, cultural geography's innovative concepts and experimental methods provide a means of making sense of these emerging environments and the impact that they have in shaping and/or disrupting our experience of ourselves and the world within the context of future cities.

Figure 3.2 Steel tree-like structures at Singapore's Gardens by the Bay attraction, towering above tourists who are walking beneath them in the foreground. Photograph by author.

HUMAN NATURE?

As we have just discussed, more-than-human approaches to cultural geography start from the idea that the relationships between people and their environments cannot be entirely reduced to an analysis of a society's representations (i.e. the systems of concepts and ideas that frame how people come to experience, understand, and value the world around them). This is not to say, however, that the social constructionist frameworks introduced in the first section of this chapter are no longer relevant. The abstract ideal of wilderness, for instance, retains a powerful influence as a representational framework that shapes how Western societies relate to non-human nature, both aesthetically *and* ethically. The popularity of reality television shows such as The History Channel's *Alone*, where contestants compete for cash prizes based on who can survive the longest in remote environments, is a case in point. For cultural geographers, shows like *Alone* offer a fascinating insight into the way our social constructions and non-representational experiences of nature rub up against one another in interesting ways. Insights about the social construction of nature are revealed most noticeably through the things the contestants say about nature, but also through a whole series of more subtle assumptions embedded in the premise of the show. These assumptions include the idea that spending time in wild spaces will teach you important things about yourself and the world and that such experiences of remoteness and isolation provide unique opportunities for personal growth and reflection.

What more-than-human approaches remind us, however, is that the world has a tendency to push back against our most familiar representational frameworks because its materiality (see **Box 1.2**) cannot be fully captured in words. Ideas and concepts such as wilderness and the wild certainly play a significant role in shaping how we humans experience non-human nature, but the familiarity that they generate is an inherently limited one from the perspective of a more-than-human world that doesn't play by linguistic rules. In the case of *Alone*, this irreducible materiality is laid bare when a particular turn of events disrupts or challenges the socially constructed framework that a contestant had previously relied upon to make sense of their environment. An unexpected downpour, a fish slipping the line at the last minute, or an unnerving visit from a hungry bear can quickly undermine a contestant's deeply held associations of wilderness with majesty, wonder, and awe. In fact, while most experiences of nature on *Alone* begin with contestants adopting the familiar Western trope of a celebratory encounter with the sublime, this often quickly fades to boredom as the monotony of the environment and the weight of social isolation take hold. It is perhaps in such moments that contestants are faced with what geographer Nigel Clark (2011: xiii) refers to as "nature's capacity to be a great deal more or a lot less than we would ask of it."

In this final section, we want to highlight a third exciting dimension to cultural geographic debates about nature. This third dimension concerns the way cultural geographers have approached the question of *human nature* – or, in other words, how we conceptualise the human in a philosophical sense. Cultural geography's willingness to engage with these philosophically challenging questions about human nature is, we would argue, another key characteristic of what it means to think geographically about the cultural significance of nature. While the question of what it means to be human is certainly of interest in other social science disciplines (sociology, criminology, and cultural studies, for example), cultural geography provides a unique perspective to the extent that it frames this question in terms of the *constitutive* relationships that take shape between people and their environments. As we noted in ***Chapter 1***, cultural geographers are fundamentally interested in the ontological primacy of relations over fixed categories such as 'the human.' This means that they approach this question of what it means to be human from the perspective that we are continually being shaped and transformed through the relations that we participate in.

The significance of social constructionist approaches within these debates is that they highlight how representations of non-human nature are often intimately tied to certain ways of thinking about the human, most notably the anthropocentric assumption that humans are unique or 'exceptional' beings when compared to the rest of nature. Despite what the science of evolution tells us, anthropocentrism retains a powerful hold over the modern worldview (Ruddick, 2017). Since its origination in the period known as the European Renaissance, Western humanistic philosophy has bolstered this seductive notion that human beings are not like anything else that exists in nature, and, by extension, that this is what being human is all about. French philosopher René Descartes (1596–1650), a key figure in the Western philosophical canon, argued that human beings were unique because they were the only beings to possess conscious minds as well as their physical bodies. Descartes believed that non-human nature (including animals) was lacking in mind and could therefore be understood as nothing more than a complex physical mechanism devoid of agency – and, in the case of animals, lacking the ability to experience suffering.

This brief excursion into Descartes's philosophy is useful because it further illustrates the cultural-geographic argument that the social constructions shaping our interactions with the environment often reflect deeply held ideas and assumptions about what it means to be human. Thus, the belief that it is the presence of consciousness that defines human nature is, in a certain sense, predicated upon Descartes' prior assertion that the rest of nature is all matter and no mind. It is important to note that there are many people around the world who would fundamentally disagree with Descartes' rather lifeless account of non-human nature. This includes the animistic worldviews of the Australian and Amerindian Indigenous groups mentioned earlier in this chapter, as well as a growing number of contemporary philosophers who are interested in exploring more capacious definitions of sentience that extend to the non-human world (see Godfrey-Smith, 2016). Descartes' philosophy is just one example of how this relationship between constructions of nature and humanistic philosophies plays out. While a full account of the historical evolution of this relationship lies beyond the scope of this book, it is worth noting that similar critiques can be applied to many of the most influential philosophers in the Western tradition, some of whom you may be familiar with if only by name. This includes Immanuel Kant's theory that the faculty of moral reasoning distinguishes human beings from the rest of nature, as well as Martin Heidegger's assertion that humans alone are temporal beings and, as such, are unique in their capacity to experience their own mortality.

For cultural geographers, the question of what it means to be human is as much a matter of geographical enquiry as it is of philosophical speculation. Where humanist philosophers like Descartes, Kant, and Heidegger sought to anchor their definition of the human in an unchanging essence (i.e. the abstract *ideal* of human nature), cultural geographers, on the other hand, have engaged with a range of *post-humanist* thinkers who emphasise the malleability of the human in a more-than-human world (see **Box 3.4**). As such, Clark's (2011: xiii) argument that nature often turns out to be "a great deal more or a lot less than we would ask of it" applies equally to the concept of *human nature*, because the boundaries between human bodies and their environments are fundamentally porous rather than fixed. Like all other beings, humans enter into uncertain relationships with their environments in order to sustain themselves, and through this process of relation, both human beings and their environments are transformed. Human nature turns out to be a lot less certain (and a lot less human) than philosophers such as Descartes or Kant might have wanted us to believe! At the same time, however, the complex folding of non-human nature within culture means that there is always much more to the human than traditionally meets the eye.

Just as cultural geographers have argued that the world's liveliness pushes back against our representational concepts, this world also resists our desire for an unchanging human nature through the transformative encounters that its materiality engenders. The kinds of transformations we are referring to here can be dramatic. Consider, for instance, how humanity's fateful encounter with fossil fuels not only transformed the physical make-up of the planet and its atmosphere but, at the same time, fuelled forms of communication and travel that enabled a kind of global consciousness to emerge across spaces and times that were previously disconnected from each other. Thus, from a cultural geography perspective, the question of what it means to be human remains fundamentally entangled with the geological materiality of coal, oil, and natural gas, generating what cultural geographers Clark and Yusoff (2014) call a 'geo-social formation.' Some transformations may be more subtle, however, working through registers of embodied feeling that tend not to manifest as grand narratives. Here, cultural geographers have explored the way that visual arts such as painting, photography, and cinema can be used to experiment with non-human perspectives, and, in the process, to reshape the affective bases through which we come to understand ourselves in relation to non-human others (Williams et al., 2019).

BOX 3.4 Posthumanism

There are two main ways of understanding posthumanism. First, posthumanism is sometimes used to describe a situation where, for better or worse, technological advances enable human beings to transcend their biological limits. This is how posthumanism tends to be talked about in popular culture (think Elon Musk and Silicon Valley utopianism more generally!). In the context of cultural geography, however, there is a second definition of posthumanism that is generally more significant: posthumanism as a critique of (and alternative to) Western humanism as the philosophical framework that dominated the humanities and social sciences for most of the twentieth century. In this second definition, the prefix 'post-' refers to humanistic philosophy rather than the human *per se*: posthumanism as an alternative to humanism that sees the world through interconnection and entanglement rather than anthropocentrism (see **Box 3.2**). Key theorists in posthumanism include Donna Haraway, Rosi Braidotti, and N. Katherine Hayles. To find out more about cultural geography's relationship with posthumanism, see Williams et al. (2019).

Cultural geography's sensitivity towards these transformations provides a much-needed critical perspective when it comes to contemporary conversations about the Anthropocene. We imagine that many of our readers will already be familiar with this term, which, in recent years, has played an increasingly significant role in shaping public conversations about environmental change. For those readers who are less familiar with the term, the key idea associated with the Anthropocene is that we are living at a time where human beings have become the principal driver of environmental change and that the impact of human activity can now be detected across the vast timescales of the planet's geological history. The concept of the Anthropocene has, however, been fiercely debated by scientists since it was first popularised by Paul Crutzen and Eugene Stoermer in 2000. A key source of disagreement among geologists relates to the issue of how to measure the geological impact of human activity and thus how to formally date the start of the Anthropocene as a geologic period. While some scientists situate the onset of the Anthropocene in the layer of artificial radiocarbons deposited through nuclear weapons testing in the 1960s, others claim that humans have been altering the chemical make-up of the Earth's atmosphere (and thus the geologic record) for the past 8,000 years.

These disagreements are probably part of the reason why, in 2024, the International Commission on Stratigraphy officially rejected the Anthropocene as a formal unit of geologic time. Despite this ruling from the geologists, the Anthropocene is likely to remain a concept that has migrated far beyond its scientific context to the sphere of public discourse and debate. Thinking as cultural geographers, it is important to critically reflect upon the various assumptions about human nature that are tied up with the concept of the Anthropocene. Who or what, we might ask, is the *Anthropos* being referred to here? The unstated assumption is that the Anthropocene refers to humankind in the most general sense of an abstract 'human nature.' A major problem with this assumption, however, is that it ignores the fact that different populations are differentially implicated in these processes of environmental transformation, whether this be in terms of their agency to enact such changes or their exposure to their emerging impacts. Is it an abstract category of human nature (i.e. *Anthropos*) that is responsible for dramatically altering the chemical composition of the planet's atmosphere, such that levels of carbon dioxide are the highest they have been in the past three million years? Or is it more accurate to say that *some* people (i.e. largely those living in Western countries) bear greater responsibility for these changes than others? Pursuing this idea further, Jason Moore (2017) argues that a better term to use to describe our current age would be the Capitalocene, substituting the uneven landscape of capitalism for the universalising notion of '*Anthropos.*'

Finally, by placing so much emphasis on the agency of human beings in their capacity to transform non-human nature, the concept of the Anthropocene is perhaps not well suited to grappling with the changing nature of human itself. As we have discussed throughout this section, there is a more-than-human dimension to human beings that arises from our relational interactions with various forms of non-human agency (this is particularly the case when it comes to the agency of technology, which we explore in ***Chapter 4***). Some of these interactions pose troubling consequences for the future health of human populations. As we write this book, discourses relating to environmental pollution are shifting towards the growing problem of microplastics: tiny particles of plastic that are accumulating not only in the environment but also, scientists have shown, within the human body. While the impacts of these particles on human beings are yet to be fully understood, scientists are concerned that some of the chemicals found in plastics are disrupting the body's endocrine system, whereas others are known carcinogens. On the one hand, this example of microplastics clearly illustrates the astonishing impact that certain forms of human activity have had in transforming the nature of our non-human environments – indeed, in transforming the very nature of 'nature'! On the other hand, the accumulation of microplastics in our bodies shows how these transformed environments also expose us to uncertain relations with new forms of non-human agency, changing what it means to be human at the cellular level. Cultural geography's more-than-human understanding of what the human is (and what it might become) thus provides an important reminder that, despite their geological impacts, human beings are not the only source of agency in the Anthropocene.

CONCLUSION

Our aim in this chapter has been to provide readers with a better sense of the significance of nature as a key concept in cultural geography. In bringing this discussion to a close, we want to reiterate that what we have provided here is a highly selective snapshot of the different areas of research that posit nature as an ongoing matter of concern for cultural geographers, rather than an exhaustive literature review. Three significant agendas were introduced, beginning with the role of representations in shaping how societies perceive, understand and value their environments (what we termed cultures of nature). Here, we paid particular attention to wilderness mentality as a persistent aesthetical and ethical ideal that continues to shape modern experiences of nature. In the second section, we noted the limits of these social constructionist approaches for making sense of the complex entanglements of nature and society that constitute cultural life. We then showed how various more-than-human approaches have been developed by cultural geographers to better conceptualise and empirically capture the myriad forms of non-human nature that shape, give life to, and sometimes threaten culture. Finally, we explored how, for many cultural geographers, a critical interest in the concept of nature extends to a more philosophical concern with understanding *human nature* in a more-than-human world. The take-home point from this third agenda is that cultural geography provides a conceptually innovative alternative to the anthropocentric logics of humanistic philosophy that have traditionally informed the study of culture in the humanities and social science disciplines.

FURTHER READING

Barua, M. *Lively Cities: Reconfiguring Urban Ecology*. Minneapolis: University of Minnesota Press, 2023.

Bawaka Country, S. Wright, S. Suchet-Pearson, K. Lloyd, L. Burarrwanga, R. Ganambarr, M. Ganambarr-Stubbs, B. Ganambarr and D. Maymuru. "Working with and learning from Country: Decentring human author-ity." *Cultural Geographies* 22, no. 2 (2015): 269–283. https://doi.org/10.1177/1474474014539248

Castree, N. *Nature*. London: Routledge, 2005.

Cronon, W. "The trouble with wilderness: Or, getting back to the wrong nature." *Environmental History* 1, no. 1 (1996): 7–28.

Wang, J. *Reimagining the more-than-human city*. Harvard: MIT Press, 2024.

REFERENCES

Allen, C. D. "On actor-network theory and landscape." *Area* 43, no. 3 (2011): 274–280. http://www.jstor.org/stable/41240503

Anderson, K. "A walk on the wild side: A critical geography of domestication." *Progress in Human Geography* 21, no. 4 (1997): 463–485. https://doi.org/10.1191/030913297673999021

Barua, M. *Lively Cities: Reconfiguring Urban Ecology*. Minneapolis: University of Minnesota Press, 2023.

Bawaka Country, S. Wright, S. Suchet-Pearson, K. Lloyd, L. Burarrwanga, R. Ganambarr, M. Ganambarr-Stubbs, B. Ganambarr and D. Maymuru. "Working with and learning from Country: Decentring human authority." *Cultural Geographies* 22, no. 2 (2015): 269–283. https://doi.org/10.1177/1474474014539248

Bosco, F. J. "Actor-network theory, networks, and relational approaches in human geography." In S. Aitken and G. Valentine (eds.) *Approaches to Human Geography* (pp. 136–146). London: Sage, 2006.

Braun, B. "Environmental issues: Writing a more-than-human urban geography." *Progress in Human Geography* 29, no. 5 (2005): 635–650. https://doi.org/10.1191/0309132505ph574pr

Braun, B. and S. Whatmore (eds.). *Political Matter: Technoscience, Democracy, and Public Life*. Minneapolis: University of Minnesota Press, 2010.

Cameron, E., S. De Leeuw and C. Desbiens. "Indigeneity and ontology." *Cultural Geographies* 21, no. 1 (2014): 19–26. https://doi.org/10.1177/1474474013500229

Castree, N. *Making Sense of Nature: Representation, Politics and Democracy*. London and New York: Routledge, 2014.

Castree, N. *Nature*. London: Routledge, 2005.

Clark, N. *Inhuman Nature: Sociable Life on a Dynamic Planet*. London: Sage, 2011.

Clark, N. and K. Yusoff. "Combustion and society: A fire-centred history of energy use." *Theory, Culture & Society* 31, no. 5 (2014): 203–226. https://doi.org/10.1177/0263276414536929

Cronon, W. "The trouble with wilderness: Or, getting back to the wrong nature." *Environmental History* 1, no. 1 (1996): 7–28.

Crutzen, P. J. and E. F. Stoermer. "The 'Anthropocene' (2000)." In S. Benner, G. Lax, P. J. Crutzen, U. Poschl, J. Lelieveld and H. G. Brauch (eds.) *Paul J. Crutzen and the Anthropocene: A New Epoch in Earth's History* (pp. 19–22). Cham: Springer, 2021.

Demeritt, D. "Science, social constructivism and nature." In B. Braun and N. Castree (eds.) *Remaking Reality: Nature at the Millennium* (pp. 172–192). London & New York: Routledge, 1998.

Dewsbury, J. D., P. Harrison, M. Rose and J. Wylie. "Enacting geographies." *Geoforum* 33, no. 4 (2002): 437–440. https://doi.org/10.1016/s0016-7185%2802%2900029-5

Duncan, J. and D. Ley (eds.). *Place/Culture/Representation*. Abingdon: Routledge, 1993.

ECT Travel. *Singapore's supertrees*, 2025. https://www.ecttravel.com/news/singapores-supertrees [Accessed 10/01/2025].

Fletcher, M.-S., R. Hamilton, W. Dressler and L. Palmer. "Indigenous knowledge and the shackles of wilderness." *Proceedings of the National Academy of Sciences* 118, no. 40 (2021). https://doi.org/10.1073/pnas.2022218118

Fletcher, T. and L. Platt. "(Just) a walk with the dog? Animal geographies and negotiating walking spaces." *Social & Cultural Geography* 19, no. 2 (2018): 211–229. https://doi.org/10.1080/14649365.2016.1274047

Ganambarr, R., M. Ganambarr-Stubbs, B. Ganambarr, D. Maymuru, S. Suchet-Pearson, S. Wright, L. Daley and K. Lloyd. "Nature culture." In K. Dombroski, M. Goodwin, J. Qian, A. Williams and P. Cloke (eds.) *Introducing Human Geographies* (4th ed.) (p. X). London: Routledge, 2024.

Gandy, M. *Natura urbana: Ecological Constellations In urban Space*. Harvard: MIT Press, 2022.

Ginn, F. "Death, absence and afterlife in the garden." *Cultural Geographies* 21, no. 2 (2014): 229–245. https://doi.org/10.1177/1474474013483220

Ginn, F. and D. Demeritt. "Nature: A contested concept." In S. L. Holloway, S. P. Rice, G. Valentine and N. Clifford (eds.) *Key Concepts in Geography* (2nd ed) (pp. 300–311). London: Sage, 2010.

Godfrey-Smith, P. *Other Minds: The Octopus and Evolution of Intelligent Life*. London: William Collins, 2016.

Head, L. *Beyond Green: The Social Life of Australian Nature*. Melbourne: Melbourne University Press, 2025.

Head, L. *Hope and Grief in the Anthropocene: Re-Conceptualising Human-Nature Relations*. London: Routledge, 2016.

Hinchliffe, S. *Geographies of Nature: Societies, Environments, Ecologies*. London: Sage, 2007.

Instone, L. "Situating nature: On doing cultural geographies of Australian nature." *Australian Geographer* 35, no. 2 (2004): 131–140. https://doi.org/10.1080/0004918042000249430

Kirsch, S. "Cultural geography I: Materialist turns." *Progress in Human Geography* 37, no. 3 (2012): 433–441. https://doi.org/10.1177/0309132512459479

Kirsch, S. "Cultural geography II: Cultures of nature (and technology)." *Progress in Human Geography* 38, no. 5 (2014): 691–702. https://doi.org/10.1177/0309132513516913

Latour, B. *Reassembling the Social: An Introduction to Actor-Network-Theory*. Oxford: Oxford University Press, 2005.

Moore, J. W. "The capitalocene, part 1: On the nature and origins of our ecological crisis." *The Journal of Peasant Studies* 44, no. 3 (2017): 594–630. https://doi.org/10.1080/03066150.2016.1235036

Neo, H. and J. Emel. *Geographies of Meat: Politics, Economy and Culture*. London: Routledge, 2017.

Peace, A. "Talking about bushfires: Difference and division in Australia's environmental crisis." *Anthropology today* 36, no. 4 (2020): 3–7. https://doi.org/10.1111/1467-8322.12588

Phillips, C., E. Straughan and J. Atchison. "Gratitude for and to nature: Insights from emails to urban trees." *Social & Cultural Geography* 25, no. 3 (2024): 363–384. https://doi.org/10.1080/14649365.2023.2177715

Pol, G. "What is Country?" *Common Ground*, Common Ground First Nations, 2023. https://www.commonground.org.au/article/what-is-country

Roberts, T. "From 'new materialism' to 'machinic assemblage': Agency and affect in IKEA." *Environment and Planning A: Economy and Space* 44, no. 10 (2012): 2512–2529. https://doi.org/10.1068/a44692

Roe, E. and B. Greenhough. "A good life? A good death? Reconciling care and harm in animal research." *Social & Cultural Geography* 24, no. 1 (2023): 49–66. https://doi.org/10.1080/14649365.2021.1901977

Rose, G. "Situating knowledges: Positionality, reflexivities and other tactics." *Progress in Human Geography* 21, no. 3 (1997): 305–320. https://doi.org/10.1191/030913297673302122

Ruddick, S. M. "Rethinking the subject, reimagining worlds." *Dialogues in Human Geography* 7, no. 2 (2017): 119–139. https://doi.org/10.1177/2043820617717847

Vannini, P. and A. Vannini. *Wilderness*. Abingdon: Routledge, 2016.

Virens, A. "Plants out of place: How appreciation of weeds unsettles nature in New Zealand." *New Zealand Geographer* 79, no. 2 (2023): 65–74. https://doi.org/10.1111/nzg.12364

Viveiros de Castro, E. *Cannibal Metaphysics*. Minneapolis: Univocal, 2014.

Wang, J. *Reimagining the More-Than-Human city*. Harvard: MIT Press, 2024.

Whatmore, S. *Hybrid Geographies: Natures Cultures Spaces*. London: Sage, 2002.

Whatmore, S. "Mapping knowledge controversies: Science, democracy and the redistribution of expertise." *Progress in Human Geography* 33, no. 5 (2009): 587–598. https://doi.org/10.1177/0309132509339841

Whatmore, S. "Materialist returns: Practising cultural geography in and for a more-than-human world." *Cultural Geographies* 13, no. 4 (2006): 600–609. https://doi.org/10.1191/1474474006cgj377oa

Williams, N. and T. Keating. "From abstract thinking to thinking abstractions: Introducing speculative geographies." In N. Williams and T. Keating (eds.) *Speculative Geographies: Ethics, Technologies, Aesthetics*. Singapore: Springer, 2022.

Williams, N., M. Patchett, A. Lapworth, T. Roberts and T. Keating. "Practising post-humanism in geographical research." *Transactions of the Institute of British Geographers* 44, no. 4 (2019): 637–643. https://doi.org/10.1111/tran.12322

4

TECHNOLOGY

INTRODUCTION

One of the central arguments of this book is that, for cultural geographers, the desire to understand and make sense of culture is framed through a conceptually rigorous appreciation of the relationships between humans and their environments. In ***Chapter 3***, we explored how this uniquely geographical sensitivity to the more-than-human dimensions of culture has led some cultural geographers to question the typically anthropocentric (and largely Eurocentric) frameworks through which nature is theoretically conceptualised, spatially situated, and ethically/aesthetically valued in the West. The significance of nature as a cultural-geographical concept means that we will be revisiting some of these important arguments in later chapters – particularly in relation to the cultural geographies of bodies in ***Chapter 5*** – but also in this chapter, which focuses on technology as a key site where the more-than-human aspects of contemporary culture are brought into sharper focus and where the very concepts of 'human' and 'environment' are called into question.

One of the challenges associated with writing about technology relates to the staggering rate of technological change that is currently shaping human societies around the world (albeit in ways that are geographically uneven in their socioeconomic impacts). The notion that we are living at a time of exponential technological change is increasingly adopted as a kind of mantra amongst the world's leading tech-corporations, who often chant it to justify their ruthless pursuit of profit at the expense of ecological sustainability

DOI: 10.4324/9781003542667-4

and the rights of workers across the globe. As critical social scientists, then, cultural geographers would encourage people to remain somewhat suspicious of these techno-utopian discourses and the performative politics that they enact. That said, the magnitude of technological change witnessed since the onset of the 1800s and its ongoing impact on culture is undeniably astonishing. The history of human evolution is tightly entangled with that of technological change, with evidence of rudimentary tool use stretching back as far as 3.4 million years (Roser, 2023). From this point, however, scientists estimate that it took a further 2.4 million years for our ancestors to harness the power of fire for cooking (Roser, 2023). Compare this to the rate of technological change over the last century: the first human flight was achieved by the Wright brothers in 1903, but it was a mere 66 years later, in 1969, that human beings first set foot on the moon. In more recent history, the rate of technological change has been further accelerated by rapid advances in semiconductor manufacturing technologies. The smartphones available to consumers in 2026 can carry out upwards of 40 trillion operations per second, housed in a platform the size of the human hand. This is roughly 20,000 times the processing power of CRAY-2, the record-breaking supercomputer of the 1980s, which, in stark contrast, was the size of a small room and weighed in at a whopping 2,500 kilograms (Adobe Acrobat Team, 2022).

An inevitable consequence of this accelerating rate of change is that the examples we will be referring to in this chapter are likely to age quite rapidly, as the speed of contemporary technological changes outstrips the time it takes for academics to think about them and to then articulate these thoughts in the form of a published manuscript. We are writing this book at a time when artificial intelligence (AI) is increasingly dominating discussions about technology and its relationship with society and culture. This is especially true for forms of so-called generative AI that power conversational chatbots such as ChatGPT, as well as 'text-to-image' applications like DALL-E (both of which are owned by Silicon Valley company OpenAI). Some of these technologies will no doubt shape your encounter with this book. Perhaps it was recommended to you by an algorithm that learned something about your interests by analysing the unimaginable amounts of data generated in/through your daily activities? Or perhaps you are using an AI-enabled application to identify and summarise the book's key arguments? Even if you are reading this book offline, it is highly likely that AI has had some role in shaping the environment around you – and, crucially, how you feel, think, and act in the world. For cultural geographers, therefore, this moment of profound technological change encapsulates "a broader cultural shift whereby AI has entered not only the consciousness of the average person, but is rapidly becoming a routine part of everyday life for many" (Maalsen et al., 2023: 1).

Cultural geographers continue to make important contributions to the study of AI as a technological innovation that is transforming culture by reshaping the interface between people and their more-than-human environments (Cockayne et al., 2017; Birtchnell and Elliott, 2018; Amoore, 2020; Lundman and Nordstrom, 2023; Lapworth and Roberts, 2024; Roberts et al., 2024). We will return to this work in greater detail later in the chapter. But whatever technologies are currently capturing the headlines, the cultural-geographical perspectives that we introduce in this chapter provide powerful tools for grappling with some of the long-standing cultural problematics associated with technology and its place in human societies – and, significantly, with making sense of and responding to technological change. Something else to note, from the very outset, is that human geographical engagements with technology tend to cut across the disciplinary subfields of cultural geography, social geography, urban geography, and what might be broadly labelled as critical geographies. Thus, urban geographers are interested in the ways AI is transforming culture at the level of lived experience through urban planning initiatives like smart cities and the social disruptions heralded by the promise of automated vehicles (Bissell et al., 2020). For critical geographers or Marxist geographers, understanding how powerful corporations are investing in technologies to manipulate the cultural production of collective memory and attention, as well as exploring new ways of resisting these processes, is a key area of concern (Kinsley, 2015). And then there is the burgeoning field of digital geographies, which brings together insights from all corners of human geography to shed light on the complexities of digital life (see Ash et al., 2019).

While acknowledging these productive overlaps, our aim is to retain a focus on the cultural dimensions of technological change as much as possible. In doing so, we want to emphasise what it is that cultural geography adds to contemporary discussions about technology and the impacts of technological change on human society. One of cultural geography's key strengths lies, we believe, in its nuanced appreciation of the capacity for technologies to transform human experience – and, therefore, the very fabric of human culture – by fundamentally reshaping the environments in which we live. Furthermore, the fact that many of these technologies operate in the background of our everyday lives, at speeds that are too fast to be registered by human consciousness, requires an understanding of culture in radically non-representational terms. From the perspective of cultural geography, then, culture is not simply a set of linguistic discourses *about* technology that requires critical interrogation; rather, cultural geographers remind us that, in many respects, *culture is itself a kind of technological production or achievement.* So, while representation, discourse, symbolism, and meaning are still important expressions of culture, they each remain unthinkable without an appreciation of the various technologies (e.g. the pigment, the pencil, the printing press, the personal computer, etc.) that make this expression possible.

To conclude this introduction, cultural geography's perspective on technology is fundamentally informed by its underlying interest in the constitutive entanglements that complicate clear-cut distinctions between people and environment, society and nature, and human and non-human. Indeed, it is this underlying interest in how the human is relationally constituted in/through its various modes of interfacing with the environment that explains why technology has remained a key object of interest within cultural geographic thought. In the following section, we provide further context by situating cultural geography approaches in relation to the intellectual climate that dominated Western philosophical debates about technology during the second half of the twentieth century. Here, we pay particular attention to the work of German phenomenologist Martin Heidegger, whose reactionary critique of modern technology as something that distances human beings from their true essence has remained hugely influential, informing both academic discussions and popular narratives.

Following on from this, we show how a cultural geography perspective enables a less reactionary, more nuanced analysis of the cultural dimensions of technology in the twenty-first century through the idea of an evolving, co-constitutive relation between humans and their technologies. This idea is unpacked through the real-world example of generational cohorts (i.e. 'Millennials,' 'Gen Z' and 'Gen Alpha') as a way of illustrating how moments of technological innovation feed into and shape the non-representational dimensions of collective experience, memory, and identity. Here, we also introduce post-phenomenology as a theoretical framework recently adopted by cultural geographers interested in the technological conditions of human subjectivity and subjective experience (Ash and Simpson, 2016).

Finally, in the third section, we turn specifically to the example of AI as a contemporary technology that looks poised to transform the non-representational dimensions of culture in significant ways. We briefly unpack a selection of innovative cultural-geographical perspectives on AI in relation to two key themes: trust and creativity. Beginning with trust, we explore how cultural geographers have turned to everyday technologies such as Google Maps to rethink what trust and trustworthiness look and feel like in a world of intelligent machines (Roberts et al., 2024). Following this, we address the issue of creativity and the impact that emerging forms of AI are having on artistic production and aesthetic tastes in contemporary societies (Birtchnell and Elliott, 2018; Nordstrom et al., 2023).

TECHNOLOGY, MODERNITY, AND CULTURE

To understand how cultural geographers have contributed to the study of technology and its societal impacts, we first need to know something about the intellectual trends and traditions that dominated discussions about technology during the twentieth century. This was a period characterised by a phenomenal rate of technological change. Innovations in telecommunications, aviation, and pharmaceuticals (to name but a few domains) were reshaping the materiality of everyday life at timescales that were now much shorter than a single generation and, in the process, crystallising new consistencies of culture through an unfolding re-organisation of space, time, organic life, and even physical matter. According to critical human geographer David Harvey, these re-organisations generated a situation characterised by "time-space compression," in which advances in communication and transport technologies brought distant places closer together while simultaneously accelerating the pace of life (Harvey, 1989). The sense of acceleration associated with the technological innovations of the twentieth century is something that most people can intuitively relate to, to the extent that it has become a key part of the way the relationship between technology and culture is narrated today. Consider, for instance, how technological interfaces like Zoom or Microsoft Teams rely upon the speed of electronic communication to shrink the space between, say, a university lecturer and an online cohort of geographically dispersed students. Space shrinks *because* these communication technologies operate at faster speeds, generating an accelerated experience of temporality as the passing of time is fragmented into shorter and shorter intervals.

And yet, other cultural geographers have argued that the situation is perhaps less straightforward, particularly when considering the impact of technologies outside the domains of communication and transport. According to Jon May and Nigel Thrift (2001: 10),

> When these more numerous developments are considered, and the connections between each traced, the picture is less of any simple acceleration in the pace of life or experience of spatial 'collapse' than of a far more complex restructuring in the nature and experience of time and space reaching through the nineteenth and in to the early decades of the twentieth century.

For May and Thrift, Harvey's argument that technologies have compressed or even collapsed our experience of spatial distance through an acceleration of everyday life fails to capture the nuances of the cultural transformations associated with the technological innovations of the late nineteenth and early twentieth centuries. Instead, May and Thrift show how collective experiences of space and time have been complicated by new technologies in ways that are not fully captured by Harvey's compression theory. A key example here are technologies associated with "light and power" (e.g. early forms of gas lighting), which, the authors argue, decoupled cultural perceptions and experiences of time from diurnal cycles of day and night, while simultaneously expanding the accessibility of urban space for many city dwellers (May and Thrift, 2001: 11). Similarly, the cinematic use of photographic and projection technologies fractured the cultural experience of space into discontinuous perspectives and enabled disparate orders of time to be captured, perceived, and thought (May and Thrift, 2001: 11).

May and Thrift's argument is important because it emphasises what might be described as the multifaceted, nonlinear, and ultimately *ambiguous* nature of the technological developments unfolding during this time. In particular, the development of military technologies, like the machine gun, radar, and nuclear weapons, exposes the ambiguity of technological progress through the global destruction and bloodshed that took place during the twentieth century. On the one hand, then, we might be tempted to paint a picture of technology as the pinnacle of human achievement, the embodiment of scientific knowledge, and the epitome of societal progress: technological machines are, by this account, the physical embodiment of reason, the distinguishing attribute that makes us human. On the other hand, the long shadow cast by the violent events of the twentieth century – including the Battle of the Somme in 1916, the Holocaust during World War II, the detonation of atomic bombs over the civilian populations of Hiroshima and Nagasaki in Japan in 1945, and the terrifying threat of nuclear winter during the Cold War – undermines the association of technological change with the ideal of progress associated with *Enlightenment* humanism (see **Box 4.1**). From this second perspective, technology appears less as a physical embodiment of human reason and more like a threat to humanity: morally, in the sense of technology's capacity to undermine our humanity through events of industrial slaughter, but also, in the wake of nuclear weapons, existentially, through its capacity to destroy both the social and ecological conditions of planetary life (see Figure 4.1).

Highlighting this fundamental ambiguity is important because it helps to explain why reactionary approaches to technology have enjoyed lasting appeal, not only in humanities and social science scholarship but also in public discourse more generally. By reactionary, we are referring to philosophical theories or worldviews that present technology as a force that detracts from, undermines, or compromises an assumed ideal of 'humanness' or 'human nature.' A defining feature of these reactionary approaches is the assertion that modern technologies have become increasingly functional and

Figure 4.1 A mushroom cloud rising above the Japanese city of Nagasaki after an atomic bomb was dropped on it by American forces on August 9, 1945. Public Domain.

utilitarian in their scope, and, for this reason, that contemporary society's cultural fascination with technology risks alienating human beings from their true nature – indeed, from what it means to be human. Such approaches are often founded in broader critiques of modernity, whereby the kinds of technologically induced transformations witnessed during the nineteenth, twentieth, and twenty-first centuries are presented as expression of cultural decadence and decline. The culture of modernity is characterised, or so these approaches suggest, by a collective forgetting of what it means to be human that culminates in the horrors of technology's destructive tendencies.

BOX 4.1 The Enlightenment

The Enlightenment refers to a period of intellectual, technological, cultural, and political upheaval that began in Europe towards the end of the seventeenth century. A key characteristic of this period was a newfound confidence in the power of reason – and, specifically, the newly established scientific method – to advance the human condition and, through technological innovation, to rebuild the world in its own image. Philosophically, the ideas of René Descartes were of critical importance in setting the stage for the Enlightenment. By reducing matter to physical extension, Descartes effectively established science's metaphysical framework and equated the act of measuring with knowing. The Enlightenment is often considered a period of optimistic humanism: through science, humans were now seen to be the makers of their own destiny, using rational knowledge to dispel the myths of religion and to build machines that could transform humanity's lot. Of course, there are many reasons to be critical of this narrative – not least because it focuses on a highly Eurocentric interpretation of progress at the expense of innovations that have taken place in other parts of the globe.

HEIDEGGER'S CRITIQUE OF WESTERN METAPHYSICS

A key thinker who has shaped reactionary approaches to modern technology, and whose work continues to have a profound impact within humanities and social science disciplines (including cultural geography), is the German philosopher Martin Heidegger (1889–1976). While a thorough analysis of Heidegger's philosophy lies far beyond the scope of this book, there are some key aspects of his approach to technology that are worth unpacking, given their significant role in shaping how the question of the relationship between technology and culture is often approached today. First, then, Heidegger's disdain for modern technology is part of a broader reaction against what he called 'Western metaphysics': an intellectual perspective or attitude which, according to Heidegger, reduces the world to calculable matter, waiting to be rationalised and put to use by human subjects (Joronen, 2008). Modern technology, Heidegger argues, is the embodiment of this metaphysics to the extent that it promotes a perception of the world as a collection of resources defined solely by their utility. In Heidegger's own words, modern technology reduces the world to a "standing reserve" of materials for human use (1993: 329).

Second, Heidegger's critique is based on the assertion that Western metaphysics – and, by extension, modern technology – are complicit in producing a situation where human beings, as a species, have forgotten what is most important about being human. For Heidegger, what is most important about being human is the capacity, through language, to pose the philosophical question: 'What is Being?.' Social scientist Ruth Irwin (2020: 366) unpacks the nuances of Heidegger's argument in the following passage:

> Openness to Being denotes the unique and special quality of humanity. However, under the sway of rationalised efficiency, humanity is increasingly forgetting to enquire into Being, and thus we lose what is most important about our humanity, and more than that, most important to planetary consciousness.

Heidegger's argument depends upon this romanticised vision of what it means to be human, which, in contrast to the calculative mode he associates with Western metaphysics, achieves its philosophical disclosure of Being through the poetics of language.

For Heidegger, then, the tendency for modern technology to reduce the world to a standing reserve prevents humans from posing the question of Being, and it does so by foreclosing what he understands to be a more poetic – and, crucially, more *authentic* – relationship with the environment. Jeff Malpas, an Australian philosopher who has written at length on the geographical dimensions of Heidegger's philosophy, notes how, for Heidegger, this authenticity is encapsulated in his concept of *dwelling*. According to Malpas (2000: 207):

> It is the disclosedness [of Being] that arises in relation to the space and place of dwelling that Heidegger also refers to as

> 'nearness' and it is precisely such nearness that technology obliterates, according to Heidegger, through its en-framing of things as mere resource and its corresponding transformation of spatiality and place.

Heidegger's concept of dwelling is complex. What we want to draw out, as a third key aspect of Heidegger's critique of technology, is the sense in which dwelling represents Heidegger's reactionary alternative to what he sees as the alienating impact of Western metaphysics. It is this concern that modern technologies distance us from what it means to be authentically human that Malpas is getting at in the extract above when he refers to the obliteration of nearness. So, while modern technology generates experiences of space and time characterised by abstraction, dwelling, for Heidegger, describes a mode of being that is rooted in the finitudes of space and time. To dwell is to make space for this question of Being to be posed in/through the 'nearness' of one's worldly entanglements: it is, in Heidegger's thinking, to be authentically human in a way that is fundamentally at odds with the time-space compression associated with modernity.

Spending time outlining Heidegger's critique is important given the impact his ideas have had, not only for academics within the humanities and social sciences, but also in popular culture more widely, as elements of his philosophy have been influential in shaping various environmental movements (including deep ecology). But Heidegger's story also illustrates the dangers of adopting such a reactionary stance towards the destabilising impacts of modern technology in contemporary culture. The emphasis that Heidegger placed on the authenticity of being rooted in a particular place – and, more specifically, of this rootedness being a defining feature of German culture, above all others – lends itself to a conservative form of nationalism that "assumes there is an organic bond between a people and the land that they inhabit" (Paddock, 2004: 245). Indeed, Heidegger remains infamous for his support of National Socialism and his capitulation to the Nazis during World War II, with some commentators arguing that his critique of Western metaphysics rehearses the anti-Semitic association of Jewish people with the less savoury aspects of modernity. In his rigorous engagement with Heidegger's so-called *Black Notebooks*, Richard Wolin

(2023: 6) makes a convincing case that, for Heidegger, "the reemergence of Being in its glory and plenitude would not take place until 'world Jewry's' disintegrative influence was eliminated."

The relationship of Heidegger's critique of modern technology to the fascist ideology of Nazism is something that will continue to be hotly debated by philosophers and those who engage with his ideas in humanities and social science disciplines for years to come. What we want to highlight, however, before moving on to the next section, is the way that Heidegger's suspicion of modern technologies is framed by a broader set of value claims regarding what constitutes an authentic human culture – and, much more disturbingly, given his political activities, what counts as a truly human life. For Heidegger, this authenticity is achieved through rootedness in place, nostalgia, and a romanticised notion of the poetic mystery of Being, all of which are things that Heidegger opposes to modern technology. The problem with this reactionary perspective, we argue, is that it ends up positioning technology as something external to culture. Put simply, Heidegger sees technology as something that *disrupts* authentic human culture. The unstated assumption here is that, through the distractions of modern technology, human beings are at risk of deviating from their 'true' nature, their 'proper' place in the world, and an 'authentic' relation to Being.

In the next section, we explore how cultural geographers have complicated this reactionary perspective by developing the theory of a co-constitutive relationship between human beings and their technologies. Instead of seeing technology as something that happens *to* culture, cultural geographers who adopt this co-constitutive framework explore how the shared memories and collective experiences that define human culture are inscribed in our material environments through technical means.

HUMANS AND MACHINES: A CO-CONSTITUTIVE RELATIONSHIP

One of the most significant contributions that cultural geography has made to the study of technology and its impact on human society lies in its departure from the kinds of reactionary logic most clearly embodied in Heidegger's thought. To fully grasp what this departure looks like, and thus to appreciate what we think is most novel and innovative about cultural geography perspectives, it is important to note that one of the key assumptions underlying reactionary approaches to technology is the idea that culture precedes or 'comes before' technology. There are two senses to this assumption, the first of which is perhaps more straightforward and refers to the *temporal* relationship between culture and technology. Here, then, to state that culture precedes technology is to assume that there was once a time in the history (or, indeed, the pre-history) of the human species where there was culture without technology. This assumption is often expressed through a kind of nostalgia for pre-industrial forms of craft and artisanship, which are presented as being more authentic modes of existence than those associated with modern technologies.

There is, however, a second sense to this idea that culture precedes technology, and this has to do with the ontological assumptions associated with this statement – that is, the often-implicit assumptions we make about reality and the nature of what exists (see previous discussions of ontology in ***Chapters 2*** and ***3***). From an ontological perspective, to state that culture precedes technology does not only mean that culture comes before technology in a temporal sense, but, more fundamentally, that an ontological category of 'the human' is a necessary condition for understanding what technology is or does. Or, put slightly differently, the evolutionary processes that enable something like human culture to emerge are assumed to occur independently of our relationship with technology.

For many cultural geographers, this commonplace assumption that culture precedes technology – whether temporally, ontologically, or a combination of the two – is problematic, not least because it downplays the active role that technological processes play in the production of memory, perception, anticipation, and thought, all of which are things we tend to associate with culture: that is, with being human. In a bid to grapple with these constitutive entanglements of human and machine, a growing number of cultural geographers have turned to the philosophical writings of *Bernard Stiegler* (see **Box 4.2**) and his innovative theory of 'technics' (Ash 2012, 2018, 2019; Kinsley, 2014; Rose, 2017). There are many dimensions to Stiegler's thought, and this is reflected in the different ways that cultural geographers have adopted and applied his ideas about technology. Nevertheless, something that unites these approaches is the idea that it is not possible to separate human beings – and, therefore, the question of culture – from technology. Humans and technology emerge at precisely the same moment (i.e. the temporal dimension) because their 'natures' are fundamentally entangled with one another (i.e. the ontological dimension). Another way of saying this is that, for Stiegler and those cultural geographers who have been inspired by his thinking, the human does not precede or 'come before' technology as we commonly assume. The reactionary notion that humanity might return to some romanticised pre-technological state, and that, in doing so, it might somehow remember a more authentic mode of existence, is, from this perspective, nothing more than a fanciful myth (albeit one that lends itself readily to fascist ideologies).

BOX 4.2 Bernard Stiegler

Bernard Stiegler (1952–2020) was a French philosopher known for his innovative writings on technology, which focus on the constitutive role of 'technics' in the production of human memory, experience, and thought. Stiegler argues that the human, unlike other animals, is born without an essence and so requires technologies to survive (what Stiegler, following Jacques Derrida, calls technical 'prostheses'). Stiegler (1998) explains this idea in the first volume of *Technics and Time*, through a retelling of a Greek myth in which Zeus instructs Epimetheus to share out qualities to the different creatures of the world in a balanced and harmonious way. Epimetheus completes this task, only to realise that he has forgotten to give any qualities to humans. To remedy this situation, Epimetheus' brother, Prometheus, comes up with a plan: he will steal fire from the god Hephaestus and give this to humans to make up for their lack of intrinsic qualities. This gift of fire, Stiegler argues, represents technics. For Stiegler, this allegory captures an important truth, namely that the birth of human beings coincides with the emergence of technics.

To understand why Stiegler makes this claim, and to appreciate what this has to do with cultural geography perspectives on technology, we need to unpack the relationship between technology and culture in his philosophy in more detail. For Stiegler, this relationship centres around the question of memory – specifically, collective memory – as a key dimension of what he terms 'technics.' As cultural geographer Sam Kinsley (2014: 372) explains, Stiegler's theory of technogenesis:

> is the idea that humans and technology co-evolved together, that you do not get one without the other. Humans are irreducibly distinct because of the reflexive transmission of complex cultures made possible by technics and the 'exteriorization' of thought.

The key term that Kinsley uses here is 'exteriorisation.' For Stiegler, exteriorisation describes how the evolution of the human depends on material supports that are no longer internal to living organisms. Technologies, according to Stiegler, are precisely these exteriorised evolutionary supports that make it possible for the human to emerge as a thinking being capable of reflexive self-consciousness. Technology is thus the ongoing process of exteriorisation that makes the interior world of human experience and subjectivity possible – or, as Kinsley (2014: 372) puts it, "the mental interior is only recognized as such with the advent of the technical exterior." This process of exteriorisation that simultaneously produces an interiorisation of human consciousness is what Stiegler calls technics.

How does this process of exteriorisation relate to memory? Well, according to Stiegler, technics produces a kind of memory (or 'retention') inscribed in the organism's nonorganic environment. James Ash (2020a: 211), a cultural geographer at the forefront of contemporary social science debates relating to technology, explains Stiegler's theory of retention in the following way:

> Drawing on the work of Husserl, [Stiegler] distinguished between primary retention (human perception) and secondary retention (human memory) and adds a third form of memory, which he terms tertiary retention. Tertiary retention is a form of technical memory, where knowledge, experience, and skill are inscribed on different technical objects (e.g., hammers, books, computer hard drives). This tertiary retention operates as a platform for knowledge and skill to be passed on, while also changing the content and quality of that knowledge and skill.

Ash's work provides an excellent resource for those who are new to cultural geography perspectives on technology and want to know more about the significance of philosophers like Stiegler for thinking about the entanglements of humans and machines. As the above quote illustrates, Ash often uses concrete examples to help readers appreciate how an abstract idea or concept, such as retention, relates to our everyday experiences of interacting with technologies. So, to borrow Ash's example, when we reach for a technical object like a hammer, we are tapping into a reservoir of collective memory that 'retains,' amongst other things, the accumulated *knowledge* represented in physical laws, the *experiences* of different material properties, and the various *skills* embodied in both the manufacture of the hammer and its use.

A key aspect of the technical memory that Ash is describing through his engagement with Stiegler's philosophy is that it involves a process of transmission (of knowledge, experience, and skill) that is no longer dependent on the biology of living organisms. The emergence of technics is significant, Stiegler argues, because it generates a new evolutionary pathway for life. Staying with Ash's example, the technical memory embedded within a hammer is something that we, the users of such a technical object, inherit when we put it to use. Technical memory is therefore not like the personal form of memory that we would ordinarily associate with the recollection of past events. The memory retained in the hammer, the book, or the computer hard drive is something that exceeds the memory of any given individual. So, to take another of Ash's examples, a book is not simply a repository of information: it is *also* a process of retention that enables thoughts, ideas, and feelings to travel across space and time – and, crucially, to outlast the biological constraints of organic life.

Ash's example of the book as a technical object leads us to another fascinating implication of Stiegler's philosophy, and this is the idea that, for human beings, technical or 'tertiary' retention underlies both the secondary retentions of human memory (i.e. personal recollection of past events) *and* the primary retentions associated with basic perception (i.e. our ability to experience ourselves as individual entities situated within the flow of time). This is a complex and somewhat counterintuitive idea! What Stiegler is saying here is that technicity provides the ontological conditions necessary for the emergence of human memory and perception. Without the externalised retentions embedded within an environment of technical objects, Stiegler thinks that our capacities for personal recollection (i.e. memory) and subjective experience (i.e. perception) would cease to exist. It is because of technics that we become capable of recalling the past as memory, and, in turn, it is through memory that it becomes possible to experience the present as a subject who anticipates the future.

Take a moment to think about this idea. In what ways do the constitutive relationships you have with technology make it possible to recall past events? And how does the technical choreography of collective memory shape the way you perceive the world around you? There are many examples, but one that stands out as particularly pertinent for cultural geographers is photography – specifically, the ways that technologically induced changes in the production, circulation, and consumption of photographic images have transformed the conditions of collective memory in the twenty-first century. Photographs and photographic technologies have always had an interesting relationship with memory. However, with the development of phone cameras, increased access to the Internet, and the global phenomenon of social media, this relationship has become even more pronounced. Social media platforms have become an enormous repository of human memory, populated by digital images that have been facially recognised, geotagged, and algorithmically categorised (Taffel, 2021). What is more, the desire to share our images in this way – and thus the pull to create future memories – is something that increasingly colours how we experience our environments in the here-and-now of the present moment. We have probably all had the experience of trying to photographically capture a landscape in a way that looks 'Instagrammable' or have used a filter to smooth out skin blemishes (perhaps without even realising it). This is one situation where the tertiary retentions that Stiegler associates with technicity create a form of collective memory (or culture) that shapes what we perceive in the present by creating new forms of anticipation.

Stiegler, like many other contemporary thinkers of technology, was significantly influenced by Heidegger's philosophy, particularly the idea that our participation in the world is facilitated and structured by a variety of tools which, for the most part, function silently in the background of our conscious awareness. Where Stiegler differs from Heidegger, however, is in his assertion that there can be no collective memory, no culture, and thus *no human* without technics. This is not to say that Stiegler blindly celebrates modern technology. In fact, Stiegler argues that our tertiary retentions, particularly those associated with information technologies, are being increasingly co-opted by the exploitative logics of capitalist accumulation in a way that undermines the capacity for collective resistance to the status quo. This is an important observation given the centrality of new technologies like algorithms and AI in undermining democratic processes, amplifying fascist desires, and shoring up authoritarian leaders around the globe (see ***Chapter 6*** for more on this topic). And yet for Stiegler, unlike Heidegger, it makes no sense to imagine a more authentic version of ourselves outside, beyond, or before our relationships with technology, because it is through technics alone that we become capable of recalling the past, sensing the present, and anticipating the future. Stiegler's theory thus provides a more politically progressive approach to the question of the relationship between culture and technology, to the extent that a renewed engagement with technics is, for Stiegler, as much a solution to contemporary forms of alienation, exploitation, and authoritarianism as it is part of the problem.

This appreciation of the impact technologies have in shaping human perception, experience, and *subjectivity* (see **Box 4.3**) has been taken up by cultural geographers working in the area of post-phenomenology (Lea, 2009), including James Ash, who draws inspiration from Stiegler's ideas. Associated with the works of Edmund Husserl, Martin Heidegger, and Maurice Merleau-Ponty, phenomenology is a philosophical movement that seeks to understand the conditions that give rise to and structure subjective experience. Cultural geographers including Ash share this phenomenological interest in experience and the different ways the world appears to consciousness as something to be perceived. But where more traditional forms of phenomenology tend to anchor the conditions of experience within the human, post-phenomenologists have drawn on philosophers including Bernard Stiegler, Don Ihde, and others to explore how a variety of material processes that are external to the human mediate the internal experiences associated with subjective consciousness. The textures of conscious experience, post-phenomenologists argue, are shaped by all sorts of technologies, objects, and materials. Post-phenomenological approaches to the cultural geographies of technology thus offer a powerful conceptual framework for understanding how technical objects contribute to "the dense scaffolding of things that enables and shapes human thought" (Ash and Simpson, 2016: 63).

BOX 4.3 Subjectivity

Often opposed to objectivity, subjectivity tends to be used by non-experts to describe someone's individual perspective on reality. Increasingly, the word subjective is used pejoratively. This is what is implied when people discount something on the basis that it is 'just subjective': subjectivity is equated with personal interpretation and objectivity with established fact. Within cultural geography, however, subjectivity is a technical term related to the philosophical problem of what it means to have an experience and how the event of having an experience changes the way things unfold. Subjectivity happens when, in certain contexts, the memories of past experiences are in-folded into the present in a way that gives rise to specific trajectories (and not others). This process sometimes overlaps with the individual person, but it can also be collective – think, for instance, of the collective subjectivity that emerges through the experience of traumatic events like wars or in the wake of disasters. Finally, while subjectivity tends to be associated with human experience, cultural geographers working with new materialist and post-humanist theories have explored the idea that matter itself has its own forms of memory, experience, and anticipation. For a more detailed account of how this more-than-human understanding of experience and subjectivity relates to debates in cultural geography, see Roberts (2024).

Thinking of technology in this way, as a relationship that produces a sense of interiority in/through human experience, has interesting implications for cultural geography. First, it foregrounds the material environment as the primary site where the experience of temporality is produced through acts of 'inscription.' For cultural geographers like Kinsley and Ash, who draw heavily on Stiegler's work, processes of inscription retain the past through the organisation of matter, thus producing the human as a cultural being endowed with collective memory. Second, and perhaps more significantly, is the way that co-constitutive approaches to the technology-human relation provide a conceptual purchase on the changing nature of the human at a time characterised by accelerating rates of technological innovation. So, if post-phenomenological geographers are correct in stating that our capacities to remember, to perceive, to anticipate, and even to think are intimately tied to the way we inscribe our material environments, then it follows that our interactions with new technologies – and, therefore, with novel forms of inscription – will produce significant transformations in the way we think of and experience ourselves as human beings. Thinking in this way short-circuits Heidegger's tendency to oppose modern technology to a more authentic mode of being encapsulated in the concept of dwelling because, as Ash (2020a: 212) explains, "technologies are always with and alongside humans, altering what they are and what they can do on a variety of perceptual and somatic registers." Even our ability to ask the philosophical question 'what does it mean to be human?' relies fundamentally on the technicity of writing as a form of inscription that exteriorises thought and enables philosophical reflection. This is something that Heidegger's romanticised notion of language tends to overlook.

The post-phenomenological analyses developed by cultural geographers remind us that technical machines have a life of their own that often far exceeds the intentions of their inventors (Keating, 2024). In other words, the gradual integration of new and emerging technologies into the material fabric of our everyday lives creates novel forms of retention that feed back into the production of the human in ways that cannot be predicted. This is the crux of what cultural geographers mean when they describe the relation between humans and technology as co-constitutive: it is the process of relation itself (what Stiegler calls technics) that comes first, not the familiar categories of 'human' and 'technology' with their conventional associations. In simpler terms, humans and technology are two sides of the same relational process, a process that is itself evolving and mutating over time.

TALKIN' ABOUT MY GENERATION

A key implication of cultural geography's co-constitutive approach to technology and the human is that major technological changes are always much more than technical achievements: they are also, as we have explored in this section, transformations of the conditions of collective memory, perception, and anticipation. These philosophical arguments might seem to be overly speculative, as if they were more suited to the world of science fiction than rigorous scholarly pursuits. And yet, the idea that the human is changing through its shifting relationships with technology is perhaps not so far-fetched when we consider the technics of intergenerational differences. For the so-called 'Millennials' born between 1981 and 1996, these changes in how humans made sense of themselves and the world around them were intimately tied to the advent of the Internet as an unimaginably vast repository of collective memory, connecting spaces and times in ways that were hitherto unimaginable. Facilitated, among other things, by the miniaturisation of computer chips and the increasing affordability of desktop computers, the rapid incursion of the Internet into people's lives can be thought of as an event where familiar forms of inscription (e.g. print media, books, libraries) were being radically disrupted through the nanoscale materiality of semiconductor technologies.

Immediately following the Millennials comes Generation Z (or the 'Zoomers' as they are sometimes called). Born between 1997 and 2012, Generation Z are often referred to by demographers as the first 'digital natives,' having been born into a world where widespread access to the Internet had already been firmly established – and, in economically prosperous parts of the world, culturally normalised. Here, again, conceptual debates in cultural geography are useful for making sense of this concept of digital natives and its broader significance for understanding the co-constitutive entanglements of human and machine. A key idea that cultural geographers have explored in relation to Stiegler's philosophy is that our individual sense of self or subjectivity is shaped by the collective memories embedded within a society's technologies (this is the concept of tertiary retention discussed earlier in this chapter). In the case of Generation Z and its digital natives, then, we could say that the tertiary retentions of the Internet played an increasingly significant role in shaping the material conditions of individual memory and experience.

This brings us up to the most recent cohort, Generation Alpha, which runs from the end point of Generation Z (roughly the mid-2010s) through to 2025. For members of this generation, regular exposure to portable touchscreen devices such as smartphones and tablets became a defining feature of early childhood, both in the home and in educational settings. The family desktop computer was quickly replaced with a multiplicity of personal devices, each connected to the Internet through advances in wireless network technologies (e.g. Bluetooth, 5G). This is a generation that has grown up with an increasingly personalised interface with the Internet, where algorithms filter and choreograph the unimaginable amounts of collective memory – the tertiary retentions of so-called 'big data' – according to your past activities, for example: which shops you entered at the mall, and which you did not; which thumbnail you hovered over on YouTube while deciding what video to watch next; where you took that selfie, and with whom; what time you went to sleep, etc. And, of course, these algorithms can be weaponised to shape anticipation and desire according to specific economic, political, and ideological agendas. Contemporary phenomena like social media echo chambers and online radicalisation are striking examples of the way technicities shape our experience of reality (and, therefore, our cultural values) in ways that are vulnerable to manipulation. For Generation Alpha, it is this intensely choreographed and individualised experience of tertiary retention that has shaped their formative years, and, crucially, how they experience the relationship between past actions, present events, and future possibilities.

Technology is not the only factor at play in the process of mapping generational boundaries. Nonetheless, we think this example of social generations provides an interesting thought experiment for grappling with the inseparability of culture and technics, as well as the idea that, as social beings, our experiences are dependent on the collective forms of memory that are inscribed in our technical environments. Of course, the boundaries between these generations are not so clear-cut, and yet, by thinking of these technological shifts as ontological transformations in the temporality of human life, we can also begin to grapple with the significance of intergenerational differences in ways that are less beholden to reactionary narratives.

CULTURAL GEOGRAPHY AND ARTIFICIAL INTELLIGENCE

One of the most significant technological innovations to have emerged in recent years is AI. As scholars in the social sciences and humanities disciplines have noted, however, the relationship between AI and culture has a much longer history. While the field of AI research was officially established in the 1950s, human cultures have long been fascinated by the allure of intelligent machines. In fact, the very idea of AI is intimately entangled with long-standing philosophical discussions about what it means to be human, and, by extension, how we understand and define foundational concepts like intelligence, agency, and free will. What this means is that the cultural geographies of AI extend far beyond recent technological innovations like machine learning, neural networks, and the large language models that power platforms like ChatGPT.

The level of excitement that has accompanied the roll-out of generative AI technologies during the early 2020s has clearly been amplified by those companies and individuals that stand to gain from their uptake, whether this takes the form of higher share prices or increased access to lucrative sources of user data. In their opening to a special issue of *Digital Geography and Society*, journal editors Sophia Maalsen, Jonathan Cinnamon, and Sam Kinsley describe how we "are undeniably in a moment of both rapid acceleration and exaggerated hype surrounding artificial intelligence" (Maalsen et al., 2023: np). This hype is problematic because it tends to obscure the oversights and shortcomings of these technologies, and, by extension, the sorts of solutions they can realistically provide. A key example here is the now well-documented tendency for large language models like ChatGPT to fabricate sources of information that appear realistic but that either do not exist or are false in some way. This well-documented phenomenon, sometimes referred to by experts as 'hallucination,' reflects the probabilistic nature of large language models, which function by predicting likely associations of words and phrases based on vast training sets of text-based data (this is why using these technologies to write essays or class papers is a risky business, especially if your professor has a decent knowledge of the academic literature!). Spotting these hallucinations can be tricky because the conversational interface developed for platforms like ChatGPT is deliberately designed to sound more authoritative and persuasive than a conventional search engine.

A more pervasive problem associated with AI technologies is their tendency to uncritically reproduce existing societal structures of inequality, discrimination, and bias. The reason for this is that the vast datasets used to train AI are ultimately shaped by the prejudices and power dynamics inherent within a given cultural milieu. In the context of recent attempts to predict the incidence and spatial distribution of crime, research shows that AI policing technologies like the Correctional Offender Management Profiling for Alternative Sanctions (COMPAS) software system tend to be biased towards Black populations, because these populations are over-represented in the training data (Broad, 2018). The reasons for this over-representation are grounded in structural racism: statistically, in the United States, Black people and other non-white minorities are more likely to be stopped and arrested than white people. Similarly, in Australia, it is a fact that Aboriginal and Torres Strait Islander people are subjected to far greater police monitoring than non-Indigenous groups and so are at a much higher risk of being arrested in the first place (Broad, 2018: 92). This over-representation of minorities skews training datasets and ultimately leads to predictive algorithms that further amplify racial stereotypes rather than challenge them.

The problem of harmful cultural stereotypes and their influence on the development of AI is particularly problematic when it comes to image recognition technologies. Cultural geographer and visual artist Trevor Paglen has explored this issue in relation to the labelling of images used to populate machine learning datasets. In collaboration with sociologist Kate Crawford, Paglen notes how image-recognition algorithms have been shaped by all manner of unsavoury stereotypes embedded within training datasets through human labelling and categorisation. This is especially the case when it comes to images of people, with the authors citing evidence of offensive stereotypes and slurs being used to label images in the influential 'ImageNet' dataset (Crawford and Paglen, 2021: 1105). The key point here is that AI's ability to categorise and label images is shaped by the way those images take on meaning within a particular culture. This includes harmful stereotypes to do with race, gender, class, etc. What is more, the commonly held assumption that these technologies are somehow more objective than human minds can lead to situations where these stereotypes slip beneath the radar of critical questioning. The data that AI is trained on, Crawford and Paglen (2021: 1107) argue, always bear the imprint of culture, and so, "[d]espite the common mythos that AI and the data it draws on are objectively and scientifically classifying the world, everywhere there is politics, ideology, prejudices, and all of the subjective stuff of history." Everywhere there is AI, there is culture.

From the early 2020s, and especially during the period of economic recovery immediately following the COVID-19 pandemic, there has been a rapid expansion in the everyday application of AI-enabled technologies. To give a few quick examples, it is becoming increasingly common for employers to use AI in the initial stages of recruitment, from shortlisting applications to automated interviews and video analysis (indeed, we anticipate that many readers will likely have had some experience of this already). Digital assistants like Siri and Alexa rely on AI to provide a more personalised, conversational interface between users and the World Wide Web. Finally, forms of generative AI are now capable of producing photorealistic imagery, raising all sorts of challenging questions regarding the supposed authenticity of photographs and the potential for new, more elaborate forms of deception and misinformation.

HOW TRUSTWORTHY IS AI?

A key issue associated with the increasing prevalence of these technologies, and one that we have explored in our own research (Lapworth and Roberts, 2023), relates to trust – specifically, the need to understand how people's perceptions of what it means to trust technology are being reshaped, transformed, and reimagined in the age of AI. The question of what it means to place one's trust in technology is, of course, not unique to AI (think of the countless technologies that you rely upon to be able to perform even the most basic everyday activities). What is new, however, is the way AI is shifting the nature of our trust in technology away from the reliable repetition of tasks towards a much more unpredictable process of computational decision-making. So, while driving a vehicle certainly involves a degree of trust on the part of the driver, for the most part, this is a form of trust based on an expectation of reliability: as drivers, we trust that the car will perform and handle in a predictable fashion when provided with a familiar set of inputs. The situation is very different in the case of AI-enabled technologies, which, through processes such as machine learning and neural networks, can modify their own algorithms in response to novel situations. This means that there is a degree of unpredictability inherent to AI that enables these technologies to respond to changing environmental cues in real time and in ways that we humans might not have anticipated.

The question of what it means to trust AI is, therefore, quite complicated. Staying with the previous example of driving a car, imagine a situation where you are driving a familiar route to a familiar destination at a familiar time. The classic example here would be a daily commute to a place of work, but it could be any number of journeys where the driver is navigating almost 'on autopilot,' controlling the vehicle without needing to actively think about or plan the route ahead. Suddenly, the navigation app linked to your smartphone lights up on the car's dashboard display: 'faster route available: turn right after two-hundred metres!' You glance ahead. Everything seems the same as it did yesterday. The traffic appears to be flowing, and the weather conditions are good. For this reason, this AI-enabled decision catches you off guard. You're not sure whether to trust this unusual recommendation because it disrupts your expectations of familiarity and predictability. The significance of this everyday example is that it illustrates how, in the wake of AI, we are increasingly faced with situations where the question of what it means to trust technology can no longer be based on characteristics like functional predictability or reliability (Roberts et al., 2025). To put it simply, trusting AI implies an expectation of unexpected behaviours (if it didn't, it wouldn't make much sense to call these technologies intelligent in the first place!).

In our own research, we have explored some of these issues relating to trust through an analysis of people's qualitative experiences using various AI-enabled navigation technologies in Canberra and Sydney in Australia, including applications such as Google Maps, Apple Maps, and Waze (Roberts et al., 2025). One of the key findings to emerge from our qualitative interviews was that users of these technologies tended to experience trust in ways that were not reducible to evaluations of functional efficacy. To put it in simpler terms, the capacity of our research participants "to trust their navigational apps was only partly captured by the functional ability of these technologies to get them from A to B" (Roberts et al., 2025: 172). Instead, the interviews showed how people conceptualised and experienced trust across a range of overlapping and sometimes contradictory contexts, which we refer to in the paper as "ontologically heterogeneous milieus" of trust. These milieus include (but are not limited to): (1) the performative impacts of the dominant *imaginaries* that shape how people experience AI through the lens of popular culture; (2) the socio-technical *ecologies* that embed our everyday technological encounters within broader relationships of power, politics and privilege; and (3) the important role of *habits and routines* in making (and sometimes breaking) our capacity to trust AI and its decisions.

Although not something explicitly articulated in the paper, our approach to AI builds on the co-constitutive conceptualisations of technology developed by cultural geographers in recent years. It does so by trying to better capture, conceptualise, and ultimately understand the fundamentally co-constitutive dimension of our relationships with these emerging technologies. Approaching AI in this way runs against the grain of our everyday manners of speaking and writing about technologies, which tend to figure technological encounters as a coming together of pre-existing categories: human and machine, mind and matter, and subject and object. The problem with these everyday figurations of human-technology relations is that they tend to operate within a framework where the human and its attributes never truly become anything other than what they already are. Instead, what we were trying to capture in our research was the sense in which the widespread adoption of AI in contemporary society is generating experiences of trust across humans and machines, that have not been seen before – experiences which, in small but not insignificant ways, disrupt universalising assumptions about what it means to be human.

CREATIVE COLLABORATIONS WITH INTELLIGENT MACHINES

Before bringing this chapter to a close, we want to finish by briefly touching on a second dimension of AI that has caught the attention of cultural geographers interested in the co-constitutive evolution of humans and machines. This second dimension is creativity. Philosophical questions relating to creativity have a long tradition within the context of the history of computer technologies, and this is particularly so when it comes to the development of AI. Indeed, while we may well be impressed by a computer's ability to crunch numbers at increasingly mind-blowing speeds, it is often only when a machine exhibits some form of creativity that it begins to seem truly intelligent. A classic example here is the DeepMind Challenge Match, which, in 2016, pitted South Korean grandmaster Lee Sedol against Google's 'AlphaGo' in a five-match game of Go. Winning four of the five matches, it was the AI player AlphaGo that emerged victorious. This result came as a surprise to many experts, given the degree of creativity and intuition required to succeed in this ancient game. Of particular interest was the now infamous 'Move 37' made by AlphaGo during the second game of the series, which Go-playing commentators have described as a move so creative that no human player would have ever considered playing it. As previously discussed with the example of navigation technologies, what this case of Google's Go-playing AI shows is that it is the capacity for contemporary technologies to act creatively by deviating from predictable scripts that shapes much of the emerging cultural discussion regarding the future of machine intelligence.

The recent hype surrounding AI has led to a proliferation of public debates and discussions about whether AI can truly be creative, and, if so, whether this points towards a form of machine sentience that demands some form of ethical acknowledgement on the part of human beings. While not shying away from these more speculative questions, cultural geography's emphasis on evolving relations of co-constitution and its interest in critically questioning universal definitions of the human offer a more concrete set of inroads into these exciting (and sometimes unnerving) debates. This is particularly the case for post-phenomenological approaches to technology, where a key concern is to understand how creativity emerges *relationally* through the co-constitution of humans and machines – here, think back to our previous discussion of Stiegler's philosophy and his assertion that technics is inseparable from human evolution. Creativity, from a post-phenomenological perspective, is not something that can be attributed to an already constituted human individual. Contrary to the long-standing assumptions of the humanist tradition, post-phenomenological geographers would argue that the creative agency associated with intelligence has never been an exclusively human affair. As humans, we think and create *with* or *alongside* technologies that are always-already shaping and reshaping how we think, what we do, and who we are.

A key strength of these cultural geography approaches is that they prevent us from getting too bogged down in the quagmires of categorical thinking. The question of whether machines exhibit intelligence through creative agency can become a bit of a distraction because it blinds us to what is actually taking place in the concrete messiness of a world where action always happens 'in-between' individuals. We will return to this relational understanding of action in ***Chapter 5***, when we discuss theories of affect and assemblage as novel frameworks for understanding how bodies act. For now, the point we want to underline is that cultural geography's preference for relational processes over and above individual categories shifts the focal point of existing debates about the creativity of technologies like AI in ways that are more attuned to what is happening, here and now, in the overlapping interfaces of human and machine. The starting point for this is understanding how the ontological conditions for creative thought and action are not locked away inside the abstract category of 'the human.' Instead, what cultural geographers like Ash and others argue is that human creativity would not be possible without technicity and the production of collective temporal experience (what Stiegler understands as culture).

Another advantage of cultural geography's co-constitutive framework is that by critically questioning the human as an unchanging, universal category, we are less likely to be drawn into reactionary arguments regarding new technologies like AI. We discussed the key characteristics of such reactionary approaches in an earlier section of this chapter, where we paid particular attention to Heidegger's influential critique of modern technology. When it comes to the question of creativity, such approaches tend to set up an oppositional relationship between, on the one hand, a purely mechanical materiality of machines and, on the other, the 'authentic,' world-disclosing creativity of human beings. These frameworks are incredibly powerful because the narratives they are based on appeal to our sense of self-importance as a species. Life would be much simpler if we could look at the world and draw a hard boundary between the creative and the mechanical. And if this boundary just so happens to demarcate the human as *the* privileged actor in a world of lifeless matter, even better! Cultural geographers tend to be suspicious of these narratives, however, and are more inclined to focus on relational grey zones rather than black and white distinctions. What this means is that, for cultural geographers, non-human materiality is often much livelier (and, by extension, more *creative*) than we ordinarily assume, whereas much of what we associate with being human takes place at the level of unconscious habit and material repetition.

Cultural geography's suspicion towards essential categories and the reactionary attitudes they support is particularly important given the polarisation of public debate relating to AI and its impact on future societies. What we tend to see in these public discussions is a gravitation towards two extremes: either a dystopian scenario where AI exceeds human intelligence and starts to act in ways that undermine the social, economic, political, and existential structures that support human life; or, a utopian future where the roll-out of AI frees human beings from the drudgery of work and solves the problems of climate change, disease, and even our own mortality. Yet neither extreme makes much sense for cultural geographers who think of the relationship between humans and machines as an evolving process of co-constitution. Utopias and dystopias may sound enticing; from a cultural geography perspective, however, the reality is less clear-cut. Technologies like AI depend on human thought and action, whether through the process of their design or in terms of the vast amounts of behavioural data that they feed upon. Conversely, for philosophers like Stiegler, the forms of collective subjectivity we recognise as human culture are only possible thanks to the technological prostheses associated with technics and the externalisations they support.

Within the context of AI's impact on creativity and the creative industries, the strength of adopting a cultural geography approach would be to emphasise that technics have always been an integral part of what it means to think and act creatively. There is, for this reason, no pure form of human creativity that can be isolated from our relationship to technology. This does not mean that creativity can be reduced to a technical achievement. The point, rather, is that our creative faculties (e.g. anticipation, imagination, speculation) will always remain entangled with the broader milieus of technologies that shape our consciousness of time, space, and self. Thus, in their 2018 publication, Thomas Birtchnell and Anthony Elliot examine the impact of AI on the audio mastering profession, as software products such as LANDR promise to automate creative tasks that were previously reserved for highly experienced individuals. While acknowledging legitimate concerns regarding the possibility of job losses within this creative profession, Birtchnell and Elliot (2018: 78) argue that the more interesting question, from a cultural geography perspective, is "how AI will become enmeshed in new assemblages of people and machines in creative endeavours rather than simply substituting directly for human expertise." Similarly, in our own research (Roberts et al., 2025), we have explored how technological processes like machine learning can be used as productive relays within a broader assemblage of creative practice, focusing on the specific example of synthetic photography as a means of challenging the tropes and clichés that dominate visual culture.

CONCLUSION

The goal of this chapter has been to introduce readers to some of the latest cultural geography perspectives on technology. In doing so, we have covered a lot of ground. So, in bringing the chapter to a close, we want to briefly consolidate what we believe are the key contributions that cultural geography brings to current debates about technology. First and foremost, then, is an understanding that the cultural dimensions of technology are not limited to the representational overlay of meaning and/or cultural significance (although this may well be an important dimension in some circumstances). Instead, a key concern for cultural geographers has been to investigate the role of technologies in mediating the non-representational aspects of culture. This leads to the second contribution: by refusing to situate the human 'before' or 'beyond' technology, cultural geography provides a means of conceptualising our relation to machines in a way that avoids falling into reactionary critiques. Third, the development of post-phenomenological frameworks is one of cultural geography's most significant and exciting contributions to the study of technology and society today. Drawing on an underappreciated lineage of philosophers of technology, cultural geographers working in the post-phenomenological tradition help us to understand how our capacities for perception, attention, and anticipation are – indeed, *have always been* – shaped by technologies operating in the background of conscious awareness. Finally, we noted how cultural geography's sensitivity to the evolving co-constitution of people and technology adds much-needed nuance to contemporary debates about AI, including the more-than-human rearticulations of trust and creativity associated with these emerging technologies.

FURTHER READING

Amoore, L. *Cloud Ethics: Algorithms and the Attributes of Ourselves and Others*. Durham: Duke University Press, 2020.

Ash, J. *Phase Media: Space, Time and the Politics of Smart Objects*. London: Bloomsbury, 2019.

Ash, J., R. Kitchin and A. Leszczynski (eds.). *Digital Geographies*. London: Sage, 2019.

Crawford, K. and T. Paglen. "Excavating AI: The politics of images in machine learning training sets." *AI & Society* 36, no. 4 (2021): 1105–1116. https://doi.org/10.1007/s00146-021-01162-8

Roberts, T., A. Lapworth, L. Koh and M. Ghasri. "Negotiating trust in AI-enabled technologies: Imaginaries, ecologies, habits." *Social & Cultural Geography* 26, no. 2 (2024): 160–178. https://doi.org/10.1080/14649365.2024.2399239

REFERENCES

Adobe Acrobat Team. *Fast-forward – comparing a 1980s supercomputer to the modern smartphone*. Adobe Blog. (November 8, 2022) https://blog.adobe.com/en/publish/2022/11/08/fast-forward-comparing-1980s-supercomputer-to-modern-smartphone

Amoore, L. *Cloud Ethics: Algorithms and the Attributes of Ourselves and Others*. Durham: Duke University Press, 2020.

Ash, J. "The age of disruption: Technology and madness in computational capitalism." *The AAG Review of Books* 8, no. 4 (2020a): 211–212. https://doi.org/10.1080/2325548X.2020.1781452

Ash, J. "Attention, videogames and the retentional economies of affective amplification." *Theory, Culture & Society* 29, no. 6 (2012): 3–26. https://doi.org/10.1177/0263276412438595

Ash, J. *Phase Media: Space, Time and the Politics of Smart Objects*. London: Bloomsbury, 2019.

Ash, J. "Smart cities and the digital geographies of technical memory." *Annals of the American Association of Geographers* 109, no. 1 (2019): 161–172. https://doi.org/10.1080/24694452.2018.1489214

Ash, J. "Technology and affect: Towards a theory of inorganically organized objects." *Emotion, Space and Society* 14 (2014): 84–90. https://doi.org/10.1016/j.emospa.2013.12.017

Ash, J. and P. Simpson. "Geography and post-phenomenology." *Progress in Human Geography* 40, no. 1 (2016): 48–66. https://doi.org/10.1177/0309132514544806

Ash, J., R. Kitchin and A. Leszczynski (eds.). *Digital Geographies*. London: Sage, 2019.

Birtchnell, T. and A. Elliott. "Automating the black art: Creative places for artificial intelligence in audio mastering." *Geoforum* 96 (2018): 77–86. https://doi.org/10.1016/j.geoforum.2018.08.005

Bissell, D., T. Birtchnell, A. Elliott and E. L. Hsu. "Autonomous automobilities: The social impacts of driverless vehicles." *Current Sociology* 68, no. 1 (2020): 116–134. https://doi.org/10.1177/0011392118816743

Broad, E. *Made by Humans: The AI Condition*. Carlton: Melbourne University Press, 2018.

Cockayne, D., A. Leszczynski and M. Zook. "#HotForBots: Sex, the non-human and digitally mediated spaces of intimate encounter." *Environment and Planning D: Society and Space* 35, no. 6 (2017): 1115–1133. https://doi.org/10.1177/0263775817709018

Crawford, K. and T. Paglen. "Excavating AI: The politics of images in machine learning training sets." *AI & Society* 36, no. 4 (2021): 1105–1116. https://doi.org/10.1007/s00146-021-01162-8

Harvey, D. *The Condition of Postmodernity: An Enquiry into the Origins of Cultural Change*. Oxford: Blackwell, 1989.

Heidegger, M. "The question concerning technology." In D. F. Krell (ed.) *Martin Heidegger: Basic Writings* (2nd ed.) (pp. 311–341). New York: Harper Collins, 1993.

Irwin, R. "Heidegger and Stiegler on failure and technology." *Educational Philosophy and Theory* 52, no. 4 (2020): 361–375. https://doi.org/10.1080/00131857.2019.1654855

Joronen, M. "The technological metaphysics of planetary space: Being in the age of globalization." *Environment and Planning D: Society and Space* 26, no. 4 (2008): 596–610. https://doi.org/10.1068/djoro

Keating, T. "Techno-genesis: Reconceptualising geography's technology from ontology to ontogenesis." *Progress in Human Geography* 48, no. 1 (2024): 49–65. https://doi.org/10.1177/03091325231209020

Kinsley, S. "The matter of 'virtual' geographies." *Progress in Human Geography* 38, no. 3 (2014): 364–384. https://doi.org/10.1177/0309132513506270

Kinsley, S. "Memory programmes: The industrial retention of collective life." *Cultural Geographies* 22, no. 1 (2015): 155–175. https://doi.org/10.1177/1474474014555658

Lapworth, A. and T. Roberts. "Habit, artificial intelligence and the ontological performance of trust." *Performance Research* 28, no. 6 (2024): 73–81. https://doi.org/10.1080/13528165.2023.2334639

Lea, J. "Post-phenomenological geographies." In R. Kitchin and N. Thrift (eds.) *International Encyclopaedia of Human Geography* (pp. 373–378). London: Elsevier, 2009. https://doi.org/10.1016/B978-008044910-4.00726-4

Lundman, R. and P. Nordstrom. "Creative geographies in the age of AI: Co-creative spatiality and the emerging techno-material relations between artists and artificial intelligence." *Transactions of the Institute of British Geographers* 48, no. 3 (2023): 650–664. https://doi.org/10.1111/tran.12608

Maalsen, S., J. Cinnamon and S. Kinsley. "Artificial intelligence, geography and society." *Digital Geography and Society* 4 (2023). https://doi.org/10.1016/j.diggeo.2023.100061

Malpas, J. "Uncovering the space of disclosedness: Heidegger, technology, and the problem of spatiality in Being and Time." In M. A. Wrathall and J. Malpas (eds.) *Heidegger, Authenticity, and Modernity: Essays in Honor of Hubert L. Dreyfus, Volume 1* (pp. 205–228). Cambridge: MIT Press, 2000.

May, J. and N. Thrift. "Introduction." In J. May and N. Thrift (eds.) *Timespace: Geographies of Temporality* (pp. 1–46). London: Routledge, 2001.

Nordstrom, P., R. Lundman and J. Hautala. "Evolving coagency between artists and AI in the spatial cocreative process of artmaking." *Annals of the American Association of Geographers* 113, no. 9 (2023): 2203–2218. https://doi.org/10.1080/24694452.2023.2210647

Paddock, T. "Gedachtes Wohnen: Heidegger and cultural geography." *Philosophy and Geography* 7, no. 2 (2004): 237–251. https://doi.org/10.1080/1090377042000285435

Roberts, T. "Matter, affect, life: A Whiteheadian intervention into 'more-than-human' geographies." *Dialogues in Human Geography* (2024). https://doi.org/10.1177/20438206241255446

Roberts, T., A. Lapworth and R. Carter-White. "Refusing cliches: Artificial imagination in the synthetic photography of Kevin Abosch." *Cultural Geographies* [early view] (2025). https://doi.org/10.1177/14744740251347940

Roberts, T., A. Lapworth, L. Koh and M. Ghasri. "Negotiating trust in AI-enabled technologies: Imaginaries, ecologies, habits." *Social & Cultural Geography* 26, no. 2 (2024): 160–178. https://doi.org/10.1080/14649365.2024.2399239

Rose, G. "Posthuman agency in the digitally mediated city: Exteriorization, individuation, reinvention." *Annals of the American Association of Geographers* 107, no. 4 (2017): 779–793. https://doi.org/10.1080/24694452.2016.1270195

Roser, M. Technology over the long run: Zoom out to see how dramatically the world can change within a lifetime. *Our World in Data*, 2023. https://ourworldindata.org/technology-long-run [Accessed 24/01/25].

Stiegler, B. *Technics and Time, 1: The Fault of Epimetheus*. Stanford: Stanford University Press, 1998.

Taffel, S. "Google's lens: Computational photography and platform capitalism." *Media, Culture & Society* 43, no. 2 (2021): 237–255. https://doi.org/10.1177/0163443720939449

Wolin, R. *Heidegger in Ruins: Between Philosophy and Ideology*. New Haven: Yale University Press, 2023.

5

BODIES

INTRODUCTION: WHAT CAN A BODY DO?

The body is perhaps the most intimate landscape available to human beings (Nast and Pile, 1998). Bodies have their own geographies, their own forms of earth-writing, characterised by spatial dynamisms and temporal rhythms. Because of this dynamism, they are also where the seeming self-evidence of philosophical dualisms like organism and environment, self and other, individual and collective, begin to buckle under the weight of visceral experience. Where does 'my' body end and the environment begin? While conventional wisdom would suggest a body ends at the skin's surface, cultural geographers explore how bodies enfold aspects of their environment in ways that are far more complex and capacious. Non-haptic senses like vision, hearing, and smell extend the spatial reach of the body beyond the limits imposed by the skin. And as with space, so with time: bodies accumulate material traces of their past, and, through habit, muscle memory, and skilled practice, they become capable of anticipating particular futures.

Many of these spatial and temporal extensions – these distributed *geographies* of the body – are supported, shaped, and amplified by technologies in ways that are impossible to foresee. Indeed, for many of the post-phenomenological geographers introduced in ***Chapter 4***, the human body is characterised by its ontological dependence upon technical prostheses (Braun and Whatmore, 2010: xvi). Those who seek to wield power are keenly aware of these deep entanglements between bodies and machines. In an age of big data, human bodies are quite literally plugged into unimaginably

DOI: 10.4324/9781003542667-5

complex systems that map out and modulate how our bodies respond to various stimuli (e.g. advertisements, public service announcements, political slogans) on visceral, often unconscious levels. This body, prosthetically extended through technology, is thus a key site for understanding and contesting the cultural geographies of power (see ***Chapter 6*** for a more detailed discussion of power and its analysis in cultural geography).

It is with cultural geography's fundamentally relational understanding of the body that we begin this chapter. To set the tone for the discussion that follows, we want to briefly return to the work of key twentieth-century French philosopher Gilles Deleuze. There are, of course, a variety of conceptual frameworks available for thinking about the body and theorising its place within contemporary culture. The most significant of these for cultural geographers – performativity, critical phenomenology, and assemblage theory – will be explored in the following sections. Yet, it is difficult to find a philosopher as invested in the challenge of thinking about the body as Deleuze was. For Deleuze, what is most interesting about our relationship with our bodies is that "we do not know what the body can do" (Deleuze, 1988: 17). This might seem like a curious assertion, but Deleuze's reasoning is unnervingly straightforward: the body achieves many extraordinary feats without our knowing. Deleuze finds this idea exciting because it means that there will always be powers of the body that extend "beyond the given conditions of our knowledge" (1988: 18). The condition of having a body is such that we find ourselves thrown into relational encounters that exceed our accumulated knowledge, encounters which, in the absence of this knowledge, force us to improvise and to think in new ways.

What, then, can a body do? Deleuze's question has resonated with cultural geographers (particularly those working in non-representational theory) and is more a provocation to be explored than a question to be answered. What it does provoke is an intense appreciation of the body's powers to persist, to relate, to make its way in the world without the interventions of a knowing self. The limited knowledge we do have of the body is representational. Scientific knowledge practices dissect the body through words and concepts (as well as scalpels!), and, like a butterfly specimen pinned to a collector's display board, the body is assigned various meanings according to the dominant conventions of signification. Through representation, we make the body mean something. But the body, insofar as it is a body, has no need for representations to do what it does. The body *bodies.* It operates without words and concepts, independently of our conscious desire for meaning.

It is perhaps not surprising, then, that the body has long been a concept of interest for cultural geographers interested in psychoanalytic theories of the unconscious (Pile, 1996; Straughan, 2014; Secor, 2025). And yet, as many psychoanalytic geographers would themselves be quick to point out, the visceral materiality of the body does not need a psychoanalytic interpretation to make itself felt. To illustrate this, try turning your mind to all the things your body is doing right now, entirely of its own accord: lungs breathing, heart pumping, intestines digesting, a prickling sensation on the surface of the skin as you coax these ordinarily unconscious processes into your perceptual field. Think about the violent contortions of living matter that have made your body what it is today, beginning as a foetus but persisting through the plasticity of your brain and wider nervous system. Think about the body's pleasures, its exuberant desires to connect and to feel and to be felt, without the need for logical justification. And, at the same time, consider the body's unavoidable exposure to suffering: there can be pain, there is most likely sickness, and there will undoubtedly be death. All this the body achieves without consciousness, representation, or meaning, and for Deleuze this is something quite amazing to behold from a philosophical point of view.

Another reason for beginning this chapter with Deleuze is that his approach to the body spotlights the tension between its everyday familiarity and its fundamental strangeness. The body is an intimate landscape, and yet, we do not know what a body – *your* body, but also *any* body – can do. In a short book on Spinoza, Deleuze (1988: 17–18) notes how a deeper appreciation of the body and its powers has been foreclosed by philosophy's obsession with cognition:

> We speak of consciousness and its decrees, of the will and its effects, of the thousand ways of moving the body, of dominating the body and the passions – but **we still do not even know what a body can do.**

The body appears as familiar and uninteresting within the specific cultural milieu associated with so-called Western philosophy, including the works of humanist philosophers like Plato, Descartes, and Kant. Deleuze reminds us, however, that the realities associated with bodily life are often strange and sometimes profoundly disturbing. The bodies that we *are* do not possess the degree of representational unity and coherence that we cognitively ascribe to ourselves as individual selves or subjects (Burdon, 2022). To borrow a phrase from artist and philosopher Erin Manning (2013), bodies are always "more than one": they interpenetrate, they form strange alliances, they ingest, they secrete, and they leak (see Longhurst, 2000). Our bodies surprise us, and they are liable to let us down. Deleuze's reminder is that, in Western cultures, we have inherited a model of individual selfhood – of 'I' and 'Other' – which is more concerned with our mind's capacity to represent the body as a concept than it is with taking seriously what it is that bodies do and what they might be capable of when exposed to new relations.

In this chapter, we will explore how a desire to take the body seriously has animated a series of interrelated but often incongruous approaches within cultural geography. We will pay particular attention to the tensions that exist between the body's dual status in society, being both a surface for the inscription of a culture's dominant representations *and* a conduit for life's more visceral, non-representational intensities. Perhaps one of the most interesting aspects of cultural geography's relationship with the body is that, similarly to Deleuze's provocation, there is something about corporeal life that keeps impressing itself as a recurring problematic for geographic thought. The body keeps coming back. The world changes, our knowledge of that world evolves, but the visceral force of the body and its uncertain capacities remain (Harrison, 2008). For cultural geographers, then, the body is an ever-present reminder that there is a part of being human that never quite fits into the representational unity of a self or subject, however much we may wish this to be the case.

This insistent force of the body is not limited to these philosophical debates concerning the corporeality of the self. Indeed, throughout the early decades of the twenty-first century, a diverse array of issues relating to bodies have continued to shape many aspects of cultural life (the evolution of medical science and the shifting cultural discourses relating to a body's health and well-being stretching back even further through the past 200 years). We emphasise this insistence of corporeality as a means of countering the common assumption that the technological innovations of the digital age (e.g. smartphones, high-speed Internet, social media, virtual reality) have generated a progressively *disembodied* form of culture. While this is often imagined to be the case in the dystopian landscapes of science fiction – the Hollywood blockbuster *The Matrix* (Wachowski and Wachowski, 1999) being perhaps the most obvious example of this disembodied aesthetic – in reality, digital technologies often intensify experiences of embodiment and the corporeality of culture in interesting ways. What is more, these intensifications of bodily life are unevenly distributed, with some bodies made to feel their corporeality far more than others within specific cultural contexts.

This issue of the differentiated and uneven realities associated with bodies and bodily capacities remains a key problematic for cultural geographers, and it is one that we will address throughout this chapter in relation to the corporeal dimensions of gender and race. For now, however, we want to bring this introduction to a close by outlining what the intensification of bodily life associated with twenty-first-century techno-cultures looks like in practice and why it matters from a cultural-geographical perspective. The first and perhaps most disturbing example is the use of AI-enabled technologies to monitor, profile, and police certain kinds of bodies within larger populations. As useful as they might be for unlocking your device or accessing online banking without needing a password, technologies such as face detection and emotion recognition have radically amplified corporeal experiences of discrimination and disadvantage for politically vulnerable minorities across the globe. This includes the mass surveillance of Uyghur people and other ethnic minority groups in the Xinjiang Uyghur Autonomous Region in northern China, where vast amounts of data relating to bodily characteristics and facial expressions "have enabled the Chinese Communist Party to undertake mass social sorting" of its population (Clarke, 2021: np). Surveillance technologies have been deployed on Palestinian people living in the Israeli-occupied territories of the West Bank and the Gaza Strip in similarly disturbing ways, rendering certain kinds of bodies far more vulnerable to state-sanctioned oppression and violence than others (Loewenstein, 2023). Furthermore, in both Xinjiang and the Israeli-occupied territories, the surveillance of minorities has played a significant role in facilitating the development of new technologies for export to lucrative international markets.

These examples of surveillance technologies in the age of AI and big data show how, for some populations, the experience of having a body is intensified within specific cultural (and spatial) contexts. Consider, for instance, how Palestinian experiences of corporeality are heightened through the knowledge that their bodies, unlike others, are recognised by the state as objects of constant surveillance and targets of socio-spatial control (Long, 2011). Here, there are significant overlaps (and important differences) with the experiences of those who identify with the LGBTIQA+ community, as well as others whose lives and lifestyles are deemed to transgress the corporeal norms dictated by patriarchal culture. For many people, then, what it means to have a body and to undergo bodily experiences is overwhelmingly shaped by a culture's dominant ideas and assumptions relating to gender, in ways that often exact a heavy toll (Brice, 2020; Todd, 2023). A culture's ideas about gender are made durable through a variety of technologies and institutions, including, for instance, architectural design and the planning of urban spaces, which are often shaped by patriarchal (and able-bodied) ideals of corporeality. During the early days of 'new spatial media' and the rise of personal location applications, feminist geographers Agnieszka Leszczynski and Sarah Elwood were quick to point out that such technologies often "(re)produce gender(ed) identities, norms, subjectivities, exclusions, and spaces in new, unprecedented ways" (2015: 13). Thus, within a patriarchal society, the geolocational visibility of non-cis-male bodies facilitated by these technologies is registered far more viscerally than it is for cis-male bodies, who are less vulnerable to gendered violence from the outset.

Finally, we can consider how emerging cultural forms associated with the rapid expansion of social media platforms are, in some cases, intensifying problematic or self-destructive relationships with our bodies. The algorithms developed by social media platforms are designed to direct people to content that may be of interest to them, based on data generated through their past activities. For the most part, these algorithms provide an incredibly powerful tool for parsing out the vast amounts of irrelevant data that constitute our online worlds. However, these algorithms have no awareness of what these past activities mean for each user. A brief pause in scrolling at the sight of a particularly disturbing image will register as user interest, thus training the algorithm to provide similar content in the future. The resulting algorithmic rabbit holes (sometimes referred to as 'echo chambers') can trigger or amplify existing psychological issues relating to the body, including unrealistic body image ideals, body dysmorphia, eating disorders, health anxiety, and obsessive-compulsive disorder (OCD). And this is to say nothing of the recent proliferation of AI-generated images and the impacts these will have on how we perceive and relate to our bodies in the decades to come.

With these brief examples, what we hope to have illustrated is the sense in which the body retains a significant place in our increasingly digital and online culture. In what follows, we will explore the different ways that cultural geographers have responded to the body as a problematic that provokes new ways of thinking about culture and the wider world. In the following section (*Fantasies of disembodiment*), we show how cultural geography's interest in the body emerged in response to an historical denigration (and exclusion) of bodily life in the pursuit of scientific objectivity. Next, we trace cultural geography's engagement with post-structuralist theories of the body, focusing on the groundbreaking work of gender theorist Judith Butler (*Bodies that matter*). As important as Butler's work has been, cultural geographers have argued for alternative approaches that place more emphasis on the body's materiality. The final section (*Excessive bodies*) explores two such responses: first, through the lens of critical phenomenology; and second, in relation to theories of affect and assemblage. We then conclude the chapter with some final reflections on the body's significance as a lightning rod that continues to enliven thought (and challenge what it means to think) within cultural geography today.

FANTASIES OF DISEMBODIMENT

Bodies have not always been welcomed by the institutions of knowledge production and their gatekeepers. Indeed, within the physical science disciplines, a desire to exclude the lived experiences associated with the reality of having a body often remains. This exclusion is believed by many to be a necessary step in ensuring that the knowledge we produce about the world is rigorously obtained, reliably accurate, and repeatable by others. Another term associated with the kind of knowledge these scientific practices are aiming towards is 'objectivity.' This term will likely be quite familiar to most readers. What might be less familiar, however, is the cultural context in which this desire for objective knowledge emerged, as well as the specific relationship to the body that it engendered. The purpose of this section is to provide a brief introduction to this context, which has been the topic of significant scholarship within cultural geography (particularly feminist geography) since the early 1990s.

What is knowledge? What is it like to know something? And by what criteria should we evaluate the veracity of what we claim to know? These questions are what philosophers and other scholars in humanities and social science disciplines call epistemological questions (see **Box 2.1** for a concise definition of this term, or ***Chapter 3*** for a more detailed discussion of the relationship between epistemology and nature). For most people in most situations, epistemological concerns might seem extremely detached from their lived realities. This is especially the case in the twenty-first century, where, through things like new technologies and medical advances, the spectacular achievements associated with scientific knowledge are virtually impossible to ignore. Why, then, given the extent to which the scientific method has increased our understanding of the world, would cultural geographers have an interest in critically questioning the foundations of what we know and how we know that we know it? And does cultural geography's willingness to explore such epistemological questions make it 'anti-science'?

The first point to underline here is that there is an important difference between, on the one hand, being critical of something in a negative or pejorative sense, and, on the other, what it means to think critically or to ask critical questions. Critical thinking, of the kind associated with epistemological issues, is about understanding how the solidity of the things and structures we often take for granted came to be as such. To put it simply, critical thinking means not taking reality at face value. Critical thinkers are, for this reason, suspicious of things like universal truths, the impact of which is to stop people thinking about the contingency of the world and to discourage them from considering how things could have ended up otherwise under different circumstances. In relation to knowledge, then, the significance of epistemology as a critical tool for cultural-geographical enquiry lies in the emphasis it places on understanding how the achievements of science are made possible by particular ideas and assumptions concerning the nature of knowledge – and, crucially for our discussion of cultural geography in this chapter, the relationship between knowledge and the body.

For cultural geographers, thinking critically about the knowledge practices associated with modern science requires an understanding of the broader cultural contexts in which they first developed. A society's epistemologies (i.e. its theories of knowledge) do not simply materialise out of nowhere; they are shaped, in space and through time, by ideas, values, and aesthetics. Science, as we noted in ***Chapter 3***, is a profoundly cultural enterprise in at least two senses: first, as an expression of its cultural context; and second, as a set of practices that generate their own cultural forms. Situating scientific knowledge in this way is not intended to detract from the reality of its achievements or the legitimacy of its claims to know reality. We write this book at a time when the rapid proliferation of misinformation, facilitated by a deliberate undermining of cultural institutions, means that the legitimacy of scientific knowledge is increasingly being questioned by those seeking to consolidate power: climate change denial and the terrifying rise of vaccine scepticism are two notable examples of this. All of this is to say that, by thinking critically about science as a form of knowledge, cultural geographers are interested in understanding the broader cultural contexts that enable science to make the knowledge claims that it does.

There are many paths that can be traced through the history of science, and it is important to emphasise that not all of these originate in, or indeed even pass through, Europe. That said, when it comes to understanding the relationship between science and the body, and thus the broader question of the place of the body in contemporary culture, it would be impossible to ignore the impact of one European philosopher in particular: René Descartes (1596–1650). A key figure during Europe's Scientific Revolution, Descartes' philosophical ideas about the world (and, crucially, the body) laid many of the key foundations for the development of modern science. Central to his so-called Cartesian worldview is the idea that reality can be broken down into two fundamentally different substances: body (*res extensa*) and mind (*res cogitans*). By the term body, Descartes was referring to the physical world of extended matter, of which the human body forms a part; mind, on the other hand, referred to consciousness or the soul as a non-physical substance. In the case of human beings, Descartes believed that body and mind were brought together through a mysterious process located, or so he thought, in the pineal gland, buried deep within the brain. Ultimately, however, Descartes would argue that it was the presence of an immaterial mind within human beings that distinguished them from the rest of nature.

When it comes to the place of the body in scientific knowledge production, two significant implications follow from Descartes' substance dualism. The first of these is that, for Descartes, the body cannot think or know. Like the rest of non-human nature, Descartes understood the body as a form of pure extension, devoid of will or agency. Indeed, he went as far as arguing that animals and even the bodies of humans were no different from the rudimentary automata used to entertain the upper classes of his day. Another way of saying this is that, following Descartes, material bodies of all kinds became *objects* of knowledge, reducible to their spatial extension and measurable qualities. The second implication is closely tied to the first, and this is that knowledge is of the mind alone. The ideal knower (the *subject* of knowledge) becomes, following Descartes, a disembodied individual or immaterial soul; its detachment from the world of bodies is the condition of its capacity to objectively know them.

In reality, of course, this ideal of a disembodied knower does not exist. To borrow a phrase coined by feminist philosopher of technology Donna Haraway (1988: 581), the Cartesian fantasy of disembodied knowledge represents the humanist "God trick of seeing everything from nowhere." And yet it is a fantasy that has persisted in shaping the underlying epistemologies of modern science in hugely significant ways, particularly through its attempts to exclude corporeal experiences such as feelings and emotions from the spaces and practices of knowledge production (for a more detailed discussion of how cultural geographers have sought to counter this fantasy through methodological experimentation, see ***Chapter 7***). Another key impact of Descartes' scientific method was that it disciplined the body by reducing it to an object of knowledge. The fantasy of the disembodied knower thus excluded the visceral landscapes of the body – in this case, the bodies of the scientists themselves – from the experimental practices associated with the scientific method. This desire to exclude or minimise the impacts of the body is something that continues to shape contemporary discourse relating to science, where the cultural trope of the scientist dressed in a white lab coat makes it easy to forget that the people doing science are also fleshy sacks of visceral matter, traversed by the corporeal dynamisms of desires, feelings, memories, and emotions.

Taking inspiration from feminist philosophers of science and technology, cultural geographers have explored how this exclusion of the body associated with these dominant scientific epistemologies reflects long-standing gender stereotypes within the cultural milieus of European thought (see **Box 5.1**). As Australian philosopher Elizabeth Grosz (1987: 4) explains, Descartes' mind-body dualism

> is commonly associated with a number of other binary pairs: nature and culture, private and public, self and other, subject and object. These help to provide the mind-body dualism with positive contents. The mind becomes associated with culture, reason, subject and self; while the body is correlated with nature, the passions, object and other. Not unexpectedly, the positive side of the opposition, mind/culture etc. is also associated with masculinity, and their opposites, with femininity.

What Grosz is arguing here is that Descartes' substance dualism was shaped by cultural ideas and assumptions related to gender: specifically, the tendency to code and devalue bodies (and, more broadly, materiality) as *feminine*. Pushing further, Grosz (1987: 5) explains how Descartes's scientific epistemology contributes to the oppression of women in society because "[p]atriarchal oppression justifies itself through the presumption that women, more than men, are tied to their fixed corporeality." This spurious and derogatory claim that women were naturally more 'in touch' with their bodies – and, by extension, less capable of rational thought – enabled early men of science like Descartes to further entrench their already dominant status in society.

BOX 5.1 Feminist geography

Cultural geography has made significant contributions to feminist politics, at the level of both theory and practice. Feminism refers to a diverse array of philosophies with a dynamic and evolving history. What mattered for the 'First Wave' feminists in the late nineteenth century (i.e. earning the right to vote) is quite different from the debates that shaped later 'Second Wave' (i.e. questioning traditional gender roles, challenging institutions, etc.) or 'Third Wave' (i.e. sex positivity, intersectionality) feminism. The genealogy of feminist ideas in cultural geography is equally diverse, beginning in the 1970s when geographers first used empirical research to shine a light on gender inequality, through to the feminist critiques of Marxist geographies that took hold in the 1980s, and then the emergence of feminist geographies of difference inspired by post-structural philosophers in the 1990s. Cultural geographers have also carried out important work critically reflecting on the gendered dimensions of geography as an academic discipline. Historically, geography has been an intellectual pursuit dominated by men and, for this reason, tended to ignore, downplay, or belittle cultural spaces associated with women's lives. Cultural geographer Gillian Rose (1993) explores how these structural inequalities find expression in the gendering of concepts like 'nature' and 'landscape' in her classic text *Feminism and Geography: The Limits of Geographical Knowledge*.

In its desire to be seen as a legitimate science, the discipline of geography and its associated practices of knowledge production have also been profoundly shaped by these gendered readings of the body-as-feminine. In her classic book *Feminism and Geography* (1993), cultural geographer Gillian Rose examines what she refers to as the inherent 'masculinism' of geography. Rose explores how the subject of geographical knowledge (i.e. the academic geographer) was often imagined through the colonial aesthetics of the male explorer, freely taking in his surroundings without ever needing to reflect on the partiality of his perspective (see Figure 5.1). Like Grosz, Rose connects this masculinist vision of geography's knowing subject to the birth of scientific epistemology and Descartes' devaluation of the body in relation to the mind. "Masculinist subjectivity," Rose (1993: 15) argues, "is a form of knowledge which assumes a knower who believes he can separate himself

Figure 5.1 North-east view from the northern top of Mount Kosciusko, 1863, by Eugene von Guérard (oil on canvas, public domain).

from his body, emotions, values, past and so on, so that he and his thought are autonomous, context-free and objective." What the work of feminist cultural geographers like Rose and others sought to emphasise, therefore, was an assertion that knowledge production is in fact always shaped by the partiality and material situatedness of our bodies.

BODIES THAT MATTER

The fantasy of disembodiment, so central to the scientific epistemology of Western science and to geography more specifically, serves as a dramatic reminder that knowledge production is never a politically neutral affair and that science's epistemological dream of achieving a universal 'view from nowhere' remains intimately entangled with patriarchal culture. In this section, we expand outwards from the preceding discussion of the body as an object of epistemological exclusion to explore broader cultural-geographical concerns with the placing (and policing) of bodies and bodily capacities in the spaces of everyday life. Here, the work of post-structuralist philosopher and gender theorist *Judith Butler* (see **Box 5.2**) has played an especially significant role in shaping how cultural geographers have approached the relationship between gender, embodiment, and identity (Kinkaid and Nelson, 2020). Butler's work, particularly their conceptualisation of gender as performativity, has both inspired and frustrated cultural geographers in its treatment of the body, and we will spend some time outlining why this is the case later in this section.

BOX 5.2 Judith Butler

Judith Butler is an American philosopher whose work has played a significant role in shaping feminist philosophy, gender studies, and political theory. While most well-known for their theory of gender performativity, Butler's work is also concerned with the broader issue of how, given a particular cultural context and its discursive regimes, certain bodies come to be recognised as *subjects* while others are not afforded this right. The technical term that Butler uses to refer to the condition of these unrecognised others is *abjection*: they are cast outside of the dominant system of norms that grants bodies the status of being subjects (i.e. being properly human). In addition to their work on gender, Butler examines this problematic in relation to war and the 'grievability' of different lives. For Butler, the violence of war is predicated on a situation where certain lives are deemed to be 'ungrievable' because they are not even recognised as properly living in the first place (this is an example of *abjection*). Butler, who is Jewish, has been a vocal critic of the Israeli Government's policy towards Palestinians, which, they argue, is based on a refusal to extend 'grievability' (and therefore humanity) to Palestinian lives (Butler, 2023).

The title of this section is named after one of Butler's most important books, *Bodies That Matter*, which was first published in 1993. In this book, Butler engages with the concept of gender, understood as a form of socially constructed identity that remains irreducible to biological sex. At the time of its publication, conversations relating to gender identity had come to play a significant role within what has now come to be known as 'Second Wave' feminism. The work of Butler and other gender theorists was (and largely still is) seen as a way of detaching gender identity from essentialist accounts of identity associated with biological sex. To put it in simpler terms, the gender theories associated with Second Wave feminism argued that a person's gender was socially constructed (see **Box 3.1**). These theories emphasised how, when understood through the conceptual framework of gender, the categories of femaleness and femininity came into focus as cultural phenomena whose meanings were contextually situated and, therefore, open to contestation.

In their earlier work, *Gender Trouble* (1990), Butler develops the concept of 'performativity' as a means of understanding how bodies – their movements, acts, gestures, and comportments – are enrolled in the *doing* of gender. As cultural geographers, Kinkaid and Emard (2024: 77) explain:

> Butler's theory of performativity posits that there is no essence to gender; it is not some stable truth to be found in or read from the body. Rather, the illusion of gender's truth is produced through a string of citations of gendered meanings, representations, and behaviours.

Gender, in Butler's (1990: 33) own words, is "the repeated stylization of the body, a set of repeated acts within a highly rigid regulatory frame that congeal over time, to produce the appearance of substance, of a natural sort of being." What Butler means by performativity here is not just that gender is a performance that we are free to choose, as if we were taking on a role in a theatrical play. Rather, their point is that the discursive frames that enable us to articulate gender actively shape the bodies that they claim to represent. In other words, it is the inherent tendency for discourses to actively produce reality (their performative dimensions) that was of most interest to Butler. This ability of discourse to produce reality is what Kinkaid and Emard are getting at in the above quotation, which states that gender's truth (i.e. its reality) is produced (i.e. performed) through a string of citations of gendered meanings, representations, and behaviours (i.e. discourses).

For Butler, however, there was a problem with the way existing feminist theory conceptualised the distinction between gender and sex. While gender was seen as a cultural phenomenon based in the performativity of discourse, it was still common to assume that sex was something biologically given or 'natural'; for the most part, sex was still understood to be a material characteristic of bodies 'prior to' or 'beyond' discourse. A consequence of this approach is that it retains a subtle form of biological essentialism: while a person's gender identity may be fluid or may differ from what was assigned at birth, their biological sex remains grounded in bodily characteristics – the presence or absence of certain sex organs, hormones, or chromosomes – that exist independently of culture and the performative power of discourse. Sex, in other words, is seen as the objective fact (i.e. nature) upon which the subjective interpretations of gender (i.e. culture) are projected.

Butler's response to this approach, in *Bodies that Matter*, was radical. They argued that this very desire to anchor sex in bodily characteristics outside or beyond discourse was itself a fundamentally patriarchal project, reflecting what Butler (1993) referred to as the regime of heterosexuality. In characteristically technical prose, Butler (1993: 30) argues that "[t]he body posited as prior to the sign, is always *posited* or *signified* as *prior*." What Butler is arguing here is that there are no aspects of the body's materiality that are not shaped in some way by discourse – and, specifically for Butler, gender as the dominant discursive regime. The very concept of biological sex is, for Butler, already gendered from the outset. Contrary to the claims of conservative critics and right-wing hysteria, this is not about denying the reality of anatomical differences. Instead, what Butler wants us to consider is *why* it is that so much of what it means to be a legitimate body is evaluated on the basis of our sex organs, hormones, and other biological markers of sexual difference. It is possible to imagine an alternative reality where biological markers such as a person's genitalia or their hormone levels were materially real, without having the power that they do in contemporary culture: a power that, for Butler (1993: 2), determines "that which qualifies a body for life within the domain of cultural intelligibility." The fact that this is clearly *not* the reality that most of us inhabit is what Butler's theory of gender performativity tries to explain.

It is at this point that the political and ethical implications of Butler's argument come into sharper focus. Instead of being something superficially added to the body, gender is the principal operation through which certain bodies are granted the legitimacy to exist in the world and to be recognised as fully human. As Butler (1993: 8) explains in relation to the gendering of newborn babies:

> Such attributions or interpellations contribute to that field of discourse and power that orchestrates, delimits, and sustains

> that which qualifies as 'the human'. We see this most clearly in the examples of those abjected beings who do not appear properly gendered; it is their very humanness that comes into question. Indeed, the construction of gender operates through exclusionary means, such that the human is not only produced over and against the inhuman, but through a set of foreclosures, radical erasures, that are, strictly speaking, refused the possibility of cultural articulation.

The incessant demand to articulate one's gender within the dominant regime of heterosexuality comes with the threat of social and cultural exclusion, where one's body is deemed not to matter as much as the bodies of others. As a discursive regime, gender is structurally dependent on exclusion: the very demand to articulate one's gender creates the possibility of abject bodies (see **Box 5.2**) that are cast outside the framework of intelligibility.

GEOGRAPHIES OF VULNERABILITY

The toll of navigating these discursive regimes can have devastating impacts for those whose lives and lifestyles do not map onto heteronormative expectations of bodies, generating particular "geographies of vulnerability" for transgender people and other members of the LGBTQIA+ community (Brice, 2020). This is not something that has been lost on cultural geographers, who have taken up and extended Butler's work to explore how public spaces like shopping malls (Doan, 2010), bathrooms (Bender-Baird, 2016) and even queer spaces (Nash, 2011) can exclude transgender people by inscribing heteronormative expectations about bodies – and what bodies are permitted to *do* – into the material fabric of the built environment. Butler's work serves as a reminder of what is at stake when it comes to the gendering of bodies, because a body that ceases to be intelligible within the dominant discursive regime is often a body which, according to that regime, no longer matters. Gender, for this reason, is very much a matter of life and death for these bodies: a point that Butler returns to time and again in their work.

The culture wars that have taken hold in relation to transgender people in countries like the United States, the United Kingdom, and

Australia provide a clear example of the dehumanising exclusions that Butler warns against. On January 20, 2025, President Donald J. Trump issued Executive Order 14168: *Defending Women From Gender Ideology Extremism and Restoring Biological Truth to the Federal Government* (Trump, 2025). The order rails against what it terms the subjective nature of gender, stating that "[i]t is the policy of the United States to recognize two sexes, male and female" and that "[t]hese sexes are not changeable and are grounded in fundamental and incontrovertible reality." We hope that our brief introduction to Butler's work illustrates just how poor Trump's understanding of gender theory is! What thinking with Butler clearly shows is that this Executive Order is appealing to biological sex as an ultimate, unquestionable truth in a way that produces certain bodies (most obviously those of transgender and intersex people) as abject or not fully human. This is also a very clear example of how scientific appeals to biological sex are themselves a product of heteronormative culture. Somewhat ironically, then, President Trump's appeal to the "incontrovertible reality" of biological sex is evidence of his complicity in the "gender ideology" he is so desperate to get rid of.

The existential burden posed by gender performativity is far less for cisgendered heterosexual people, given that the design of public spaces and institutions is overwhelmingly suited to facilitate the intelligibility of heterosexually gendered bodies. That said, the patriarchal nature of these heterosexual regimes means that the bodies of cisgendered heterosexual women are scrutinised, judged, and policed to a far greater extent than those of cisgendered heterosexual men. While clearly privileged, cisgendered heterosexual men are not entirely exempt from the demands of gender performativity either. The ubiquity of social media and algorithmically targeted digital content has created new arenas for the discursive scripting of bodies, including emerging forms of ephemeral media like Facebook 'Reels,' TikTok clips, and GIFs. The demand for bodies – including cisgender male bodies – to perform their gender in ways that are intelligible within the discursive regime of heterosexuality is alive and well on these platforms: a fact that can be seen through the growing prevalence of body-image issues among young males who are trying to emulate the gendered aesthetics of muscularity, strength, and bodily discipline/control. The statistics are alarming, with a recent parliamentary inquiry in Australia suggesting that approximately one third of men are dissatisfied with their body size or shape (Victorian State Government, 2004).

EXCESSIVE BODIES

Butler's theory of gender performativity highlights the extent to which our bodies are shaped through their ongoing encounters with discursive regimes, underlining the ethical and political implications for how a given culture determines what bodies signify – and, ultimately, which bodies matter. For Butler, then, the idea that there is a pure body 'beyond' or 'outside' discourse is a trap that prevents us from seeing how bodies are shaped by a discursive regime of intelligibility. Even those individuals who find themselves excluded from the framework of cultural intelligibility are excluded *because* of discourse, Butler would argue. But as some cultural geographers have pointed out, Butler's focus on the discursive materialisation of bodies has very little to say about the viscerality of bodily experience (Nelson, 1999). What is it like to be a body? What is it like to tremble, to sweat, to feel anxious, to experience joy, to dance, or to age? Do we only experience the materiality of our embodiment through discourse (i.e. through systems of knowledge and power that define their cultural intelligibility)? Or is there something about the body that *exceeds* signification? And, if this is the case, how does the body's excessiveness make itself felt, non-discursively, in the overlapping registers of perception, experience, and thought?

This idea that there are aspects of bodies and embodied experience that take place in non-discursive registers is where some cultural geographers, who are interested in the body and are otherwise sympathetic to Butler's political project, end up parting ways with gender performativity as a conceptual framework. Before looking at the alternative pathways that have emerged in the wake of cultural geography's encounter with Butler, it is worth noting that Butler did in fact anticipate this critique and went to some length explaining that they did not intend to deny the existence of a physical world beyond/before discourse. As gender theorists Margrit Shildrick and Janet Price (1999: 7) explain:

> To say that a body is a discursive construction is not to deny a substantial corpus, but to insist that our apprehension of it, our

> understanding of it, is necessarily mediated by the contexts in which we speak.

The problem, however, is that Butler's theory lets language set the ultimate boundaries on human experience, including the experiences through which we come to apprehend or understand ourselves as embodied beings. For Butler, then, there is nothing 'beyond' discourse because our ability to experience the body – indeed, our ability to experience anything at all – is always mediated by the contexts *in which we speak*, which means there can be no experience of the body that isn't already shaped by discourse.

As we shall see in the remainder of this section, Butler's focus on the materiality of discourse at the expense of other aspects of material life is something that cultural geographers have pushed back against (Nelson, 1999; Jacobs and Nash, 2003). Much of this work has developed either directly out of or in close conversation with non-representational theory, which, as we outlined in ***Chapter 2***, comprises a diverse body of work that seeks to question subject-centred accounts of society and culture within (but also beyond) cultural geography. The body has remained a key area of interest for non-representational theory since the term was first coined by British cultural geographer Nigel Thrift in the early 2000s (Thrift and Dewsbury, 2000). Non-representational theories of the body diverge from Butler in two important ways: first, by shifting focus towards its materiality, non-representational theory affirms the primacy of the body vis-à-vis the discourses that capture and shape it; and second, perhaps more significantly, non-representational approaches see this materiality of the body as *itself* a form of thinking and/or knowing that happens before we are identified (and positioned) as subjects within discursive regimes. Cultural geographers working within the orbit of non-representational theory have developed a range of innovative concepts for grappling with the materiality of embodied thought, including habit (Dewsbury and Bissell, 2015), skill (Patchett and Mann, 2018), and attunement (Latham and Wagner, 2021).

In what remains of this section, we now turn to two approaches that attempt to reincorporate the excessiveness of the body into cultural geography research, namely critical phenomenology and assemblage theory. Both approaches have risen to prominence within twenty-first-century cultural geography, and, while there are significant conceptual differences between them that we will explore, they are both animated by the conviction that there is more to the body than can be captured by discourse. Similarly, critical phenomenology and assemblage theory emerged at a time when non-representational theorists were beginning to experimentally broaden the register of empirical experience to include the pre-conscious push of bodily intensities or 'affects.' Affects are the relational forces that shape, move, and direct our attention before we are fully conscious subjects, unfolding through the "vague moods and atmospheres associated with a tightening of the gut, the shivering of the skin, and modulations of pulse" (Roberts, 2012: 2517). Again, there are important differences (and lively disagreements) in the way critical phenomenologists and assemblage theorists have engaged with the affective life of the body (see **Box 5.4**); yet, common to both of these approaches is a hunch that those affects and impulses that stir the viscera are fundamentally indissociable from what it means to experience and know the world. Let's now explore each of these in turn, beginning with critical phenomenology.

CRITICAL PHENOMENOLOGY

An interest in phenomenology has accompanied the conceptual and methodological landscape of cultural geography since Carl Sauer's seminal works on cultural landscapes in the early twentieth century. Phenomenology encompasses a heterogeneous lineage of twentieth-century European philosophers, including Edmund Husserl, Martin Heidegger, Maurice Merleau-Ponty, and Jean-Paul Sartre. While the differences between each of these thinkers are significant, what they share is an underlying commitment to first-person experience as the starting point for philosophical enquiry. Phenomenology is thus concerned with *phenomena*, or the way things appear to consciousness. This means that the starting point for phenomenological inquiry is neither reality (i.e. ontology) nor knowledge (i.e. epistemology), but rather the world as it appears in/through first-person experience. In the 1970s, phenomenology's attention to lived experience was adopted by humanistic geographers, where key thinkers like Yi-Fu Tuan shifted the focus of cultural geography away from a previous focus on the spatial distribution of human cultures towards "the relationship between geography, experience and meaning" (Hepach and Kinkaid, 2024: 2). For cultural geographers influenced by phenomenological philosophy, the body – and, crucially, the *lived experience* (see **Box 5.3**) of embodiment – becomes a key locus in the mediation of this relationship.

BOX 5.3 Lived experience

Lived experience refers to a research approach that situates a person's qualitative experience of something (e.g. an event, situation, phenomenon, condition, identity) at the centre of its approach to knowledge production and, crucially, as a form of political intervention that seeks to provide a voice to marginalised research subjects. Lived experience research is primarily phenomenological in that it is concerned with phenomena as they are experienced by individuals or groups in specific cultural and socio-spatial contexts. So, instead of seeking an objectively verifiable account of whatever it is that happened to a research subject, lived experience approaches focus on the way an event or situation plays out within the context of the research subject's experience. From this perspective, the way a research subject recounts their experience and the particular words and phrases they use to make sense of that experience are what a lived experience researcher is primarily interested in capturing. For an excellent example of what this approach to research looks like in practice, see Duff and Hill (2022).

'Critical phenomenology' refers to a more recent set of debates across the humanities and social science disciplines, emerging in the twenty-first century and informed by cutting-edge insights from cultural geographers. Like the traditional phenomenologists before them, critical phenomenologists are fundamentally interested in lived experience. However, critical phenomenologists place much more emphasis on the *differential* nature of embodiment and the impact this has in shaping people's experiences and worlds. Cultural geographer Eden Kinkaid (2020: 168) explains this key difference in the following extract:

> A critical phenomenology of social space serves as a starting point for articulating the ways that different kinds of bodies – marked by race, gender, sexuality, disability, and other forms of

social difference – encounter space differently, embodying and enacting its ruptures and contradictions.

The work of Kinkaid and others addresses what has often been seen as a significant problem associated with traditional phenomenology, which is that, in making universal claims about the nature of human experience, there is an assumption that the world appears in the same way to all bodies, in all spaces, and at all times. So, whereas traditional forms of phenomenology tend to speak in terms of *the* body or *the* subject, the critical phenomenology developed by cultural geographers like Kinkaid (2021: 310) reminds us that "bodies and subjects have histories, histories formed in a field of power."

One of the most glaringly obvious issues with traditional phenomenology is that its universalising claims about the structures of human experience and consciousness are based on the lived experience of individuals who would have enjoyed a highly privileged position within their cultural milieu. What do you notice about the list of phenomenological philosophers that we included at the beginning of this section? Most obviously, they are all men. They are also all white (specifically European), middle-aged, and employed by universities as professional academic philosophers. These factors shape how the world appears to their individual consciousnesses, structuring the possibilities of lived experience in significant ways. An interesting example of this can be seen with the kinds of objects that tend to crop up as examples in philosophical texts. These often include things like chairs and writing desks, both of which reflect the kind of privileges associated with the life of a tenured academic (including having the space and time to philosophically reflect on what it means to experience these inanimate objects!). In short, if we take phenomenology's commitment to phenomena seriously, then we need to understand that the stillness and stability of the philosopher's embodied state is a rather uncommon (and extremely privileged) basis for exploring how the world appears to consciousness in first-person experience.

Within cultural geography, critical phenomenological approaches have been developed to address this unacknowledged privilege and to expand the remit of phenomenological approaches to include a more diverse collection of lived experiences. Kinkaid (2020: 181) refers to this key dimension of critical phenomenology as "the spatial politics of nonnormative embodiment." Drawing on Sara Ahmed's critique of Merleau-Ponty's phenomenology, Kinkaid (2020: 181) describes how the possibilities of lived experience that dominate a given cultural milieu tend to be orientated around those bodies that conform to culturally mediated norms of "whiteness, masculinity, and heteronormativity." Bodies that deviate from this norm are often faced with a profound disconnect between their lived experience and the way society is oriented around the movements, gestures, and practices associated with normative bodies. This is what Kinkaid, following Ahmed, refers to as the *disorientation* of minority subjects. Some examples of the disorientation experienced by these minorities include, for instance, the experience of feeling 'out of place' for women breastfeeding in public spaces (Boyer, 2012); embodied feelings of anxiety experienced by members of marginalised communities working in universities (Todd, 2021); and the various ways migrant bodies are made to experience themselves as 'other' in specific socio-spatial contexts like nightclubs and shopping centres (Simonsen and Koefoed, 2020).

These efforts to look beyond the dominant orientations of lived experience are not just inclusionary gestures. The political objective of critical phenomenology goes much further than this by seeking to challenge and disrupt the universalising assumptions inherent within these orientations of experience. Approaching phenomenology from the perspective of non-normative embodiment is a form of political resistance to the extent that it produces disorientation among the majority. As Simonsen and Koefoed (2020) explain in relation to the embodied orientations of sexuality:

> 'Straight' and 'queer', then, are not only sexual orientations; they are ways of being in the world, and to be queer in a world that is normatively straight is often to be disorientated towards it – and also to be perceived as disorientating.

For Kinkaid (2021: 307), too, the politics of attending to these marginalised perspectives lies in the ability for cultural geographers and others to "illuminate how spaces and worlds are formed around the bodies of normative subjects," in such a way that the neutrality of these orientations can no longer be assumed.

When they do arise, expressions of non-normative embodiment often reveal how forms of inequality are at play in the most everyday of activities. One such activity is participation in sports. Here, work in critical phenomenology draws our attention to the way culturally coded expectations relating to gender place limits on the movements, gestures, and athletic achievements of non-male sportspeople. Political philosopher and feminist theorist Iris Marion Young (1949–2006) provides a compelling account of this phenomenon in her classic essay 'Throwing Like a Girl' (1980). Young's essay explores how differences in the experience of motility and spatiality arise from patriarchal assumptions relating to femininity in ways that limit women's sporting capacities. According to Young (1980: 143):

> For many women as they move in sport, a space surrounds them in imagination which we are not free to move beyond; the space available to our movement is a restricted space.

The contemporary relevance of Young's argument was dramatically illustrated in 2019, when professional Australian rules football player Tayla Harris was subjected to a horrific barrage of sexual Internet 'trolling' after being photographed mid-match performing a spectacular kick for goal (Gillett, 2020). What this example shows is that there are certain forms of movement – in this case, maximising a kick's power by extending the kicking leg high above the head – that are constrained by sexism and the patriarchal expectations placed on women's bodies, expectations that extend into the upper reaches of athletic performance and the culture of professional sports even today.

To summarise, then, cultural geographers working in this space of critical phenomenology are interested in understanding what the lived experience of embodiment is like for different bodies as they move through socio-spatial contexts and navigate cultural norms. Of particular interest here are what Kinkaid (2021: 301) refers to as "marginalized forms of embodiment" – in other words, what it is like to be a body that differs significantly from the bodies of normative subjects (i.e. male, white, heterosexual). Critical phenomenologists share Butler's concern for the way bodies and bodily capacities are shaped by cultural norms; however, their focus on the lived experience of embodiment creates more space for the excessiveness and unruliness of bodies in their irreducibility to discursive regimes. This is because lived experience, although undoubtedly shaped by discourse, takes place through forms of relational embodiment (e.g. orientation, attunement) that are far more expansive and capacious than can be captured through discursive means.

ASSEMBLAGE AND AFFECT

Another important conceptual framework that cultural geographers have adopted in their analyses of bodies and embodiment is assemblage theory. Taking inspiration from Gilles Deleuze and his long-time collaborator Felix Guattari, cultural geographers who turn to theories of assemblage tend to emphasise the fundamentally relational dimensions of the body (Dewsbury, 2011). We can think about the body's relationality operating at different scales. At one level, each body is the product of relational processes that pre-exist the individuality of the 'self' or the 'I' that we take ourselves to be. *The body is multiple from the start.* Consider how your body expresses a relational assemblage of DNA, microbes, viruses, etc., that takes place beneath the level of conscious perception. This is what we might call the 'infra-individual' assemblage of the body (the prefix infra- meaning below or beneath). For assemblage theorists, however, the body is also shaped by processes of assemblage that operate above the level of its individuality, plugging it into relations with a whole host of bodies beyond its corporeal boundaries. Bodies become what they are in/through the relations that they enter into. Indeed, the body's unconscious *desire* to relate is, for assemblage theorists, an ontological characteristic of corporeality. We use the term 'supra-individual' assemblage to capture this dimension of corporeality whereby bodies are constantly exceeding their individuality to assemble with others (supra- meaning above or over).

One of the key challenges posed by such theories of assemblage is that they redirect our attention towards those aspects of corporeality that precede and exceed a body's individuality. Erin Manning (2013), an artist and philosopher whose work has been adopted by cultural geographers interested in assemblage theories, vividly articulates this sentiment when she describes bodies and embodied experience as being "always more-than-one." What makes Manning's work particularly challenging is that the corporeal experience of being "always more-than-one" takes shape through subtle movements, forces, and associated intensities of feeling that are often difficult to articulate in words – especially when operating within the conventions of academic writing. At the infra-individual level, then, we might consider how the seemingly unified experience of conscious perception is in fact assembled from a multiplicity of micro-perceptions, swarming within the body. Think, for instance, of the barely perceptible shift in awareness that takes place at the very onset of a viral infection, where the body begins to assemble itself differently in response to the microbial hijack occurring deep within its cells. At the same time, consider how these infra-individual assemblages overlap with (and are folded into) the body's supra-individual dimensions; once the virus has taken hold, there are the collective feelings of awkwardness and unease that restructure bodily encounters when you succumb to a cough or a sneeze on public transport.

These shifting intensities of feeling are what cultural geographers refer to as *affects* (see Dewsbury, 2009; McCormack, 2014). Cultural geographers have engaged with the concept of affect from a variety of perspectives and philosophical lineages, and to do justice to this variety would take us far beyond the scope of this introductory text (see **Box 5.4**). The concept of affect that we are referring to here emerges from a philosophical lineage that originates with Baruch Spinoza in the seventeenth century, passes through Gilles Deleuze in the twentieth century, and has been reinterpreted by Brian Massumi in more recent years. As cultural geographer Paul Simpson (2020: 74) notes, Massumi's work provides a "common reference point" for many of the cultural geographers interested in affect. In his translator's introduction to Deleuze and Guattari's influential book *A Thousand Plateaus*, Massumi defines affect as a "pre-personal intensity corresponding to the passage from one experiential state of the body to another" (2004: xvii). The key word in this definition is *passage*: affect is a change in the body's readiness or capacity to act, produced in/through a process of assemblage. This emphasis on passage is what distinguishes affect from the related notion of bodily affections. Whereas affections are the body's way of registering the causal impact of the things that it encounters in the world, affect maps the shifts in intensity that constitute the background tonality of an assemblage: affect as the transitions in-between the affections of lived experience.

BOX 5.4 Affect and emotion

Within cultural geography, the history of affect as a concept is one that has been marked by periods of intense debate – and, at times, passionate disagreement. While many cultural geographers share a commitment to the importance of capturing the intensity of feelings in their research, the development of non-representational theory in the early 2000s generated a rift between an emerging interest in non-conscious affects and existing work on the cultural geographies of emotion. For some feminist geographers, the conceptualisation of affect as a form of 'pre-subjective' feeling by many non-representational theorists reflected geography's long-standing masculinist suspicion of emotion and a desire for objectivity (Thien, 2005). Others expressed concerns about the seemingly 'universalist' claims of affect theory (Tolia-Kelly, 2006). Non-representational theorists responded to these critiques by emphasising the importance of affect as a concept for articulating the more-than-human materiality that courses beneath recognisable emotions, as well as its centrality in the networking and assemblage of political power in capitalist society (McCormack, 2006). Thinking with affect has also produced many exciting methodological innovations within cultural geography (see Dewsbury, 2010), which we explore in greater detail in ***Chapter 7***.

Another important dimension of Massumi's definition is the idea that affect is *pre-personal*. What Massumi is getting at here is the way affects tend to take hold of us before we are able to rationalise them through our cognitive faculties. This interpretation of affect as pre-personal distinguishes it from emotion, which, according to Massumi, refers to affects that have been categorised according to existing cultural norms of signification. In Massumi's own words:

> Emotion is qualified intensity, the conventional, consensual point of insertion of intensity into semantically and semiotically formed progressions, into narrativizable action-reaction circuits, into function and meaning. It is intensity owned and recognized.

Affects, understood as pre-personal intensities, are the raw materials from which recognisable emotions are socially constructed. In and of themselves, affects do not represent or signify anything beyond the corporeal intensity that they express (they are, quite profoundly, non-representational). This emphasis on the pre-personal or pre-individual (Keating, 2019) dimension of affect also generates new ways of understanding contemporary forms of social organisation and power, in ways that are no longer dependent on discourse and the signifying capacities of the body (as they tend to be for Butler).

For theorists like Massumi, then, the socio-spatial ordering of bodies takes shape through the pre-personal modulation of collective affects within relational assemblages. These assemblages include discursive elements – what Deleuze and Guattari call 'signifying materials' – but they are never fully determined by their signifying logics. Assemblages are productive rather than representational, and what they produce are unconscious investments of *desire* that shape how bodies interact within a given assemblage (Roberts, 2021). Here, the word desire is not simply a matter of sexual or erotic desire (although it could well include this in specific situations); desire, in the sense that Deleuze and Guattari use it in their theorisation of assemblage, refers to an unconscious drive for connection that flows through all bodies, human or otherwise. The modulation of collective affects that characterises a given assemblage thus produces a consistency of desire. In other words, assemblages align a body's unconscious desire for connectivity in particular directions and away from others. This is why, for Deleuze and Guattari, oppressive formations of power (e.g. patriarchy, racism, fascism) do not function through the top-down imposition of ideologies (i.e. through discourse) but, instead, emerge through material assemblages of desire.

Within cultural geography, the work of Arun Saldanha stands out as a key example of how concepts like assemblage and affect can be used to rethink the politics of bodies in ways that are more sensitive to materiality. Drawing on the work of Felix Guattari, Saldanha criticises the social constructivist approaches of theorists like Judith Butler on the basis that they overlook the body's materiality. Here, Saldanha's main interest is to theorise race as a material formation that cannot be reduced to the performative effect of discourse, arguing that "the structures of racism and sexism encompass much more than just mental categories" (Saldanha, 2006: 15). Race, for Saldanha, is not a fact of nature, but neither is it simply a discursive category imposed by human minds on otherwise passive bodies. Instead, Saldanha theorises race as an assemblage of desire, where bodies are aggregated according to the stickiness or 'viscosity' of affect.

The practical implications of Saldanha's project are made clear in his empirical research into Goa's rave scene, where he explores how racial (and class-based) assemblages of desire are produced through the a-signifying, non-representational force of music. According to Saldanha, music's capacity to generate affects that glue certain aggregates of bodies together (and not others) illustrates the shortcomings of social constructivist frameworks, such as Butler's, which limit their analysis of power to the signifying logics of discourse. Much of music's force lies in its a-signifying, non-representational dimension; however, this does not make it immune to power. As Saldanha (2005: 716) explains:

> Music weaves some bodies together, and excludes others. Music is not a representation or a formal system. It is physical, affecting the body directly, akin to taking drugs or getting a tattoo. Music is a force.

The collective experience of music is a good example of affect because it so obviously makes bodies *move* (see Figure 5.2). In what has since become a classic paper in cultural geography, Saldanha (2005: 717) explores how, within the context of Goa's psytrance party scene, the force of music "mobilizes bodies, objects, flows, entire landscapes by unhinging potentialities that no one knew were there." And so, as the dawn breaks over Anjuna beach, and the DJs dig out their more psychedelic cuts, Saldanha uses the concept of assemblage to explain how it is predominantly the white bodies of Israeli tourists that, through the viscosity of musical affect, are rhythmically mobilised on the throbbing dancefloor. This is how race is materialised according to Saldanha: not as something inherent within or essential to bodies but as an assemblage of desire that amplifies certain affective encounters over others.

Theories of assemblage and affect are deliberately challenging: they are intended to disrupt our habitual assumptions about the

Figure 5.2 A view over a crowd of people dancing at a music event with laser lights shining above their heads. Photograph taken by author.

body, what it is, and what it can do. If we had to boil their conceptual complexities down to a single take-home point, it would be something like this: your body's capacities to tap into new gradations of feeling and intensity are shaped by the assemblages you participate in and the consistencies of desire (and coagulations of power) they produce. Assemblages give our bodies direction, purpose, and meaning. This is something that capitalism knows all too well. If a company like Apple can assemble desire in such a way that its employees really *feel* a sense of affinity with the brand and willingly strive to 'go the extra mile' for little recompense, this is because their desire has been assembled in such a way that their servitude to an exploitative system becomes an aspiration – and, indeed, one that is viscerally felt as a form of affect. This is power understood as an assemblage of desire. Yet, at the same time, the only way to resist power is to experiment with assemblages that compose desire differently. This is assemblage as a process of resistance: a creative retooling of desire that frees up new possibilities for bodies to affect and to be affected (see ***Chapter 6*** for an in-depth analysis of this 'micropolitical' approach to resistance in cultural geography).

To conclude this discussion of assemblage and affect in cultural geography, a key difference between these theories and the critical phenomenology introduced in the preceding section hinges on the status of lived experience. For cultural geographers working with concepts of assemblage and affect, appeals to lived experience as the starting point for thinking about the body can only take us so far. The main reason for this is that the first-person perspective associated with subjective consciousness only provides a tiny snapshot of what the body is doing, what its desires are, what kinds of assemblages it is participating in, and what it may or may not be capable of becoming. The challenge for cultural geographers working with Deleuze-inspired theories of affect is to approach, experience, and know the body from the perspective of the wider assemblages of desire that shape it beyond the limits of lived experience (see Buchanan, 2026).

CONCLUSION

In this chapter, we have traced the body's cultural-geographical reverberations through a variety of philosophical perspectives. The ontological and epistemological assumptions that differentiate these perspectives mean that they are not always easy theoretical bedfellows. So, whereas Butler's theory of gender performativity provides cultural geographers with a sophisticated framework for understanding how bodies are shaped by discourse, it has little to say about those experiences of embodied materiality that go beyond or exceed signification. And while critical phenomenology and assemblage theories both attempt to address this significant shortcoming, the way they conceptualise the non-discursive dimensions of bodily life differs significantly. For critical phenomenologists, the body becomes a way of materialising the subject (i.e. the body-subject), whereas for assemblage theorists, the body's excessive materiality (i.e. the body as 'more-than-one') focuses on pre-individual affects before and/or beyond the subject.

In concluding this chapter, it seems fitting to return to the body as the site where these very different problematics overlap and intermingle. The conceptual frameworks that we have outlined have enabled cultural geographers to articulate these corporeal problematics and their significance within contemporary culture. Moreover, cultural-geographical approaches recognise that the way we think about and conceptualise the body feeds back into our embodied experiences – and, in some instances, changes what our bodies are materially capable of. Put more simply, cultural geography reminds us that our theories *about* the body are also *of* the body. Whether it was Butler's emphasis on discourse or Deleuze and Guattari's theory of assemblage, we hope that this chapter has shifted the way *your* body orients itself in its world in a way that produces new tonalities of embodied experience, however subtle and fleeting these might be.

FURTHER READING

Butler, J. *Bodies that Matter: On the Discursive Limits of "Sex"*. New York: Routledge, 1993.

Deleuze, G. *Spinoza: Practical Philosophy.* San Francisco: City Lights, 1988.

Dewsbury, J. D. "Affect." In R. Kitchin and N. Thrift (eds.) *International Encyclopaedia of Human Geography* (pp. 20–24). Oxford: Elsevier, 2009.

Rose, G. *Feminism and Geography: The Limits of Geographical Knowledge.* Polity, 1993.

Saldanha, A. "Trance and visibility at dawn: Racial dynamics in Goa's rave scene." *Social & Cultural Geography* 6, no. 5 (2005): 707–721. https://doi.org/10.1080/14649360500258328

REFERENCES

Bender-Baird, K. "Peeing under surveillance: Bathrooms, gender policing, and hate violence." *Gender, Place & Culture* 23, no. 7 (2016): 983–988. https://doi.org/10.1080/0966369X.2015.1073699

Boyer, K. "Affect, corporeality and the limits of belonging: Breastfeeding in public in the contemporary UK." *Health & Place* 18, no. 3 (2012): 552–560. https://doi.org/10.1016/j.healthplace.2012.01.010

Braun, B. and S. Whatmore. "The Stuff of Politics: An Introduction." In B. Braun and S. Whatmore (eds.) *Political Matter: Technoscience, Democracy, and Public Life* (pp. ix-xl). Minneapolis: University of Minnesota Press, 2010.

Brice, S. "Geographies of vulnerability: Mapping transindividual geometries of identity and resistance." *Transactions of the Institute of British Geographers* 45, no. 3 (2020): 664–677. https://doi.org/10.1111/tran.12358

Buchanan, I. *Assemblage Theory and Affect*. London: Bloomsbury, 2026.

Burdon, G. "On being affected: Desire, passion, and the question of *conatus* after Spinoza and Deleuze." *Transactions of the Institute of British Geographers* 47, no. 3 (2022): 682–694. https://doi.org/10.1111/tran.12526

Butler, J. *Gender Trouble: Feminism and the Subversion of Identity*. New York: Routledge, 1990.

Butler, J. *Bodies That Matter: On the Discursive Limits of "Sex"*. New York: Routledge, 1993.

Butler, J. "The Compass of Mourning." *London Review of Books* 45, no. 20 (2023). https://www.lrb.co.uk/the-paper/v45/n20/judith-butler/the-compass-of-mourning

Clarke, M. "Turning ghosts into humans: Surveillance as an instrument of social engineering in Xinjiang." *War on the Rocks* (November 2, 2021). https://warontherocks.com/2021/11/turning-ghosts-into-humans-surveillance-as-an-instrument-of-social-engineering-in-xinjiang/

Deleuze, G. *Spinoza: Practical Philosophy.* San Francisco: City Lights, 1988.

Dewsbury, J. D. "Affect." In R. Kitchin and N. Thrift (eds.) *International Encyclopaedia of Human Geography* (pp. 20–24). Oxford: Elsevier, 2009.

Dewsbury, J. D. "The Deleuze-Guattarian assemblage: Plastic habits." *Area* 43, no. 2 (2011): 148–153. https://doi.org/10.1111/j.1475-4762.2011.01006.x

Dewsbury, J. D. "Performative, non-representational, and affect-based research: Seven injunctions." In D. DeLyser, S. Herbert, S. Aitken, M. Crang and L. McDowell (eds.) *The SAGE Handbook of Qualitative Geography* (pp. 321–334). London: SAGE, 2010.

Dewsbury, J. D. "Witnessing space: 'knowledge without contemplation'." *Environment and Planning A: Economy and Space* 35, no. 11 (2003): 1907–1932. https://doi.org/10.1068/a3582

Dewsbury, J. D. and D. Bissell. "Habit geographies: The perilous zones in the life of the individual." *Cultural Geographies* 22, no. 1 (2015): 21–28. https://doi.org/10.1177/1474474014561172

Doan, P. L. "The tyranny of gendered spaces – reflections from beyond the gender dichotomy." *Gender, Place & Culture* 17, no. 5 (2010): 635–654. https://doi.org/10.1080/0966369X.2010.503121

Duff, C. and N. Hill. "Wellbeing as social care: On assemblages and the 'commons'." *Wellbeing, Space and Society* 3 (2022): 100078. https://doi.org/10.1016/j.wss.2022.100078

Gillett, C. "Tayla Harris and her parents speak out about abuse and threats over AFLW photo." *ABC News* (June 2020).

Grosz, E. "Notes towards a corporeal feminism." *Australian Feminist Studies* 2, no. 5 (1987): 1–16.

Haraway, D. "Situated knowledges: The science question in feminism and the privilege of partial perspective." *Feminist Studies* 14, no. 3 (1988): 575–599. https://doi.org/10.2307/3178066

Harrison, P. "Corporeal remains: Vulnerability, proximity, and living on after the end of the world." *Environment and Planning A: Economy and Space* 40, no. 2 (2008): 423–445. https://doi.org/10.1068/a391

Hepach, M. G. and E. Kinkaid. "Geography and phenomenology." In N. de Warren and T. Toadvine (eds.) *Encyclopedia of Phenomenology*. Cham: Springer, 2024. https://doi.org/10.1007/978-3-031-25900-5_149-2

Jacobs, J. M. and C. J. Nash. "Too little, too much: Cultural feminist geographies." *Gender, Place & Culture* 10, no. 3 (2003): 265–279. https://doi.org/10.1080/0966369032000114037

Keating, T. "Pre-individual affects: Gilbert Simondon and the individuation of relation." *Cultural Geographies* 26, no. 2 (2019): 211–226. https://doi.org/10.1177/1474474018824090

Kinkaid, E. "Is post-phenomenology a critical geography? Subjectivity and difference in post-phenomenological geographies." *Progress in Human Geography* 42, no. 2 (2021): 298–316. https://doi.org/10.1177/0309132520909520

Kinkaid, E. "Re-encountering Lefebvre: Toward a critical phenomenology of social space." *Environment and Planning D: Society and Space* 38, no. 1 (2020): 167–186. https://doi.org/10.1177/0263775819854765

Kinkaid, E. and K. Emard. "Judith Butler." In M. Gilmartin, P. Hubbard, R. Kitchin and S. M. Roberts (eds.) *Key Thinkers on Space and Place* (3rd ed.) (pp. 76–82). London: Sage, 2024.

Kinkaid, E. and L. Nelson. "On the subject of performativity: Judith Butler's influence in geography." In A. Datta, P. Hopkins, L. Johnston, E. Olson and J. M. Silva (eds.) *Routledge Handbook of Gender and Feminist Geographies* (pp. 92–101). London: Routledge, 2020.

Latham, A. and L. B. Wagner. "Experiments in becoming: Corporeality, attunement and doing research." *Cultural Geographies* 28, no. 1 (2021): 91–108. https://doi.org/10.1177/1474474020949550

Leszczynski, A. and S. Elwood. "Feminist geographies of new spatial media." *The Canadian Geographer* 59, no. 1 (2015): 12–28. https://doi.org/10.1111/cag.12093

Loewenstein, A. *The Palestine Laboratory: How Israel Exports the Technology of Occupation Around the World.* Brunswick: Scribe, 2023.

Long, J. "Geographies of Palestine-Israel." *Geography Compass* 5, no. 5 (2011): 262–274. https://doi.org/10.1111/j.1749-8198.2011.00419.x

Longhurst, R. *Bodies: Exploring Fluid Boundaries.* London: Routledge, 2000.

Manning, E. *Always More Than One: Individuation's Dance*. Durham: Duke University Press, 2013.

Massumi, B. "Notes on the translation and acknowledgements." In G. Deleuze and F. Guattari *A Thousand Plateaus* (pp. xvii-xx). London: Continuum, 2004.

McCormack, D. "For the love of pipes and cables: A response to Deborah Thien." *Area* 38, no. 3 (2006): 330–332. https://www.jstor.org/stable/20004550

McCormack, D. *Refrains for Moving Bodies: Experience and Experiment in Affective Spaces*. Durham: Duke University Press, 2014.

Nash, C. J. "Trans experiences in lesbian and queer space." *The Canadian Geographer* 55, no. 2 (2011): 192–207. https://doi.org/10.1111/j.1541-0064.2010.00337.x

Nast, H. J. and S. Pile. "Introduction: MakingPlacesBodies." In H. J. Nast and S. Pile (eds.) *Places through the body* (pp. 1–14). London: Routledge, 1998.

Nelson, L. "Bodies (and spaces) do Matter: The limits of performativity." *Gender, Place & Culture* 6, no. 4 (1999): 331–353. https://doi.org/10.1080/09663699924926

Patchett, M. and J. Mann. "Five advantages of skill." *Cultural Geographies* 25, no. 1 (2018): 23–29. https://doi.org/10.1177/1474474017739024

Pile, S. *The Body and the City: Psychoanalysis, Space and Subjectivity*. Abingdon: Routledge, 1996.

Roberts, T. "A constructivism of desire: Conceptualising the politics of assemblage with Deleuze and Guattari." *Area* 53, no. 4 (2021): 691–698. https://doi.org/10.1111/area.12735

Roberts, T. "From 'new materialism' to 'machinic assemblage': Agency and affect in IKEA." *Environment and Planning A: Economy and Space* 44, no. 10 (2012): 2512–2529. https://doi.org/10.1068/a44692

Rose, G. *Feminism and Geography: The Limits of Geographical Knowledge.* Polity, 1993.

Saldanha, A. "Reontologising race: The machinic geography of phenotype." *Environment and Planning D: Society and Space* 24, no. 1 (2006): 9–24. https://doi.org/10.1068/d61j

Saldanha, A. "Trance and visibility at dawn: Racial dynamics in Goa's rave scene." *Social & Cultural Geography* 6, no. 5 (2005): 707–721. https://doi.org/10.1080/14649360500258328

Secor, A. "Spacetimeunconscious." *Dialogues in Human Geography* 15, no. 2 (2025): 177–194. https://doi.org/10.1177/20438206231191763

Shildrick, M. and J. Price. "Openings on the body: A critical introduction." In J. Price and M. Shildrick (eds.) *Feminist Theory and the Body: A Reader* (pp. 1–14). Edinburgh: Edinburgh University Press, 1999.

Simonsen, K. and L. Koefoed. *Geographies of Embodiment: Critical Phenomenology and the World of Strangers.* London: Sage, 2020.

Simpson, P. *Non-representational Theory*. London: Routledge, 2020.

Straughan, E. R. "The Uncanny in the Beauty Salon." In P. Kingsbury and S. Pile (eds.) *Psychoanalytic Geographies* (pp. 295–306). Farnham: Ashgate, 2014.

Thien, D. "After or beyond feeling? A consideration of affect and emotion in geography." *Area* 37, no. 4 (2005): 450–454. https://www.jstor.org/stable/20004485

Thrift, N. *Non-representational Theory: Space, Politics, Affect*. London: Routledge, 2008.

Thrift, N. and J. D. Dewsbury. "Dead geographies – and how to make them live." *Environment and Planning D: Society and Space* 18, no. 4 (2000): 411–432. https://doi.org/10.1068/d1804ed

Todd, J. "Exhaustion, exhausting temporalities, and young trans people's everyday lives in the UK." *Annals of the American Association of Geographers* 113, no. 3 (2023): 771–789. https://doi.org/10.1080/24694452.2022.2134087

Todd, J. "Experiencing and embodying anxiety in spaces of academia and social research." *Gender, Place & Culture* 28, no. 4 (2021): 475–496. https://doi.org/10.1080/0966369X.2020.1727862

Tolia-Kelly, D. P. "Affect: An ethnocentric encounter? Exploring the 'universalist' imperative of emotional/affective geographies." *Area* 38, no. 2 (2006): 213–217. https://www.jstor.org/stable/20004528

Trump, D. "Defending women from gender ideology extremism and restoring biological truth to the federal government." *Federal Register* 20 (January. 2025). https://www.federalregister.gov/d/2025-02090

Victorian State Government. "VicHealth Response." *Parliamentary inquiry into issues relating to the development of body image among young people and associated effects on their health and wellbeing*, 2004. https://www.vichealth.vic.gov.au/sites/default/files/VicHealth-Body-Image-Response.pdf

Wachowski, L. and L. Wachowski (dirs.). *The Matrix* [motion picture]. Warner Bros, 1999.

Young, I. M. "Throwing like a girl: A phenomenology of feminine body comportment motility and spatiality." *Human Studies* 3, no. 2 (1980): 137–156. https://www.jstor.org/stable/pdf/20008753.pdf

6

POLITICS

INTRODUCTION: CULTURAL POLITICS

What is the relationship between the cultural and the political? Tracing the etymology of the word 'culture' reveals that its original meaning was invested in a set of concepts and problematics that we commonly associate with politics. One of the roots of culture is the Latin word '*cultura*' which relates to cultivation: to tend, guard; to till, cultivate. This sense is obviously still retained in contemporary words like 'agri*culture*' and 'aqua*culture*' which relate to the processes of cultivating or rearing crops (in the former) or aquatic organisms (in the latter). It is in the 1800s that we see the word increasingly crosses over to the human domain, where it becomes associated with the 'improvement and refinement of the mind,' primarily through education. Here, then, culture comes to be understood in terms of "varied practices for the inculcation of values, beliefs, routines of life, and forms of conduct" (Barnett, 2001: 11). Culture thus becomes an important medium for politics and a governmental technique for producing certain kinds of human subjects (how they think, behave, and relate to each other).

These connections between culture and the production of human subjects help explain why questions of politics became central to the emergence of new cultural geography in the 1980s. One of the motivations for this body of work was a critique of what its advocates saw as the 'apolitical' character of discussions of culture in 'traditional' (Sauerian) cultural geography. Earlier work had often focused on describing cultural landscapes, regional traditions, and the spatial distribution of cultural traits, treating culture as relatively

DOI: 10.4324/9781003542667-6

stable and politically neutral. In contrast, and as we saw in ***Chapter 2***, new cultural geography placed greater emphasis on questions of power and representation. Here, the terms 'politics' and 'power' come to be understood in a much broader sense than their more everyday association with governments, elections, or formal state institutions. Instead, new cultural geographers explored how power operates through everyday practices, cultural meanings and identities, and spatial formations in ways that shape whose perspectives are represented, how places are interpreted, and how social differences are produced and resisted across space. This shift involved a growing interest in a cultural politics of signification, which, in the words of Anderson (2017: 501), aimed to "disclose, critique, and intervene in representational-referential systems with the hopes of minimising or ending their symbolic violences."

Attempts to characterise what such a cultural politics entails vary across theoretical perspectives and empirical contexts. However, we can follow Anderson (2017) in identifying three key tasks that have structured much recent discussion of the politics of culture in geography. The first is tracing how power operates through cultural objects and systems of representation and how social transformations are bound up with concomitant mutations in forms of power. The following part of the chapter therefore examines several influential 'genres' of power that geographers have used to analyse historical and contemporary forms of domination. In particular, we highlight the influence of Michel Foucault on cultural geographic understandings of power – especially his genealogies of sovereign, disciplinary, and biopolitical modes of power – and the distinct subjectivities and spatialities they produce. We then explore more recent work that explores how the techno-cultural shifts currently affecting societies – such as the rise of software platforms and smart devices – are generating different forms and experiences of 'control' that demand new ways of thinking politics and subjectivity.

The second task of cultural politics, Anderson (2017: 502) notes, is to "disclose and critique the symbolic and material violences" of dominant cultural realities and to unpack how this violence is enacted through the process of othering. Here, we focus on work in cultural geography on *nationalism* as a key theme for understanding how political collectives are formed through the inclusion and exclusion of particular kinds of subjects. In part three of the chapter, we contrast dominant approaches that interpret nationalism as an ideological construct reproduced through spectacular events – such as annual memorials and national parades – with approaches that emphasise the more banal and affective processes through which national atmospheres are produced. These atmospheric approaches highlight how nationalism is as much an intensive feeling in the body as it is an idea in our heads. Finally, cultural politics also seeks to "give attention to, cultivate, and sometimes create representations that break with existing formations and enable resistances of alternatives" (Anderson, 2017: 502). In the final section, we explore how recent engagements with the concept of *micropolitics* have enabled cultural geographers to conceive of power beyond the already-articulated interests, identities, and institutions that typically frame conventional political analysis. Instead, micropolitics draws our attention to intensities and forces that move within and between bodies (see also the discussion of assemblages and affects in ***Chapter 5***), constituting the often-unconscious machinery of action and desire. For some cultural geographers, such micropolitical forces and events are where "our true changes take place" (Deleuze and Parnet, 2006: 93), opening possibilities for new modes of relation, experience, and creative forms of life.

MODES OF POWER: SOVEREIGNTY, DISCIPLINE, BIOPOLITICS, AND CONTROL

We usually think of 'power' as the capacity of powerful actors to exert their influence and will over that of the powerless, forcing them to do things they might not otherwise want to do. This kind of power is something we often associate, historically, with monarchs, and, today, with states and governments. The image below is an iconic emblem of this 'Sovereign' modality of power. It is the Royal Coat of Arms. Many readers will likely be familiar with this image, given its ubiquity as a symbol on British passports and its adornment atop important buildings in the United Kingdom and across Britain's former colonial territories. It is the emblem of the British monarch and is intended to exert a sense of authority over the people who gaze upon it. Along the bottom of the emblem are the French words *Dieu et mon droit*, translated literally as 'God and my right' – or more sensically in English as 'my God-given right.' This motto, said to have first been used by King Richard I (1157–1199) as a battle cry, signals the divinely appointed right of the monarch to rule over His or Her subjects.

Figure 6.1 The Royal Coat of Arms at Old Parliament House, Canberra (Photograph by Author).

Sovereignty can therefore be understood as a mode of power involving obedience to a central authority – indeed, this is how the term tends to be used in everyday contexts. The historian and philosopher, Michel Foucault, notes that while we typically conceive sovereignty as a stable and absolute form of power, when we look historically, it is actually something that has evolved significantly over time as a result of various social and political transformations, such as the emergence of parliaments and the checks they placed on Royal power. Through historical examples, Foucault shows how sovereign power isn't something that operates continuously in people's lives and experience but rather intermittently, such as in periods where the monarch rallies the citizenry to fight against a rival power or through the gathering of annual taxes of food, goods, or money. Due to its intermittent nature, Foucault notes how sovereign power is also often applied spectacularly, most obviously through the spectacle of gory, public executions for the punishment of crimes. Foucault famously opens his book *Discipline and Punish* with a graphic account of the public mutilation and execution in eighteenth-century France of Damiens for the crime of attempting regicide of King Louis XV. Damiens was the last person in France to be 'hanged' (to within an inch of death), 'drawn' (where the prisoner is disembowelled while still alive and 'emasculated' by having their genitals cut off), and then finally 'quartered' by horses. Describing the last part of this horrific triptych, Foucault (1991: 4) quotes:

> The horses tugged hard, each pulling straight on a limb, each horse held by an executioner. After a quarter of an hour, the same ceremony was repeated and finally, after several attempts, the direction of the horses had to be changed, thus: those at the arms were made to pull towards the head, those at the thighs towards the arms, which broke the arms at the joints. This was repeated several times without success. He raised his head and looked at himself. Two more horses had to be added to those harnessed to the thighs, which made six horses in all. Without success.

Foucault characterises this sovereign expression of power as the authority of letting live and making die. Through his grizzly retelling of Damiens' execution, Foucault shows his readers how the power of the sovereign thus lies in their capacity to seize the life of a subject and end it when they deem necessary. Sovereign power continues to exist today, even in its more overtly violent forms, including wars and the use of capital punishment in many contemporary states and jurisdictions. But Foucault argues that what we see over history is that the traditional sovereign model of power increasingly becomes supplemented by other modalities and techniques of power, which produce effects and elicit obedience in very different ways.

It is hard to overestimate just how influential the philosophy of Foucault has been to cultural geographic (and, indeed, broader humanities and social scientific) understandings of power. There are three main aspects of Foucault's thinking on power that have been especially impactful for cultural geographers. The first relates to his attempt to deindividualise the question of power: in other words, to "cut off the head of the king" (Foucault, 1998: 89). Power, for Foucault, isn't something an individual possesses but is rather a diffuse and omnipresent force that is exercised through social relations and institutions. In the words of geographer Clive Barnett (2001: 15), Foucault spatially reorients the analysis of political rule from the individual sovereign "to a multitude of locations, decomposing power into the relationships between political rationalities, technologies, and practices." Second, Foucault challenges a repressive theory of power which would see it as only something that works to constrain an essentially free individuality. Instead, Foucault argues that power is *productive*: it elicits conduct, incites behaviour, and enacts new forms of subjectivity. Power, then, to the extent that it enables certain forms of relation, is also not the antonym of freedom: "power relations are only possible in so far as the subject is free" (Foucault, 2000: 342). Finally, and of particular interest to geographers, is the point that Foucault (2000: 361) was interested in the "fundamental" role that space (its production, organisation, and division) plays in the exercise of power. As he writes, "problems of space are common to all three modes of power: sovereignty, discipline, security" (Foucault, 2007: 12). In tracing a historical genealogy of modes of power, Foucault thus paid explicit attention to the various spatial archetypes (asylums, prisons, factories, and schools) that made such formations of power possible.

DISCIPLINARY SPACES

Foucault's overarching aim was therefore to expand existing theorisations of power beyond the traditional emphasis on sovereign authority. He initially does this by arguing that what we begin to see from the seventeenth century onwards in Europe is a gradual shift from sovereign power to a new mode of power that he calls *disciplinary*. In part due to demographic shifts and growth in population size, the intermittent and spectacular nature of sovereign power begins to encounter the limit of its effectiveness as a form of mass control. The brutality of public executions of the kind Damien was subjected to increasingly inspired popular revolts across Europe. Disciplinary power, on the other hand, offered a less dramatic and (importantly) continuous mode of social control because it sought to insert itself directly into people's everyday lives: into the spaces in which they live, learn, work, and socialise. Distinguishing between the aims of sovereign and disciplinary modes of power, the geographer Margo Huxley (2008: 1638) summarises how, for Foucault, "sovereignty acts to annul disobedience and rebellion, and the public spectacle serves to deter others, while discipline seeks to form and reform habits and comportments to produce docile, regulated, and productive individuals." Disciplinary power therefore refers to the behaviour of subjects not to a rule or a law, but rather to *norms of regularity* that seek to positively guide and direct conduct towards specific goals and aims.

Foucault argues that the development of disciplinary power is linked to the flowering of various 'spaces of enclosure' in the seventeenth and eighteenth centuries: new institutional sites (like the military barracks, the school, the hospital, and the asylum) that attempted to discipline and 'normalize' the bodies and minds of the individuals who entered (or were confined) to them. Such sites achieve this in three main ways. The first is through the organisation of space. The emergence of institutional spaces like schools and hospitals is associated for Foucault with the invention of new spatial and architectural forms, which enabled authorities to isolate bodies from each other, to constrain their movements and actions, and to facilitate continuous monitoring. The second approach is through the organisation of time. We also see in these same sites the emergence and use of disciplinary technologies – like timetables and bells – which dictate where individuals should be at any given time of the day or night. And finally, through a whole host of techniques that attempt to organise the actions and behaviours of bodies. These same institutions also therefore included various disciplinary practices that involved a micrological attention to the movement and posture of bodies in an attempt to quite literally take control of the habits of the body and to inculcate certain standardised and graceful behaviours (such as handwriting drills at primary/elementary school and precision drills and marching in the military).

For Foucault (1991), the spatial archetype of disciplinary power was the prison. Prisons interested Foucault because they were sites of quite radical disciplinary innovation. Many of the techniques and methods developed in prisons (such as individualised containment, timetables, and the structuring of prisoners' days around meals, work, and rest) were taken up by other institutions, like reformatories, hospitals, and boarding schools. He also notes the surprising fact that many of the most famous philosophers of the eighteenth and nineteenth centuries actively worked on aspects of prison design, including the English moral philosopher Jeremy Bentham. Indeed, Foucault dedicates a large section of *Discipline and Punish* to an analysis of the distinctive spatiality of disciplinary power in

Bentham's imagining of a new type of prison architecture: *the Panopticon*. Bentham's plan for the panopticon sought to overturn previous models of how to contain dangerous individuals. For example, in the mediaeval period, we famously see the use of dungeons in which criminals were abandoned to spend their time shrouded in darkness. Foucault argues that the panopticon reversed the principles of the dungeon. Instead of the dungeon's darkness, the panopticon was designed to be flooded by light (hence 'pan' (meaning 'all') and 'opticon' (meaning 'seeing')). It was conceived as a circular building in the centre of which was an observation tower with blacked-out glass that contained the prison guards. Around the edges are the prisoners' individual cells, at the back of which are very large windows that let light flood in.

Bentham argued that the panopticon was a more efficient mode of controlling prisoners for a number of reasons. First, the prisoners now had light and fresh air, which helped to make the prisons more sanitary, and the prisoners themselves more healthy and able to carry out prison work. The panopticon is therefore emblematic of a shift in what we could term the moral philosophy of prisons, from being understood as spaces of punishment and exile, to spaces of reform of prisoner's character. But the light also benefited the prison guards in the central observation tower who could easily see inside any cell at any time. Foucault argued that while this may seem like just a minor reform of prison architecture, it was actually a significant shift in disciplinary power because in the dungeon the prisoner was not visible and even had a degree of privacy. In the panopticon, there is no privacy, and due to the design of the space, the prisoners could never tell exactly when they were being observed and when they weren't. What this produces, Foucault suggests, are self-governing inmates who regulate their own behaviour under the fear that they are always potentially being watched. So, the panopticon is more than just a new kind of disciplinary space. It also entailed a new technology of power based on visibility and surveillance, and a new sense of the subject as self-governing and self-disciplined.

The panopticon was never built exactly to Bentham's original plan, but elements did inspire the construction of prisons in parts of the world, most notably The Round House in Fremantle, Western Australia. Geographers have also explored how the surveillant gaze embodied by the panopticon continues to be part of our everyday landscapes of power. An example here is the CCTV cameras that are ubiquitous in cities around the world. The number of cameras and the spaces they keep under surveillance has grown massively in recent decades. The geographer, Hille Koskela (2000), has argued that CCTV cameras can be understood to operate according to a kind of panoptic logic of power, in which urban residents are constantly observed but never entirely sure when or by whom. One of the main arguments used by proponents of CCTV is its purported effectiveness to reduce incidences of crime and make cities 'safer' places in which to live. Koskela (2000), however, notes the ambivalent feelings of fear and security generated by cameras, especially for women, as it can generate feelings of being 'under control' (the object of someone's gaze) rather than necessarily being 'in control.'

BIOPOLITICAL SPACES

In the first volume of his *History of Sexuality (The Will to Knowledge*), Foucault (1998) develops his earlier reflections on disciplinary power by suggesting that it constitutes one of the poles of a broader and emergent form of power that he calls *biopower*. The two poles that make up biopower – this new power over life – are first an *anatomo-politics of discipline* in which we see the emergence of techniques (like routines and timetables) that facilitate (as we saw above) the moulding and surveillance of individual bodies. The second pole is what he terms a *biopolitics of the population*. Here, from the nineteenth century onwards, states increasingly began to target (and create knowledge about) the species body of the population as a whole, which Foucault argues includes various demographic policies aimed at regulating things like birth rates, life spans, health status, the spread of disease, and the distribution of wealth.

Underpinning these demographic policies is the development of new human sciences that take human life as their object of study, including demography, sociology, political economy, and psychoanalysis. The purported aim of these biopolitical knowledges and policies, Foucault argues, is to achieve an overall equilibrium that protects the security of the population as a whole from internal biological risks and dangers. In particular, Foucault focuses his discussion of biopolitics on how 'sexuality' increasingly became an obsession of European governments, especially in the nineteenth century. The reason sexuality becomes so prominent in state policy, Foucault contends, is because its effects are situated on both poles of biopower. It concerns both the micro level of bodily behaviours (including regulation of things like masturbation, polygamy, unrestrained passions, and hidden desires) as well as the macro level of population health (relating to policies around pro- or anti-natal policies and also colonial anxieties around racial 'mixing'). Due to its biopolitical importance, then, Foucault describes how sexuality becomes an index of the moral and biological health of the nation, and thus a central target of governmental policy, economic interventions, and ideological campaigns in the Victorian era.

In the context of biopolitics, Foucault notes that the concept of the 'norm' comes to play a critical role. Whereas the sovereign power over life and death operated on the basis of a binary legal code and the punishment of those who transgressed the law, biopolitics marks a shift in which the 'law' is more and more displaced by a politics of the 'norm.' Biopolitical strategies thus function through the continuous and regulatory logic of calculating, measuring, and comparing bodies and populations according to norms of standards. As Foucault (1998: 144) summarises:

> It is no longer a matter of bringing death into play in the field of sovereignty, but of distributing the living in the domain of value and utility. Such a power has to qualify, measure, appraise, and hierarchize, rather than display itself in its murderous splendor; it does not have to draw the line that separates the enemy of the sovereign from his loyal subjects. It effects distributions around the norm.

What emerges is a 'normalising' society that classifies individual and collective bodies according to how they measure up and rank against a pre-established norm. In a medical context, we might think here of Body Mass Index (BMI) charts that classify a 'healthy' range of weight/height ratios and classify bodies as overweight or underweight according to this norm line. Newborn babies are also subject to frequent and regular checks of weight and have charts plotted of their growth in the first years based on average percentiles. Such norms, Foucault argues, are 'technologies of the self': a set of techniques and practices that enact subjects who increasingly govern themselves, monitoring and regulating their behaviour based on these normalised criteria and expectations.

Cultural geographers have been especially interested in thinking about the role that space plays in biopolitical control. In doing so, some geographers have also looked beyond Foucault to engage with other theoretical lineages of thinking on the biopolitical. Richard Carter-White and Claudio Minca (2020), for instance, discuss the philosopher Giorgio Agamben's theories of biopolitical 'spaces of exception,' in which individuals are stripped of their political rights and reduced to what he terms 'bare life.' Carter-White and Minca (2020: 2) note that the archetypal biopolitical space of exception for Agamben is the camp, understood as a "space operating outside the normal state of law in a delimited or extraterritorial location." Geographers have applied Agamben's theory of the camp to analyses of the many detention and concentration camps that proliferated in the early 2000s during the US War on Terror, such as Guantanamo Bay in Cuba. Guantanamo, as a detention camp deliberately located outside of US legal jurisdiction, allowed the US government to hold prisoners indefinitely, creating a space of exception where due process and legal rights were suspended. Following Agamben, Guantanamo manifests the spatial logic of the camp, "oriented around the isolation, division, and management of groups or individuals through extreme and often violent forms of control" (Carter-White and Minca, 2020: 2).

Other cultural geographers have sought to expand biopolitical analysis beyond just a concern with the regulation or management of *human* life. For instance, Steve Hinchliffe and Nick Bingham (2008: 1541), in a study of the more-than-human biopolitics of the 2005 Avian Flu outbreak in Egypt, note how "all kinds of things become much more interesting when we stop assuming that 'we' are the only place to begin and end our analyses." Their article explores how the approach to dealing with the spread of the H5N1 virus sought to identify the source of the outbreak in the 'premodern' animal husbandry techniques of farmers in countries of the Global South, where millions of birds were culled. Hinchliffe and Bingham (2008) note that to better understand and manage disease requires studying the heterogeneous agents (human and non-human) involved in their production. Rosemary-Claire Collard (2012) also deploys the concept of biopolitics in her study of encounters between humans and cougars on Vancouver Island, Canada. Her work explores the material and discursive processes through which cougars are 'made killable' due to their perceived threat to human biosecurity. They are made killable, Collard (2012: 31–32) notes,

> when they threaten human or domestic animal life, when they lurk stealthily in the shadowy borderlands between wild and domestic spaces and throw the split between these two cougar-human worlds into question, and when they demonstrate not only the fragility and porosity of boundaries but also the vulnerability of human life.

A final line of cultural geographic inquiry draws on the work of the Cameroonian historian, Achille Mbembe (2003), who develops the concept of *necropolitics* as an important extension to Foucault's account of biopolitics. While biopolitics is defined as a mode of power that operates through the regulation and optimisation of life, Mbembe proposes that modern forms of sovereignty are equally defined by their capacity to expose specific populations to death. Mbembe "re-spatialises" Foucault's and Agamben's discussion of biopolitics, shifting focus from the institutions and camps of Europe to the racial and colonial logics of the slavery plantation and occupied territories (Peters et al., 2025: 470). 'Necropolitics' thus comes to describe how colonial states deploy fear, violence, and infrastructural blockages to create "deathworlds": spaces in which specific groups are forced to endure conditions of life that confer on them "a status of living dead" (Mbembe, 2003: 21). For cultural geographers, this perspective has proven particularly useful for analysing spatialised regimes of violence through studies of things like environmental pollution, settler colonialism, and militarised border regimes. For instance, Brigstocke et al. (2023) explore the "necropolitical violence of borders" in the context of the favela settlements of Rio de Janeiro, demonstrating how borders don't just impede mobility but also become sites through which some lives are rendered expendable through policies of abandonment. The concept of necropolitics therefore helps extend cultural geographic analyses of politics beyond the governance of life towards considerations of how power also operates through the differential production of death across populations.

SPACES OF CONTROL

Recently, cultural geographers have explored the question of whether our contemporary digital and networked societies are associated with the emergence of a new regime of power that is quite different to the disciplinary societies discussed by Foucault (Krivy, 2018). A key inspiration here is a short essay written by Deleuze (1992) entitled 'Postscript on Societies of Control.' Deleuze argues that by the 1980s, the disciplinary society so carefully sketched by Foucault had begun to be superseded by what he calls (drawing on the American science fiction writer William Burroughs) 'control societies.' Deleuze distinguishes between control and disciplinary societies along several axes. First, he notes a shift in the technologies underpinning power, from the thermodynamic and 'homeostatic' machines of discipline that seek to impose order and normalisation to cybernetic computers and machines of control, running on information that elicit complexity and indeterminacy while submitting them to constant surveillance and statistical quantification. Second, each society elicits different forms of resistance: from the sabotage and entropy of discipline to hacking, piracy, and viruses in the age of digital control. And third, Deleuze argues we see a spatial shift from disciplinary sites of containment (schools, asylums, and factories) towards a mode of power based on "continuous control and instant communication" (Deleuze, 1992: 7). The spatial avatar for this new type of power is what Deleuze (1992: 7) calls the cybernetic (or what might today be referred to as the 'smart') city:

> . . . imagine a city where one would be able to leave one's apartment, one's street, one's neighbourhood, thanks to one's (dividual) electronic card that raises a given barrier; but the card could just as easily be rejected on a given day or between certain hours; what counts is now the barrier but the computer that tracks each person's position . . . and affects a universal modulation.

Reading this passage today, it is remarkable how prescient Deleuze is in describing the logics of design and governance that underpin contemporary 'smart urbanist' city planning (Krivy, 2018). Deleuze's point is that control is not exercised through hierarchical, top-down management (like with discipline) but rather through the pattern analysis of myriad electronic traces and the subtle shaping (or 'nudging') of microbehaviours via what Deleuze calls "universal modulation" (Deleuze, 1992: 7).

Deleuze argues that control societies are also bound up with the production of a radically different conception of the human subject. He argues that the 'individualities' of disciplinary societies (the discrete subjects that are separately confined in institutions) have transformed into control's "dividuals" which endlessly accumulate and re-combine into "samples, data, markets" (Deleuze, 1992: 5). The etymological roots of the word 'individual' speak to its supposedly in-divisible nature: that it is a whole that cannot be divided into smaller parts. But Deleuze makes the point that in societies of control, we are instead identified and produced as 'dividuals': our personalities are increasingly being divided into an array of data points (such as our consumer behaviours, our political beliefs and voting patterns, our desires, etc.) that can be analysed, mined, segmented, correlated, and then sold back to us. Whereas the individual prides itself on its supposedly unique and inalienable characteristics, Deleuze notes that as dividuals we are continuously detached from and attached to other dividuals based not on similarities of identity but rather by machinic operations and algorithmic classifications of behaviour.

In discussing Deleuze's theory of control, however, there has been a tendency to misread the concept as a primarily negative, restrictive, and limiting form of power. What distinguishes control, for Deleuze, is instead its profoundly generative and productive character. Here, we can see how Deleuze inherits Foucault's thesis of the productive nature of power and applies it to a new techno-cultural milieu. It is an enabling form of power in the sense that it enables specific actions and behaviours, seeking to channel and direct these in specific ways. Control thus operates through what we might term (following Massumi) a series of "enabling constraints" that set the generative conditions for the emergence of specific kinds of different types of behaviour and interactivity (Massumi,

2009: 15). As the political theorist Alex Williams (2015: 216) puts it, "the immense power of control rests not just in its ability to modulate behaviour to goals known in advance, but also in its ability to relatively constrain an open-ended range of contingent behaviours, which cannot be identified in advance."

Williams highlights *the platform* as arguably the archetypal technology and spatiality of contemporary control. The platform is a concept used by businesses like Google, Microsoft, and Meta to understand their operations of creating environments for user-generated content. Williams notes that this was a core advance of Web 2.0 systems over its predecessors: rather than writing content themselves, technology companies began to develop the spaces (or 'sandboxes') within which users could create their own offerings, from social interactions and blog posts to multimedia content and product reviews. The control function of the platform arises precisely at the interface between enablement and constraint. Content is constrained in the sense that it must be possible within the system's protocols and rules (from legal user agreements through to the capacities of particular configurations of code and the technical capabilities of physical substrates like server spaces and communications infrastructures). But within this constraint, there is a considerable degree of openness to contingency: to a vast range of unexpected behaviours that may be conducted upon them. Economically, web-based platforms have proven to be an extremely profitable means of extracting value from a diversity of human behaviours, while also serving to shape and transform these behaviours in turn.

Williams (2015: 220) talks about the unique power of platforms in terms of what he calls "generative entrenchment." He draws this idea from the philosopher William C. Wimslatt, who describes it as a "feature of a structure . . . that has many other things depending on it because it has played a role in generating them" (Williams, 2015: 219). Take, for example, the case of a computer operating system like Windows:

> In the case of Windows, its role in generating (acting as the basis for) multiple computer programmes means that they depend, to some extent, on the continued existence of the operating system. Windows is generatively entrenched because it has generated an entire ecosystem of programmes, products, and

> services which use the operating system as their basis. In turn, this panoply of dependent entities has served to entrench Windows. For example, in a business context, competition between complementary elements (say, between PC manufacturers or application developers) will reduce costs of complements and increase the likelihood of uptake of the platform by end users. This is all in the nature of operating systems – their success depends on their use by other programmes. It is also in the nature of platforms more generally – the more generative the platform, the more entrenched it will become.

In sum, and following Williams, technical platforms can be understood as a clear materialisation of the modulatory logic of control described by Deleuze: a modality of power that tightly weaves together both constraint and enablement and necessity and contingency. Despite the progressive and emancipatory connotations that we usually give to terms like 'enablement' and 'contingency,' Deleuze argues that we should not lose sight of the fact that control is the latest in the genealogy of governance and domination sketched by Foucault. Its regime of power is instead much more supple – and the subjects it produces more pliable and flexible – than that which characterises disciplinary spaces and societies.

NATIONALISM

In an era marked by rising populist movements, contested borders, and resurgent identity politics, nationalism has re-emerged as a powerful force in our contemporary world. Nationalism has long been an important concern in cultural geographic research, not least for the way in which it brings into sharp relief the question of how space, territory, and identity intersect. The study of nationalism in cultural geography offers critical and important insights into how political identities are mobilised to assert claims over territory, to redraw boundaries (both symbolic and material) over space, and to reinforce – or potentially subvert – the modes and structures of power discussed in the previous section.

The ways in which cultural geographers have approached nationalism have also undergone important transformations that mirror some of the broader theoretical shifts we've discussed in other chapters. These shifts have often centred around unpicking the different processes that come to constitute a subject's sense of belonging to (or, conversely, their sense of being excluded from) a national community. A key reference point for understanding the production of national identities (not just within cultural geography, but across the humanities and social sciences) is the work of Benedict Anderson, and especially his landmark book, *Imagined Communities: Reflections on the Origin and Spread of Nationalism* (Anderson, 1983). Anderson's central argument is that the nation is not a 'real' or 'natural' thing, but rather a cultural or *ideological* construct (see **Box 6.1**). As reflected in the title of his book, the nation is best understood as an *imagined community*. It is *imagined*, Anderson argues (1983: 6), because "the members of even the smallest nation will never know most of their fellow members, meet them, or even hear of them, yet in the minds of each lives the image of their communion." And it is a *community*, because "regardless of the actual inequality and exploitation that may prevail, the nation is always conceived as a deep, horizontal comradeship" (Anderson, 1983: 7). This imaginary fraternity is an incredibly powerful force. One so powerful, Anderson contends, that it makes it possible for so many millions of people to kill and willingly die for their nation.

BOX 6.1 Ideology

Defined as a set of beliefs, ideas, or convictions (consciously or unconsciously held) that link a particular group of people together and shape how they think and act. Discussions of the concept in geography and the wider social sciences have tended to be based on the more pejorative sense of the concept encountered in the philosophy of Karl Marx, who conceives it "as a representation of the imaginary relationship of individuals to their real conditions of existence" (Althusser, 2015: 181). For Marx, ideology creates a 'false consciousness' – or distorted worldview – that prevents the proletariat (working classes) from recognising their exploited position within the capitalist system. The French Marxist, Louis Althusser, argued that ideology is propagated through 'Ideological State Apparatuses,' including the media, education institutions, the family, and religion.

Anderson's book traces what he sees as the origins of "national consciousness," placing particular emphasis on the emergence of "print capitalism" (the circulation of books and newspapers) that helped shape a shared language amongst otherwise disparate communities. But Anderson (1983: 145) also spotlights the more spectacular events of national bonding (e.g. National Day parades, military displays, the singing of national anthem at memorial ceremonies) which generate experiences of simultaneity (Anderson, 1983: 145):

> At precisely such moments, people wholly unknown to each other utter the same verses to the same melody. The image: unisonance. Singing the Marseillaise, Waltzing Matilda, and Indonesia Raya provide occasions for unisonality, for the echoed physical realization of the imagined community.

Geographers developing Anderson's ideas have foregrounded how specific spaces (both real and imagined) come to be highly symbolic focal points for the performance and expression of national identity. An example here is the Civilian War Memorial in Singapore, which is situated adjacent to the Padang, itself a highly significant and emblematic site of Singapore's colonial history. The emergence of new nations is often accompanied by a frenzy of nation-building activities: the creation of new flags, the writing of new anthems, and the construction of monuments and memorials are all examples of such activities. And this is the case with the Civilian War Memorial, which was constructed by Lee Kuan Yew's government in 1963, the same year that Singapore split from its short-lived merger with Malaysia to become an independent country. The site memorialises the impact of Japan's occupation of Singapore during World War II on the citizenry, and especially the estimated 25,000 to 50,000 civilians (predominantly Chinese Singaporeans) who were killed in mass executions by the Japanese and whose remains were summarily disposed of in mass burial sites across the island. But the site isn't just a memorialisation of a past event. It also served as a highly symbolic statement of how the fledgling nation wanted to articulate its identity. And this symbolism is reflected in the site's very design and materiality. The monument itself is composed of four stone pillars reaching into the sky, each pillar representing the shared experience of the four 'major racial groups' that were recognised to comprise Singapore: Chinese, Malay, Indian, and Eurasian. Inscriptions around the monument are also written in the four 'official languages' recognised in Article 153 of the Singapore constitution: English, Mandarin, Malay, and Tamil. But it is on the 15th of February of every year that the nationalist contributions of the site are in full flourish. This date is Total Defence Day, a day of commemoration first marked in 1998, which uses the anniversary of the fall of Singapore as a reminder of the 'duty' of all sectors of the economy and society, and all citizens, to defend Singapore from threats to its national sovereignty, both external and internal. As part of the day, a memorial service takes place at the War Memorial Park, and wreaths commemorating the fallen are laid at the base of the Civilian War Memorial monument by local students, religious leaders, and politicians. Trumpets are sounded. Anthems are sung. Fighter jets fly overhead.

Events like Total Defence Day are obviously quite bombastic and symbolically charged occasions for building what Anderson (1983: 37) calls a "national consciousness." But are attending memorial services like these once a year really sufficient for cultivating the kinds of nationalist fervour that people would be willing

Figure 6.2 The Civilian War Memorial, Singapore (Photograph by Author).

to give up their lives for? This is a question raised by Michael Bilig (1995) in another text that has been influential for thinking about nationalism in cultural geography: *Banal Nationalism*. Critiquing Anderson's emphasis on spectacular displays, Bilig (1995: 8) argues that "because the concept of nationalism has been restricted to exotic and passionate exemplars, the routine and familiar forms of nationalism have been overlooked . . . 'our' daily nationalism slips from attention." Nationalism, Bilig's argument goes, isn't just about the rousing singing of the anthem at memorial ceremonies or national day parades. It is also something that plays out more on the register of the unconscious and the everyday: from wearing national team colours at football games, to the appearance of national insignias and royalty on money, to daily weather reports which present the forecast against the image of a national map. Paying attention to these (and a multitude of other) banal practices demonstrates the extent to which nationalism is something that is often so hard to pin down, and also as something that is very difficult to resist. The nation becomes, following Bilig, almost like a "background noise that is always already there and which erupts from time to time" (Closs Stephens, 2016: 184). While cultural geographers have found value in Bilig's emphasis on the endemic and everyday qualities of nationalism, some geographers, like Rhys Jones and Peter Merriman (2009), have challenged the tendency in Bilig's work to maintain a kind of categorical separation between "hot" (i.e. spectacular, the focus of Anderson) and "mundane" practices of nationalism. They argue, instead, that the hot and mundane are usually folded together. An example here would be things like street names, which are both banal parts of people's routine geography of moving through the city, but also highly symbolic in that they often reference key figures of a nation's historic memory.

Other geographers have also sought to challenge the emphasis that both Anderson and Bilig place on the symbolic and representational in the study of nationalism, at the expense of the more embodied and sensuous registers of 'doing' nationalism. Nationalism, these authors argue, is not just an idea in our heads, but an intensity or feeling felt in the body. Angharad Closs Stephens (2016: 183–184), for instance, turns to non-representational work on the concept of *affective atmospheres* to loosen the hold that concepts of identity, essence, and belonging have in conventional studies of nationalism, and instead attends to the transmission of felt intensities that circulate between bodies and that congeal around particular objects and materials in particular spaces and times (see **Box 6.2**). As she puts it (Closs Stephens, 2016: 183–184):

> I use the idea of national affective atmospheres as an opening for engaging with the ways in which national feelings touch us, take hold and become infectious: how they are felt through bodies but surpass any individual body. How, then, might such seemingly 'banal' feelings – moods that we simply 'go along with' – be identified as always already political and as laden with power and resistance?

Closs Stephens applies this concept of nationalism as an affective atmosphere to an analysis of the London 2012 Olympic Games. She notes how the "national feeling" of the games didn't emanate from a single sovereign source but rather arose from multiple constituencies "as part of a nebulous, diffuse atmosphere" (Closs Stephens, 2016: 182). Pivotal here, in building feelings of national excitement and anticipation, was the national torch relay, which saw around 8,000 torchbearers carry the torch around all areas of the United Kingdom in the lead-up to the games.

BOX 6.2 Affective atmospheres

Affective atmospheres usually refer to collective and distributed 'moods' or 'feelings' that emerge from the interactions between people, objects, and spaces. The concept emerged in cultural geography as a means for engaging with the more 'transpersonal' quality of affects (see ***Box 5.4***) beyond a tendency in affect theory to focus on the feelings of individual subjects or bodies. Derek McCormack (2008: 413) defines an affective atmosphere as "something that registers in and through sensing bodies while also remaining diffuse, in the air, ethereal." While recognising the way in which feelings can be shared, work on affective atmospheres has sometimes struggled to articulate the actual processes through which affects move through (and are differently experienced) by bodies. Ash (2013), for instance, draws on the concept of "perturbation" to explore how affective forces move between technologies in ways that produce atmospheres that shape human behaviour.

A precise timetable and map of the journey were uploaded to the Internet, and approximately one-third of the British population turned out to watch the relay and cheer on the torchbearers. The relay was an important part of emplacing the 'hot' national event of the Olympics in the everyday lives of the population. The British Broadcasting Corporation (BBC) also played a crucial role in transmitting the affective atmosphere of the games with live blog updates on the BBC News website and the day's torch highlights shown every day on their flagship breakfast and evening news programmes. Closs-Stephens argues that these local, micro-experiences of the games enabled by the torch relay worked to ensure that national affective atmospheres penetrated every corner of society while also making it difficult to voice critical perspectives that went against the national mood.

Returning to the example of war commemoration, Shanti Sumartojo (2020) has applied this concept of national affective atmospheres in her non-representational ethnography of the ANZAC (Australian and New Zealand Army Corps) Day dawn service, held annually at the Shrine of Remembrance in Melbourne, Australia. Understanding national memorial events like this through the lens of affective atmospheres, she argues, helps foreground the more non-representational and multisensorial dynamics of commemoration – or, put simply, how people *feel* in commemorative sites. These non-representational elements in relation to the ANZAC Day service include things like: the affects of darkness in the early morning and the breaking light of dawn; the oscillations between sombre music and contemplative silence; the shuffles and noise of bodies moving together; and then the moments of collective stillness.

The concept of affect also draws attention to the ways in which commemorative atmospheres are always felt and experienced differently by different people. We are always – in the words of theorist Brian Massumi (2015: 115) – "differentially attuned" to affective atmospheres, with each person "taking the event from a different angle and moving out of it following their own singular trajectory." There is, therefore, always something unpredictable and excessive to the way bodies will experience the supposedly 'same' commemorative event. This is important because it can help illuminate how "feelings can be a form of resistance, subverting or loosening our connection to state narratives" (Sumartojo, 2020: 535). Drawing on

Figure 6.3 Olympic torchbearer in College Green, Bristol, UK, May 2012 (Photograph by Author).

her autoethnographic notes of attending the ceremony, Sumartojo explores how experiences of bodily discomfort (feeling cold, tired, or frustrated by a lack of hot beverages) can render the intended meanings of the state more complex and can even open up new understandings and perspectives on commemorative stories. An attention to concepts of affect and atmosphere in the study of nationalistic events, then, can help foreground how other ways of feeling "are always already present, shadowing and troubling unifying affective atmospheres," and how bodily experience offers a site of *resistance* against the status quo and the possibility for questioning how the imagined community of nationhood shapes culture (Closs Stephens, 2016: 193).

RESISTANCE

Cultural geographers argue that resistance, like power, has a historical and spatial genealogy. Much of this work focuses on organised forms of political resistance associated with social movements. Social movements, as Walter Nicholls (2007: 627) writes, are "collective forms of contentious politics activated for the purposes of achieving political goals through non-traditional means (e.g. protests, boycotts, public campaigns rather than strictly electoral politics)."

Traditionally, the literature on social movements distinguishes between 'old' and 'new' forms. Old social movements emerged in Western industrial societies from the 1850s to the 1950s, organised primarily around class struggles against economic inequalities. Their main goals included redistributing wealth and improving material conditions – wages, education, healthcare, and welfare. They drew support from urban workers and targeted economic and political elites, laying the foundations for trade unions and left-wing parties (e.g. the Labour Party in the United Kingdom), which enabled reforms such as the welfare state, two-day weekends, and paid holidays. Since the 1960s, we see the emergence of 'new social movements,' which are seen to encompass things like environmentalism, feminism, peace activism, and civil rights movements. A key difference lies in their aims. As Fainstein and Hirst (1995: 183) write:

> While the 'old' social movements emanated from the class structure of industrial capitalism and aimed at uprooting the material inequalities produced by the capitalist mode of production, the 'new' social movements cut across classes and are guided by non-material (cultural, symbolic) considerations.

Whereas old movements focused on economic redistribution, new social movements emphasised recognition of injustice and the transformation of social and cultural life. It was the growing middle class in industrialised nations that formed the core demographic of new social movements. Although economically secure, many middle-class participants sought autonomy over their identities and lifestyles against the increasing colonisation of daily life by capitalism and the state. Globalisation further introduced complex social divisions beyond class, including race, gender, sexuality, disability, and other differences. New social movements thus focus on how economic relations intersect with these other axes of difference, broadening resistance studies beyond Marxist approaches to include fields such as cultural geography.

Another important difference between old and new social movements that is of specific interest to cultural geography concerns the *spaces of political action.* Old movements focused on iconic sites of power – parliaments, factories, government buildings – while new movements engage everyday spaces like shopping malls, transport hubs, and public events. In part, this shift reflects the fact that new movements are less concerned with seizing control of the political and economic apparatus and more with changing cultural values and attitudes around specific issues. Public opinion is a crucial arena for this, and attracting media attention is therefore vital. In recent decades, new movements have employed quite spectacular forms of protest in public space – flash mobs in malls or airports and mass bike rides through squares – to capture public and media attention.

However, recently, geographers have questioned whether the old/new typology is helpful for analysing contemporary activist movements. A case in point is the Occupy Movement, which began in Zuccotti Park, New York, in 2011 and spread globally, challenging inequality, corporate greed, and the undue influence of the financial sector on government. Occupy obviously shared many features with new social movements: non-hierarchical networks; no central leader; and a heterogeneous support base including reformist liberals, anti-capitalists, anarchists, communists, and union activists. It was media-savvy, particularly on social media platforms like Facebook and Twitter (now 'X'). And while the focus of its discourse was a powerful critique of neoliberal capitalism, it was also geared towards transforming social values as well as prefiguring alternative political futures.

Yet Occupy also reflected older movements' class concerns. The exploitation of the masses by the economic elite was nearly summarised in its slogan, 'We are the 99%.' It targeted iconic economic sites – Wall Street in New York and the European Central Bank in Frankfurt. However, it also had features distinct from both 'old' and 'new' movements. In particular, here, there was the refusal to make any specific demands. This was based on the belief that demands can easily be co-opted by political parties and that they legitimise the existing state as a willing and capable agent of making change. As Langman (2013: 521) notes:

> The movements of the 21st century link new social movement concerns with identity and culture to the realities of neoliberal capitalism. . . . We cannot analyze these movements using twentieth-century tools and concepts.

Contemporary activism also produces *new spaces of resistance*, which, since the late 1990s have increasingly included digital spaces of the Internet and social media. The Internet-based social movement – Anonymous – exemplifies this, having emerged in 2003 on the popular image board 4chan. Anonymous gained international notoriety for its protests against the Church of Scientology, support for the Arab Spring of the early 2010s, involvement in the WikiLeaks revelations, and cyberattacks on corporations and governments. Anonymous is a very interesting case study for theorising the cultural geographies of resistance because it defies much of the conventional wisdom of social movement theory. For instance, the literature on social movements suggests that shared beliefs and solidarities are an essential part of all forms of collective action. This is not the case for Anonymous, whose participants (called 'Anons') are keen to emphasise that the movement has no foundational ideology and doesn't represent any particular interest or identity. The network is loosely associated with actions ranging from political activism to disruption 'for the lulz,' a 4chan term for amusement. Part of the uniqueness (and appeal) of the group is also its emphasis on anonymity, serving as an antidote to the personalised and self-obsessed cultures of social media. This anonymity extends to street protests, where protestors have typically worn Guy Fawkes masks from the movie *V for Vendetta*, which has since become the *de facto* symbol for the group.

How might we theorise resistance in such contexts? Uitermark (2017) draws on the philosophy of Deleuze and Guattari, as well as ideas from the science of complexity theory, to theorise the unique power dynamics and political potentials of Anonymous. He uses the concept of *self-organisation* to describe how collective resistance emerges autonomously and reproduces without a central leader. He also applies Deleuze and Guattari's concept of the *rhizome*, which is contrasted with hierarchical, 'tree' models of organisations based on centre and periphery. Rhizomatic structures emerge from "decentralized networks and heterogeneous impulses" (Uitermark, 2017: 406), explaining Anonymous's horizontal, fluid organisation. However, such networks are not completely horizontal. Power can concentrate temporarily in clusters. One example is LulzSec, a group of hackers who in 2011 executed high-profile cyberattacks on Sony, News International, and the Westboro Baptist Church. LulzSec represented a temporary concentration of influence before its members were arrested.

Understanding movements like Occupy and Anonymous requires conceptual tools that better capture the unpredictable and contingent dynamics of contemporary forms of activism. Uitermark (2017: 415) suggests many contemporary movements function as "movement-brands": recognisable signifiers circulating through digital networks, mobilising activists around diverse objectives worldwide. Viewing social movements as emergent, self-organising, and rhizomatic helps explain the unpredictable dynamics and potentials of resistance in today's digital and networked age.

MICROPOLITICS

One of the concepts that have proved crucial in recent years for creatively reimagining both power and resistance is that of *micropolitics*. The concept has its origins in the philosophy of Deleuze and Guattari, where it emerges in the context of their analysis of the different kinds of "segmentarity" (Deleuze and Guattari, 1987: 208) that compose us as political subjects. As they put it in *A Thousand Plateaus*, "every society, and every individual, are thus plied by two segmentarities simultaneously: one molar, the other molecular" (Deleuze and Guattari, 1987: 213). The first type of segmentarity is thus what they refer to as the *molar line of segmentarity*. This kind of segmentarity operates through cuts of identity that follow the major oppositional binaries of society (men-women, adults-children, teachers-students, and bosses-workers). They demarcate and dictate how we should act at particular times and places. When we narrate the story of our lives, it is often the story of moving from one molar segment to the next: our childhood with our families, then our days at school, then our years at work, and then retirement (if we are lucky!). These segmentarities are described as 'rigid' because they stabilise our identities and enforce social control, reminding us of our place: "School tells us, 'you're not at home anymore'; the army tells us 'you're not at school anymore'" (Deleuze and Guattari, 1987: 209). An analysis of these molar lines of segmentarity, and the identities they produce, is the focus of much traditional political theory and constitutes the domain of what Deleuze and Guattari (1987: 213) call "macropolitics."

However, these molar identities and associated macropolitics are traversed by a more fluid and supple form of segmentarity that Deleuze and Guattari (1987: 209) term "the molecular." The molecular lines of our lives are those that "trace out little modifications, make detours in our expected paths, sketch out rises and falls" (Deleuze and Parnet, 2006: 93). If the molar line can be understood as the 'cut' that segments bodies around categories of identity (like race and gender categories), then the molecular is the 'crack up': forces and events that bubble imperceptibly below the surface of our lives and which work to unravel the binds of our constituted subjectivities. This unravelling could be a sudden and dramatic event in your life (e.g. the loss of a family member or encountering an act of state violence) or something more slow-creeping, building and building until a threshold is crossed and you "can no longer stand what you put up with before, even yesterday" (Deleuze and Parnet, 2006: 95). Imagine a lawyer in the United Kingdom, fresh out of their undergraduate geography degree, working in London on a training contract with a Magic Circle law firm. Their profession can be understood as a rigid molar segment through which they structure their lives and identity (as a young, well-dressed, educated, and legal professional). But under the surface, molecular forces are always moving. They find themselves increasingly bored and restless at work, daydreaming of travelling the world as a photographer, while they browse what their friends are up to on social media. The long hours are taking their toll, and they are finding it harder and harder to get out of bed every morning. They find themselves increasingly irritated, even repulsed, by conversations with colleagues. One day, these intensities and emotions reach a crescendo in the middle of a meeting: 'Screw it! I've had enough. I'm quitting this fucking job!.'

If the molar line is a plane of organisation and hierarchy, then the molecular line constitutes a plane of 'becoming' that creates a new distribution of desire and attitude, and, by extension, new capacities for being affected by the world. For Deleuze and Guattari (1987: 213), this means producing new creative possibilities of life:

> The two segmentarities [molar and molecular] are always in presupposition. In short, everything is political, but every politics is simultaneously a macropolitics and a micropolitics. Take aggregates of the perception or feeling type: their molar organization, their rigid segmentarity, does not preclude the existence of an entire world of unconscious micropercepts, unconscious affects, fine segmentations that grasp or experience different things, are distributed and operate differently. There is a micropolitics of perception, affection, conversation, and so forth.

Thinking politics, for Deleuze and Guattari (1987), thus concerns the constant intersection of both these forms of segmentarity. The problem with traditional (i.e. macropolitical) interpretations of political events is that they are overwhelmingly focused on molar concepts (like identity) and categories ('Left' and 'Right') in ways that occlude the molecular forces and unconscious desires that such events can give rise to. Deleuze (2006) argues that this was the case with the May 1968 student protests in France, which ultimately confused the molar grouping of the Left (unions, parties, and politicians) as it did not fit the conventional categories of class struggle. The significance of May '68, for Deleuze, is best grasped as a kind of 'molecular revolution,' its effects playing out on the unconscious level of affects, perceptions, and desires. Instead of investing in the identities and relations of the past, the 'event' of May '68 lay in its capacity to generate a shift in sensibilities (and an associated explosion of experimentation in sexuality and art), a new collective perception of what was intolerable (including the refusal of work and old political categories), and a molecular upheaval in how people relate to the question of what is possible.

With growing interest in the micropolitical across cultural geography and the wider social sciences (see Sharpe, 2020; Merriman, 2018; Lapworth, 2019), it is important to correct a few common misconceptions. The first is the idea that the 'micro-' in micropolitics refers to that which is small or insignificant in contrast to the supposed larger-scale or more significant character of a 'proper' macropolitics. Micropolitics, as Jellis and Gerlach (2017: 564) are keen to emphasise, "cannot be allied to any particular scale or register of significance." The difference between a micropolitics and a macropolitics, then, is better understood as being of a *qualitative* rather than quantitative nature. Micropolitics relates questions of power and resistance to the more affective and inventive potentials of political thinking and encounters. This difference in inventiveness is something captured by Himada and Manning (2009: 5) when they write:

> What is usually constituted as the real thing – Politics with a capital P – is far less rigorously inventive, precisely because it operates in the sphere of representation where pre-composed bodies are already circulating. The micropolitical is that which subverts this tendency in the political to present itself as already fully formed. All politics is infested with micropolitical tendencies. This is what makes the political an event. . . . Like the microperception that tweaks the event of perception, the micropolitical is the force of the political event that potentially unmoors it.

Scott Sharpe, J-D Dewsbury, and Maria Hynes (2014) have explored this inventive potential through a discussion of the micropolitics of humour in the performances of British stand-up comedian Stewart Lee. They note how one of the challenges raised by micropolitics is how it shifts thinking about resistance beyond traditional representational logics of *opposition*. The problem of oppositional logic (e.g. the oppressed rising up against the oppressor, the proletariat against the bourgeoisie) is that in defining yourself against something, you remain bound to it because you share its terms. This leads, to invoke the terminology of Deleuze, to a *reactive* politics – one that resists, critiques, and negates but which can rarely create the new. Micropolitics, Sharpe et al. (2014) argue, is instead an affirmative mode of thought and practice. Not affirmative in the sense of saying 'yes' "to something given to us ready-made that we could affirm." Instead, a micropolitics of affirmation is about "an openness to the future, the shape of which is as yet unknowable" (Sharpe et al., 2014: 116). Sharpe et al. (2014: 117) illustrate this with the stand-up routines of Stewart Lee and, in particular, his use of repetition and other performative devices to creatively modify the audience's habits of anticipation:

> Through the demands he makes upon his audience, Lee persistently affirms the capacity for transformation that is built into and vitalizes the performative situation. To the extent that Lee habituates his audience through the performance, it is certainly not the case of giving them what they expect, of saying 'yes' to the comfortable, even prejudicial, ways of thinking that much laughter among audiences to comedy materializes. Rather, it is through the production of new sensibilities that Lee habituates the audience to their capacity for change.

The politics of Stewart Lee's humour, then, pertain not simply to the molar question of the representational content of his jokes (the identities or regressive attitudes that he lambasts). Its transformative potential instead plays out on a different register of experience, concerning the capacity of comedy to affectively rewire our bodily habits of attention to new potentials of thought and action.

Sharpe et al.'s (2014) analysis of Stewart Lee's comedy highlights a common trend in discussions of the micropolitical within cultural geography, which tends to emphasise its transformative and liberatory potentials. This is where we encounter a second misconception, which is the idea that micropolitics and the molecular are inherently 'good' or 'positive' things (with macropolitics then conversely being the 'bad' or 'negative' term of the couplet). Deleuze and Guattari are clear that molecular forms of segmentarity have their own dangers which can be just as devastating as those we discover at the molar level. This is clear in their discussion of the problematic of *fascism* (Deleuze and Guattari, 1987: 215), which they argue is always both macropolitical and micropolitical:

> what makes fascism dangerous is its molecular or micropolitical power, for it is a mass movement: a cancerous body rather than a totalitarian organism . . . only microfascism provides an answer to the global question: why does desire its own repression, how can it desire its own repression? The masses certainly do not passively submit to power; nor do they 'want' to be repressed, in a kind of masochistic hysteria; nor are they tricked by an ideological lure. Desire is never separable from complex assemblages that necessarily tie into molecular levels, from microformations already shaping postures, attitudes, perceptions, expectations, semiotic systems, etc. . . . it is easy to be antifascist on the molar level, and not even see the fascist inside you, the fascist you yourself sustain and nourish and cherish with molecules both personal and collective.

The crucial point here is the way in which Deleuze and Guattari shift the analysis of fascism from an identitarian terrain to a *processual* one. While we usually associate fascism with large-scale, molar political movements (like National Socialism and the Nazi Party in 1930s Germany, or the neofascism of groups like the Proud Boys in the USA), Deleuze and Guattari argue that fascist tendencies are always working everywhere, even at the most micrological level of our everyday behaviours, social interactions, and thought processes (see **Box 6.3**). And understood as a process rather than an identity category, fascism is not something restricted to Right wing politics (although we could argue that Right wing movements often generate conditions more favourable to its crystallisation). Deleuze and Guattari (1987: 215) make the point, then, that microfascisms can also be "secreted" by Leftist organisations, especially those that become animated by reactive desires for repression and control (like we can arguably see in some contemporary forms of 'Cancel Culture').

BOX 6.3 Fascism

Commonly defined as a far-right, ultranationalist, and authoritarian political ideology that prioritises the defence of a specific (national and/or racial) community over the rights of individuals and which often deploys military force and persecution to quash opposition and dissent. As a state form, it is usually associated historically with twentieth-century regimes like Hitler's Nazi Germany (1933–1945), Mussolini's Italy (1922–1943), and Franco's Spain (1936–1975). There has been a growing interest in the study of fascism in human and cultural geography in recent years, stimulated in part by the rise of various far-right ideologies (and forms of 'neofascism') across the world. Such geographical work has highlighted the fundamental spatial character of fascism, with how it produces, controls, and imagines space and territory being a crucial aspect of its power. Recent work has expanded this focus by considering new spaces of far-right politics, including social media platforms and online forums, in explorations of emerging digital geographies of fascism (Luger, 2024). See Ince (2019) for an overview of recent key themes in the geographical study of fascist and anti-fascist politics.

A contemporary analysis of fascism must thus attend to the ways in which it takes root at both molar and molecular poles of political life. Brian Massumi (2025) adopts this 'bi-polar' approach in his study of Donald Trump's presidency. What Trumpism highlights, Massumi argues, is how fascism is not just located in the institutions of state and government but is also distributed throughout the social body in its entirety: in how we speak, desire, and relate. A crucial part of Trump's success in winning votes across such a broad spectrum of American voters lay in his capacity to act as a body that captured and relayed the affective energies of the public, especially through his use of social media (especially the platform formerly known as Twitter) and at his raucous rallies (Massumi, 2025: 63):

> The Trump media circuit formed a self-amplifying, self-reinforcing feedback loop. In a recursive loop of this kind, it is no longer possible to assign an originating subject of the utterance. A statement doesn't so much trace back linearly to a source as loop the loop. Trump began gearing up for his presidential

> campaign saying now what he truly thought, in keeping with a deeply held ideological position and moral outlook, but what he thought his potential supporters desired to hear. This is closer to ventriloquism than to full speech.

A properly 'antifascist' politics, therefore, requires a constant vigilance to the fascistic tendencies that can inhabit the power of our most everyday interactions and intimate encounters. All politics, as we've seen, are macropolitics and micropolitics. And, as Deleuze and Guattari are keen to remind us, regaining control of the institutions and organs of the state from regressive parties and politicians will achieve nothing if it isn't accompanied by a "constant guerrilla campaign" (Deleuze, 1995: i) waged against "the fascism in us all, in our heads and in our everyday behavior, the fascism that causes us to love power, to desire the very thing that dominates and exploits us" (Foucault, 2004: xiii).

CONCLUSION

In this chapter, we explored the rich vein of cultural geographic scholarship exploring the relation between politics and cultural life. As we've seen, one of the key contributions of cultural geography has been to demonstrate how politics operates not just 'from above,' through the actions and institutions of the state and government. Instead, cultural geographers also seek to think politics 'from below,' exploring how its effects and relations are distributed across multiple sites of our lived experience, including, for example, everyday spaces and practices of the city; in spectacular and banal performances of *nationalism*; in our encounters with media and art; and across contemporary digital and online platforms. In unpacking the relation between politics and experience, we began the chapter with a discussion of cultural geography understandings of 'power.' We highlighted how much of this work continues to owe a debt to the philosophy of Foucault and, in particular, his notion of the *productive* nature of power. A historical genealogy of modes of power, then, is also a genealogy of the different kinds of *subjects* produced by power: from the obedient, fearful subjects of sovereign power to the docile and regulated subjects of discipline to the normalised and self-regulating subjectivities of contemporary biopolitics. Finally, we explored recent engagements with Deleuze and Guattari's (1987) concept of 'micropolitics,' and how such work contributes to cultural geography's ongoing efforts to expand the envelope of what counts as the 'political.' We highlighted how the concept shifts the focus from the already-individuated, sovereign subjects of traditional political theorising to instead engage with the more pre-individual and unconscious forces of affect and desire that give political thought and action so much of its transformative and inventive potential. We argue that these engagements with such cutting-edge theoretical concepts continue to position cultural geography as one of the most innovative subdisciplines for grasping the changing nature of political power in the twenty-first century, offering new insights into the conditions that made the rise of neo-nationalist and neo-fascist politics possible, as well as helping sharpen attention to the sites and practices where such formations might be resisted and undone.

FURTHER READING

Anderson, B. *Imagined Communities: Reflections on the Origin and Spread of Nationalism*. London: Verso, 1983.

Closs Stephens, A. "The affective atmospheres of nationalism." *Cultural Geographies* 23, no. 2 (2016): 181–198. https://doi.org/10.1177/1474474015569994

Foucault, M. *Discipline and Punish: The Birth of the Prison*. London: Penguin, 1991.

Massumi, B. *The Personality of Power: A Theory of Fascism for Anti-Fascist Life*. Durham, NC: Duke University Press, 2025.

Sharpe, S. J-D. Dewsbury and M. Hynes. "The minute interventions of Stewart Lee: The affirmative conditions of possibility in comedy, repetition and affect." *Performance Research* 19, no. 2 (2014): 116–125. https://doi.org/10.1080/13528165.2014.928527

REFERENCES

Althusser, L. *Reading Capital: The Complete Edition*. London: Verso, 2015.

Anderson, B. "Cultural geography I: Intensities and forms of power." *Progress in Human Geography* 41, no. 4 (2017): 501–511. https://doi.org/10.1177/0309132516649491

Ash, J. "Rethinking affective atmospheres: Technology, perturbation and space times of the non-human." *Geoforum* 49 (2013): 20–28. https://doi.org/10.1016/j.geoforum.2013.05.006

Barnett, C. "Culture, geography, and the arts of government." *Environment and Planning D: Society and Space* 19, no. 1 (2001): 7–24. https://doi.org/10.1068/d236

Bilig, M. *Banal Nationalism*. London: Sage, 1995.

Brigstocke, J., M. Froes, C. Cabral, L. Malanquini and G. Baptista. "Biosocial borders: Affective debilitation and resilience among women living in a violently bordered favela." *Transactions of the Institute of British Geographers* 48, no. 3 (2023): 587–602. https://doi.org/10.1111/tran.12601

Carter-White, R. and C. Minca. "The camp and the question of community." *Political Geography* 81 (2020): 1–11. https://doi.org/10.1016/j.polgeo.2020.102222

Collard, R. C. "Cougar-human entanglements and the biopolitical un/making of safe space." *Environment and Planning D: Society and Space* 30, no. 1 (2012): 23–42. https://doi.org/10.1068/d19110

Deleuze, G. *Negotiations 1972–1990*. New York: Columbia University Press, 1995.

Deleuze, G. "Postscript on societies of control." *October* 59 (1992): 3–7. https://www.jstor.org/stable/778828

Deleuze, G. *Two Regimes of Madness: Texts and Interviews 1975–1995*. New York: Semiotext(e), 2006.

Deleuze, G. and F. Guattari. *A Thousand Plateaus: Capitalism and Schizophrenia*. Minneapolis, MN: University of Minnesota Press, 1987.

Deleuze, G. and C. Parnet. *Dialogues II*. London: Continuum, 2006.

Fainstein, S. and C. Hirst. "Urban social movements." In D. Judge, G. Stoker and H. Wolman (eds.) *Theories of urban politics* (pp. 181–204). London: Sage, 1995.

Foucault, M. *The History of Sexuality Vol 1: The Will to Knowledge*. London: Penguin, 1998.

Foucault, M. *Power: Essential Works of Foucault 1954–1984*. London: Penguin, 2000.

Foucault, M. "Preface." In G. Deleuze and F. Guattari (eds.) *Anti-Oedipus: Capitalism and Schizophrenia* (pp. xiii-xvi). London: Continuum, 2004.

Foucault, M. *Security, Territory, Population: Lectures at the College de France, 1977–78*. London: Palgrave Macmillan, 2007.

Himada, N. and E. Manning. "From noun to verb: The micropolitics of making collective." *Inflexions* 6 (2009): 1–17. https://www.inflexions.org/n3_From-Noun-to-Verb-The-Micropolitics-of-Making-Collective-Interview-between-Nasrin-Himada-and-Erin-Manning.pdf

Hinchliffe, S. and N. Bingham. "Securing life: The emerging practices of biosecurity." *Environment and Planning A: Economy and Space* 40, no. 7 (2008): 1534–1551. https://doi.org/10.1068/a4054

Huxley, M. "Space and government: Governmentality and geography." *Geography Compass* 2, no. 5 (2008): 1635–1658. https://doi.org/10.1111/j.1749-8198.2008.00133.x

Ince, A. "Fragments of an anti-fascist geography: Interrogating racism, nationalism, and state power." *Geography Compass* 13, no. 3 (2019): e12420. https://doi.org/10.1111/gec3.12420

Jellis, T. and J. Gerlach. "Micropolitics and the minor." *Environment and Planning D: Society and Space* 35, no. 4 (2017): 563–567. https://doi.org/10.1177/0263775817718013

Jones, R. and P. Merriman. "Hot, banal and everyday nationalism: Bilingual road signs in Wales." *Political Geography* 28, (2009): 164–173. https://doi.org/10.1016/j.polgeo.2009.03.002

Koskela, H. "The gaze without eyes: Video-surveillance and the changing nature of urban space." *Progress in Human Geography* 24, no. 2 (2000): 243–265. https://doi.org/10.1191/030913200668791096

Krivy, M. "Towards a critique of cybernetic urbanism: The smart city and the society of control." *Planning Theory* 17, no. 1 (2018): 8–30. https://doi.org/10.1177/1473095216645631

Langman, L. "Occupy: A new social movement." *Current Sociology* 61, no. 4 (2013): 510–524. https://doi.org/10.1177/001139211347974

Lapworth, A. "Guattari and the micropolitics of cinema: The desiring-machines of Satoshi Kon." In T. Jellis, J. Gerlach and J-D. Dewsbury (eds.) *Why Guattari? A Liberation of Cartographies, Ecologies and Politics* (pp. 187–201). London: Routledge, 2019.

Luger, J. " 'Where #freedom and #patriotism live:' Linking digital media to far-right geographies." *Political Geography* 114, (2024): 103195. https://doi.org/10.1016/j.polgeo.2024.103195

Massumi, B. "Of microperception and micropolitics." *Inflexions* 6, (2009): 1–20. https://www.inflexions.org/n3_Of-Microperception-and-Micropolitics-An-Interview-with-Brian-Massumi.pdf

Massumi, B. *The Politics of Affect*. Cambridge: Polity Press, 2015.

Mbembe, A. "Necropolitics." *Public Culture* 15, no. 1 (2003): 11–40. https://muse.jhu.edu/article/39984

McCormack, D. "Engineering affective atmospheres on the moving geographies of the 1897 Andree expedition." *Cultural Geographies* 15, no. 4 (2008): 413–30. https://doi.org/10.1177/1474474008094314

Merriman, P. "Molar and molecular mobilities: The politics of perceptible and imperceptible movements." *Environment and Planning D: Society and Space* 37, no. 1 (2018): 65–82. https://doi.org/10.1177/0263775818776976

Nicholls, W. "The geographies of social movements." *Geography Compass* 1, no. 3 (2007): 607–622. https://doi.org/10.1111/j.1749-8198.2007.00014.x

Peters, F., N. Clare and T. Davies. "Necropolitics and geography." *Progress in Human Geography* 49, no. 5 (2025): 466–488. https://doi.org/10.1177/03091325251348613

Sharpe, S. "Untoward laughter and the micropolitical: Social action, politics and the will after the sovereign subject." *Cultural Geographies* 27, no. 1 (2020): 55–69. https://doi.org/10.1177/147447401986620

Sumartojo, S. "New geographies of commemoration." *Progress in Human Geography* 45, no. 3 (2020): 531–547. https://doi.org/10.1177/0309132520936758

Uitermark, J. "Complex contention: Analyzing power dynamics within Anonymous." *Social Movement Studies* 16, no. 4 (2017): 403–417. https://doi.org/10.1080/14742837.2016.1184136

Williams, A. "Control societies and platform logic." *New Formations* 84–84 (2015): 209–227. https://doi.org/10.398/NEWF:84/85.10.2015

7

METHODS

FROM INTERPRETATION TO EXPERIMENTATION

The previous chapters of this book have unpacked a whole series of conceptual and philosophical shifts (including more-than-human geographies, non-representational theory, and post-phenomenology) that have (re)shaped the subdiscipline of cultural geography over the last two decades. What emerges from these, as we've seen, is the increasing sense that much of the world that we as cultural geographers write about is beyond human control, conscious understanding, and interpretative representation. In dedicating our final substantive chapter to the topic of research methods, the point we want to emphasise is that such recent theoretical turns do not just raise important and difficult challenges for how we *think the world*, but also for how we go about *practising research* within it. Like several other cultural geographers writing today (see Whatmore, 2006; Williams et al., 2019), we similarly refuse to invest in the long-standing and antagonistic division between the supposedly abstract and distanced work of 'theorising' and what is often assumed to be the more concrete and engaged work of 'practising.' In this chapter, we thus present theory and practice not as separate enterprises, but instead as things that are always intimately interwoven. Here, once again, we take heed from the writings of Deleuze (2005: 268), for whom philosophical theory should always be grasped as "itself a kind of practice, just as much as its object . . . it is a practice of concepts, and we must judge it in light of the other practices with which it interferes."

Another rationale for turning to the topic of methods in this chapter is that it speaks quite explicitly to some of the more political

DOI: 10.4324/9781003542667-7

and ethical dimensions of cultural geography that we explored in ***Chapter 6*** and will return to in the *Epilogue.* The choice of research methods – as feminist, post-colonial, and other progressive strands of geography have so powerfully emphasised – is never innocent. They are often based on a whole series of deep-seated, often unconscious assumptions regarding what we believe exists in the world (i.e. ontology) as well as the 'appropriate' or 'correct' procedures that determine how we come to know it (i.e. epistemology). And these assumptions come to shape what we consider to be worthy of legibility and sayability in the work we produce: what subjects, bodies, or agencies we make visible or invisible, said or unsaid, in our research.

In this chapter, we want to push further in arguing that methods don't only reflect such already given assumptions about what we think the world is. They should, we argue, also be understood as *techniques* that materially intervene in, and reshape, the processes through which different worlds appear. In other words, cultural geographers are attuned to the ways that research methods actively construct, rather than merely represent, worlds. This more *constructivist* sense of method is nicely captured by the philosopher, Jacques Rancière (2009: 114), when he writes:

> A method means a path: not the path that a thinker follows but the path that he/she constructs, that you have to construct to know where you are, to figure out the characteristics of the territory you are going through, the places it allows you to go, the way it obliges you to move, the markers that can help you, the obstacles that get in the way. Examining a method thus means examining how idealities are materially produced. . . . Ideas always are material realities, taking over bodies, giving them a map of the visible and orientations for moving.

We argue that the distinction Rancière draws here between method as a 'path to be followed' and method as a 'path to be constructed' reflects some of the significant transformations we've seen in how cultural geographers approach the question of research methods. These methodological discussions have often targeted a particular *interpretative* model of social science research that seeks to interview 'knowing' subjects, record their 'authentic' opinions, rigorously thematise and code this 'data,' and present 'accurate' accounts of everyday life in research outputs. What this gives rise to are modes of questioning and interpretative procedures that are known in advance, forging a stable methodological territory that can be re-used again and again in relation to different situations and scenarios. This is a problem, as Dewsbury (2009: 332) argues, because it produces styles of research that end up being impervious – and even resistant to – the difference and novelty that are precisely what make our social world so alive, invigorating, and exciting.

Emerging out of such critiques of interpretative social science, and the 'dead geographies' it produces, has been a range of more *experimental* styles of geographic research over the last decade. Here, the experimental is usually invoked to describe modes of research practice that are characterised by a willingness to take risks and to try new things, as well as a more creative apprehension of the researcher as someone who embraces the challenge of charting new and unforeseen trajectories in thought. This experimentalist ethos, as Dewsbury (2009: 322) notes, is one that conceives research as something "creative of problems not solutions." Methods, then, come to be evaluated less in terms of the extent to which they accurately capture the supposed truth of an event and more in terms of their capacity to problematise consensual styles of thinking and taken-for-granted habits of acting. Experimental methodologies then, as the anthropologist Annemarie Mol (2002: 121) puts it, draw their worth not simply from how they "live up to the real,' but instead are worthwhile for their ability to invent new and creative of ways for 'living with the real.'"

In this chapter, we draw on recent examples of methodological innovation to explore both the creative possibilities and some of the challenges and pitfalls associated with this shift towards experimental styles of research in contemporary cultural geography. We follow Whatmore (2006) in spotlighting two key demands of the experimentalist imperative in cultural geographic research. The first of these relates to the "urgent need to supplement the familiar repertoire of humanist methods that rely on generating talk and text with experimental practices that amplify other sensory, bodily and affective registers and extend the company and modality of what constitutes a research subject" (Whatmore, 2006: 606–7). In the next section, we thus explore how cultural geographers are creatively experimenting with both traditional (such as interview and archival methods) and more recent (sound, moving images, and embodied methodologies) research methods in order to decentre human control over research and embrace the multisensory, more-than-human, and non-representational textures of our encounters with the world. The second demand relates to the onus of experimental practices on 'redistributing expertise' and 'engaging knowledge practices and vernaculars beyond the academy' (Whatmore, 2006: 607). Here, then, the chapter will also address the growing interest in collaborative methodologies, where cultural geographers are engaging with social groups and institutions to explore new creative possibilities for the production and dissemination of cultural geographic knowledge.

PUSHING THE SENSES

'TALK AND TEXT'

You might assume, after reading the introduction to this chapter, that engaging the non-human, affective, and non-representational dimensions of social and cultural life necessarily calls for the abandonment of old methodologies and the wild invention of a whole range of new research techniques. But perhaps it is a little unfair of Whatmore (2006: 607) and others to disparage traditional "talk and text based" practices in geography as inevitably bound to humanist philosophies and methodologies that deaden the kind of geographies we can write. Instead, we find ourselves in agreement with Alan Latham (2003: 2000) when he writes:

> Rather than ditching the methodological skills that human geography has so painfully accumulated, we should work through how we can imbue traditional research methodologies with a sense of the creative . . . pushed in the appropriate direction, there is no reason why these methods cannot be made to dance a little.

Thus, the conceptual shifts that we've addressed in this book do not necessarily entail a refusal of any specific method but instead demand an experimental and creative refounding of their methodological assumptions (i.e. how they work and what they are for).

Let's take *the interview*. Interviews are by far one of the most widely used *qualitative methods* in cultural geography (see **Box 7.1**). This is unsurprising given their capacity to generate in-depth accounts of the interpretations, experiences, attitudes, and understandings held by specific individuals and social groups. Most geographical methods courses taught at university will usually have at least one week of content dedicated to interviews and other talk-based methods (like focus groups). The limitations of interview methods, however, are well known. Principal amongst these relates to the extent to which they can capture life "as-it-happens" (Dowling et al., 2016: 683). Interviews usually involve decontextualised conversations, in which people reflect on events or experiences that happened in a different time or space from that of the interview itself. At first glance, then, interviews, as representations of experience, would appear to be ill-equipped to deal with contemporary cultural geography's emphasis on the material, affective, and immediate dimensions of life.

BOX 7.1 Qualitative methods

Qualitative research methods involve the collection of 'non-numerical' data to gain insight into the complexities of people's experiences, meanings, and perspectives on a particular topic. They are often contrasted with *quantitative methods* that focus on numerical data and statistical analyses to test scientific hypotheses. Some examples of the main qualitative methods used in cultural geography include interviews, focus groups, ethnography, textual and discourse analysis, action research, and visual methods.

However, the same theoretical turns have inspired other geographers to experiment with what these methods might be able to do if we shake up some of the limiting assumptions associated with their more conventional uses. Some of this work has involved "supplementing the interview" by collecting a range of additional sensory information to enrich our apprehension of the meanings and experiences discussed in the interview conversation (Dowling et al., 2016). Examples here include the collection of written, photo, or sound diaries from research participants before or after the interview to enliven the sense of the spaces and places under discussion. New online and communicational technologies are also profoundly reshaping what is possible to do with interviews. Geographers have explored how social media (like Facebook and Twitter) and video call platforms (like Zoom and Teams) are changing the temporalities and spatialities of interview research, providing researchers unprecedented access to participants and their in-the-moment experiences (Koh and Lapworth, 2024). However, geographers have also emphasised that such online methods present their own unique challenges (from the interruptions of lag and dropped connections to the difficulties of catching subtle verbal and nonverbal cues on video compared to face-to-face) as well as distinct ethical implications that must be attended to, such as issues relating to privacy.

Other cultural geographers have returned to the interview conversation itself as a site of non-representational encounter. David Bissell (2023), for instance, has recently critiqued some of the conventional habits involved in the writing-up of interviews, and especially the 'quotation' as the default presentational mode of interview data in geographical research. He argues that the preoccupation of researchers with the "words on the page . . . overlooks and loses some of the most significant experiential dimensions of the interview encounter itself" (Bissell, 2023: 194). In contrast, Bissell experiments with a more narrative style of presenting interviews, one based on short vignettes that offer impressionistic captures of the emotions and feelings that are generated by the interview and experienced by the interviewer and interviewee. Elsewhere, Bissell (2023: 192) has argued that this culture of quotations is underpinned by a "know-and-tell illusion," where the voices we capture during interviews are purported to be the 'authentic' expressions of the participants' own thoughts and feelings. Instead, Bissell (2015: 151) argues that speech is "impersonal" in the sense that it is not the willed expression of a sovereign individual – in this case, the speaking subject. Rather, what emerges in an interview is the expression of the specific material and affective environments in which the event of speaking happens. The analytical focus, here, therefore falls less on what voices say (the semantic content of speech) and more on the various ambient forces and processes beyond the individual that shape how speech emerges and the work it does in transforming the social relations and spaces in which it occurs.

Another suite of traditional methods that have undergone experimental and creative reimagining in the hands of cultural geographers is *archival research.* Part of this has involved engagements with post-structuralist philosophy (especially the ideas of Michel Foucault and Jacques Derrida) to think of the archive not as a site that would preserve "memory," but rather as an active process involved in the ongoing (re-)construction of memory (H. Lorimer, 2010). Cultural geographic research has explored these ideas in particular through greater attention to the partial and incomplete nature of archiving and how creative engagements with such fragments can be a means to amplify some of the absences that 'haunt' the official or institutional histories being told by the archive (Mills, 2013). Caitlyn Desilvey's research on a Montana homestead, for instance, developed a kind of salvage methodology that assembled and reanimated a range of archival fragments – including fragments of paper, photographs, discarded objects, and other remains and ephemera – to describe how "the salvage of memory makes do with materials at hand, and uses this material to craft stories about people and places that might otherwise go untold" (DeSilvey, 2007: 421–422). Cultural geographers have also been involved in cross-disciplinary re-evaluations of what exactly counts as 'an archive.' One area of innovation has been to engage with a wide variety of non-textual and non-written forms – including images (Yusoff, 2007), urban ruins (Edensor, 2005), and material objects (Lorimer and Whatmore, 2009) – as archives of past material and embodied practices themselves. A fascinating example here is Merle Patchett's (2019) engagement with avian taxidermy specimens and their archiving of global histories and geographies of colonial violence, animal trade, and cultural fashion. Describing her sensual and affective encounter with the plume and feather of an ostrich (dyed black and transformed into fashion items), Patchett shows how such objects not only archive the birds "prior livingness," but also confront us emotionally with the "event of death," as well as the "hazardous working conditions of plumage sweatshops in London and New York, and the willowing work carried out by tenement children that produced the tiny knots for the plumes that pay" (Patchett, 2019: 651).

JUST THE WAY I'M FEELING: EMBODIED METHODOLOGIES

While the *body* has long been a key conceptual concern for cultural geographers (see ***Chapter 5***), it is only in the last decade or so that we see an explicit engagement with the impact of such arguments in relation to qualitative research practice. Feminist and post-colonial debates around *positionality* in the 1980s and 1990s encouraged cultural geographers to reflect critically on how aspects of our embodied identity (including things like the researcher's race, age, gender, and sexuality) differently affect how we are situated in hierarchies of power and privilege and how this positioning then shapes how we come to understand and engage with people through our research (see **Box 7.2**). However, other vitally important aspects of our bodily existence – including our senses of touch, smell, and taste; voice and intonation; instinctual gestures and habitual reactions; what we wear and how we move; the emotional pulls of anxiety or excitement about our research – tended to be ignored or downplayed in such accounts. These more material and corporeal dimensions of the body are not superficial concerns, for they are the very means by which we negotiate the world and "array the field into a space of empirical action" (Dewsbury and Naylor, 2002: 257). Writing at the turn of the millennium, Mike Crang (2003: 257) noted how, despite the obsession with 'the body' in academic discourse, it remained something of a "ghostly absence" in geographical research. The body was thus something that cultural geographers often conducted research on, but only very rarely something that research was conducted through.

In the wake of Crang's provocation, an array of papers emerged that sought to take the body seriously as the subject of research rather than just an object of knowledge. We see, in the early 2000s, the body featuring prominently in the turn to emotion in the context of feminist geographies. The emotional body as an "instrument of research" was a key theme in Longhurst et al.'s (2008: 214) work on migrant women and food in New Zealand. Reflecting on a shared group lunch with their research participants at a migrant resource centre, the authors explore how their own embodied and visceral reactions to different foods (e.g. the involuntary sense of unease or disgust at unusual food combinations) speak to how emotional experiences and encounters deliver us to our research and those whom we research.

BOX 7.2 Positionality

Positionality refers to the way in which a person's identity (e.g. their gender, race, sexuality, class, and nationality) shapes the way in which they come to experience and interpret the world. It has been an important concept in methodological discussions in human geography, which highlight how the researcher's positionality can profoundly affect every aspect of the research process: from how research questions are initially formulated, to the literature and theories that are drawn on, to the communities and groups that are included in the research, to decisions around the ways in which research outcomes are presented and disseminated. Much qualitative geographic research (including that conducted for undergraduate dissertations) will contain a positionality statement that declares aspects of the researcher's identity and biography they believe relevant to their research. However, such confessional and declaratory approaches risk stabilising the researcher as a stable and coherent subject, missing how subjectivity is constantly emerging through the shifting relations, encounters, and processes that make up fieldwork. For further discussion of different approaches to positionality in the wake of feminist and post-phenomenological geographies, see the article by Eden Kinkaid (2022).

The body as a research tool has also become a central preoccupation of non-representational geographies. As Dewsbury powerfully sets out in his manifesto for non-representational styles of geographical research, the body here becomes "thought through and presented in the research itself as the locus of sensory appreciation prior to the resulting sensation's interpretation via existing knowledge, discourse, practice, and bodily discipline that structure the somatic experience" (2009: 327). Non-representational geographies thus offer a profound reimagining of the body beyond social grids of identity and intelligibility, emerging from the conceptual debates and tensions discussed in ***Chapter 5***. Bodies, in non-representational research, are not stable identities or static objects, but instead are best apprehended as volatile processes or assemblages that are constantly undergoing change through their encounters with the world and with other (human and non-human) bodies. To grasp this volatility, non-representational researchers remind us that the defining characteristic of a body is that it is an entity that *feels* and *moves*: it feels as it moves; it is moved as it feels.

While the body as a locus of feeling is integral to the feminist emotional geographies mentioned earlier, non-representational research is distinct in offering greater attention to the precognitive and non-reflexive dimensions of sensate encounters with the world. This attention to the unconscious, microscale of bodily intensities and forces, as several cultural geographers demonstrate, does not mean a retreat from big societal issues, but rather a creative re-posing of the problem. An example here is the work of geographer Sasha Engelmann (2023) on the lived, embodied experience of changing weather and climate. Engelmann highlights how, for cultural geographers, the weather is not an abstract background but rather "an immersive forcefield that weights and presses on bodies in different ways" (Engelmann, 2023: 525). Developing these conceptions, Engelmann reflects on her collaborative, artistic project – *open-weather* – which explores the relation between the intimate experience of weather through the body's sensorium and the global 'weather-machines' of science (i.e. the global technical infrastructures of devices and satellites that sense, record, and monitor weather). She highlights the political potential of artistic practices to subvert scientific tools for monitoring the climate, foregrounding instead "the power relations in the capture of weather, and complicating the distinction between local experience and global records of environmental processes" (Engelmann, 2023: 536). The result, she argues, is the development of alternate senses of a changing climate, based not on total and global capture, but rather on "collaging and composing" other ways of experiencing and knowing the elemental forces of weather (Engelmann, 2023: 537).

Recent cultural geographic work has also produced a greater attention to the *kinetic* dimensions of embodied research. Bodies are constantly moving to, through, and out of research sites. Cultural geographers have analysed the experiences associated with a range of bodily movements and practices – including walking (Bassett, 2004), running (Cook et al., 2016), skateboarding (Stratford, 2016), dancing (McCormack, 2002), driving (Merriman, 2009), and even skydiving (Urry, 2014) – and how they each enact their own unique qualities and intensities of relation between bodies and spaces. Paul Simpson's (2017) work on the cycling body shows the capacity to connect this kind of embodied research to broader issues, such as, in this case, around the evaluation of urban policies and initiatives around cycling. In this work, Simpson pays particular attention to 'cycling infrastructures' (including urban materialities like road systems, shared foot and cycle paths, and barriers) and how these broker interactions between cyclists and other urban inhabitants and how such interactions can generate felt atmospheres that are more or less convivial for cyclists. Several of his research participants, for instance, highlighted the disconcerting experiences generated by traffic-calming islands "that often resulted in unwelcome proximity [between bikes and cars] for these cyclists" (Simpson, 2017: 432). While shared pedestrian and cycle infrastructures are often a focus of urban policies (to keep cyclists away from severe accidents on the roads), Simpson's research shows how cyclists often reported "unintended confrontational atmospheres between pedestrians and cyclists through its design" (Simpson, 2017: 441). Attending to the felt experience of urban mobilities, Simpson contends, is just as important as more quantitative metrics (around things like journeys made) for evaluating the effectiveness of specific urban policies.

However, such work has also raised important questions around how we capture and express the felt intensities of movement within the context of a subdiscipline that remains predominantly textual in its presentation of research findings. As a result, some geographers have begun experimenting with other, non-linguistic, techniques and mediums of expression to "enliven the repertoire of ways in which geographies are creatively enacted" (McCormack, 2002: 483). In the following sections, we will spotlight some of the innovative work being conducted by geographers with both sound and moving-image methodologies to creatively present and evoke bodily practices and movements.

COMFORT IN SOUND

Geographic interest in sound has grown steadily since the 1990s, particularly in the wake of Susan J. Smith's (1997) clarion call for geographers to pay more attention to the relation between space, politics, and sound. Smith's (1997) argument grew out of a dissatisfaction with the *ocularcentrism* of geographical accounts of art and culture that foregrounded the visual domain at the expense of other sensory modalities that shape how we understand and experience the world, including the sonic dimension of cultural life. Since Smith's landmark paper, an increasing body of work has emerged exploring how sonic practices and performances are involved in the construction of space, identity, and power (Burdon, 2025). However, in their review of this burgeoning subfield of sonic geographies, Gallagher and Prior (2014: 267–268) note how the bulk of geographical work on sound has remained "methodologically conventional, using techniques such as interviews, ethnography, archival research, discourse analysis, and has been disseminated via traditional written publications." The result is that sound has been "largely erased in human geography," becoming transferred into verbal-textual forms deemed more appropriate for conventional research outputs, like journal articles and books (Gallagher and Prior, 2014: 270).

Geographers have engaged with a few main types of methodological approach when analysing the sonic aspects of our world (Gallagher and Prior, 2014: 272–274). The most common is sonic *ethnography*. If ethnographic methods in human geography involve the production of rich observational accounts of specific places and practices of interest, then sonic ethnographies draw greater attention to the role that sound and music play in creating the meaning and experience of such places or practices (see **Box 7.3**). Such techniques are usually based on the collection of audio recordings (of ambient sounds or of talk amongst research participants) intended to supplement visual and textual observations. However, Gallagher and Prior (2014: 272) note how such research often "silences its own audibility" by still transcribing the sonic qualities of places into written accounts. They also tend to reproduce what the sound theorist Michel Chion (1999: 5) has called "vococentrism," which privileges the human voice as the ultimate source of meaning. Some cultural geographers have sought to disrupt the vococentrism of traditional sonic ethnography through engagement with the notion of *soundscapes* (Duffy et al., 2016). The concept of soundscape initially emerged in the writing of the Canadian composer, R. Murray Schafer (1977), whose work was interested in how specific acoustic environments (such as the mechanical acoustics of industrial workplaces, or the traffic-dominated soundtrack of modern cities) come to affect people's psychological and socio-cultural well-being, in most cases negatively.

Methodologically, soundscape studies entail a shift in attention from the human voice to the complete range of audible sounds occurring in a particular environment. Boyd and Duffy (2020), for example, adopt an immersive, soundscape approach as part of a research project on the therapeutic qualities of permaculture practices. The authors produced a sound work from the raw field recordings, arranging and juxtaposing sounds to emphasise particular moments or experiences: the squelching sound of making mulch from newspaper; the barely audible voices of children playing; the distant noise of traffic. These created soundworks, presented as embedded audio tracks alongside textual ethnographic descriptions, were designed to amplify the affective and immersive qualities of a cacophony of human and non-human sounds, many of which barely register consciously but which are vital elements in constituting the experience of permaculture practices.

BOX 7.3 Ethnography

Ethnography (sometimes referred to as 'participant observation') is a type of qualitative method that seeks to produce 'thick description' of specific cultural groups or practices. While ethnographic methods focus on the production of (usually written) observational data, they can also draw on interviews and conversations, sound and video recordings, sketches and drawings, and photographs to build an immersive sense of the space or practice being researched. Ethnography originally emerged in anthropology as the staple method for researching 'exotic' and 'foreign' peoples and places in ways that often reinforced racist imaginaries and constructions of colonial power. In cultural geography, conversely, ethnography has mainly been used in the study of more 'local' spaces of everyday life, including analyses of spaces like cafes and restaurants, music events, plane, and train travel. Human geographers have been at the forefront of methodological debates related to the practice and potential of ethnographic methods. Feminist geographers, for instance, have long experimented with forms of 'auto-ethnography' that focus on the researcher's own experiences and understandings in the course of the research process to probe more deeply into questions of power, identity, and difference. Non-representational geographers have sought to give greater attention to the researcher's body (its volatile affects and materiality) in ethnographic research methods. Non-representational styles of ethnography give, as Dewsbury (2009: 327) puts it, the researcher "confidence of using [their] body directly in the field as a recording machine, knowing that writing these nervous energies, amplitudes, and thresholds down is feasible as such jottings become legitimate data for dissemination and analysis."

A third approach to research with sound in cultural geography relates to *soundwalking* methods. Toby Butler (2007: 360) describes soundwalks as excursions or trails "that use recorded sound . . . played on a personal or mobile media to experience places in new ways." Like soundscape techniques, soundwalks also entail practices of active listening to the sounds present within an environment. But whereas soundscape studies are usually focused on faithfully capturing the audible ecology of a particular location, soundwalks instead attempt to transform our sonic experience in ways that enable a creative re-animation and re-interpretation of place. Gallagher and Prior (2014: 278) note that the soundwalk therefore enacts a more experimental approach to the "doing of geography," one that:

> Intervenes in places, producing immersive experiences through which audiences can move; exposing hidden features of places or subverting accepted meanings; inviting ways of knowing places that are spontaneously performed rather than fixed in representation.

Nina Williams' (2019) work offers an excellent illustration of the experimental potentials of soundwalk methodologies for cultural geographic research. Reflecting on field recording experiments conducted with her students around Bristol in the United Kingdom, Williams (2019: 648) highlights how soundwalks can be generative of "altered modes of attention" that render audible a range of non-human agencies and forces that comprise our research sites, but which usually appear inaudible from the perspective of our everyday habits of comprehension. Working with sound recordings in this way, she argues, shifts the emphasis from *hearing* (as a kind of cognitive process of deciphering and interpreting the world based on already-given frameworks) to *listening* (as a more embodied and physiological process that enhances our receptivity to what else is happening in our research encounters). Understood in these terms, sonic methodologies are thus not only about developing "new ways of communicating, documenting or representing research environments, but rather about engendering new ways of relating to them" (Williams, 2019: 649).

VISUAL AND IMAGE-BASED METHODOLOGIES

From viral videos on TikTok to the latest blockbuster show on Netflix, our contemporary world is a thoroughly audiovisual one. As Jamie Lorimer (2010: 240) puts it, we live in a world in which both still and moving images have become "the primary media through which we make sense of the world and the boundaries between images and that which they imagine are increasingly blurred." Cultural geographers have long been interested in the important role that moving images play in our cultural life and, since the turn of the new millennium, have developed a range of innovative methodologies that help us gain insight into how such imagery shapes and reshapes the everyday knowledges, practices, and sensibilities of different subjects.

One of the most influential approaches to researching visual materials in cultural geography is the critical visual methodology approach developed by Gillian Rose (2023). Rose (2023: 3) argues that the meaning of an image is constructed in relation to four main "sites." First, the site of production, which concerns the origins, processes, and intentions behind the making of an image. Second, the site of the image itself, which relates to the visual content and composition of an image. Third, the site of circulation, which concerns the movement of an image across different spaces and media and how its meaning changes in relation to its different materialisations. And finally, the site of audiencing, which considers how the meaning of an image is interpreted by different audiences and users.

While influential, Rose's critical visual methodology continues a long tradition of approaching images through the discursive frames of signification and representation. The emphasis of such approaches often falls on what images show (the content and identities they express), with much less attention paid to the more performative, material, and affective capacity of images to alter how people think and feel. Carter and McCormack (2006: 235) capture this more non-representational power and potential of visual imagery when they write that "rather than ideological or symbolic signs, images [are] bodies of affective intensity with the capacity to affect other kinds of bodies."

In recent years, then, cultural geographers have begun experimenting with new methodological approaches that shift attention from the representational meanings to the non-representational affects of images. Here, we can point to two main approaches for analysing the affective dimensions and dynamics of visual images. The first relates to cultural geographers generating their own images "as a means of witnessing various forms of knowledge, skill, and embodied practice that can escape text- and talk-based approaches" (J. Lorimer, 2010: 242). Paul Simpson (2011), for instance, utilised video recordings in the context of his auto-ethnographic research into the embodied practice of street performing (or 'busking'). Watching these recordings back upon returning from his performances, Simpson highlights how video can draw greater attention to some of the minutiae of his embodied movements, non-verbal communication with other people, and affective encounters between human and non-human bodies that he wasn't consciously aware of during the research event itself. But Simpson also cautions that while video can show such affective relations, it is unable to capture precisely how these were felt by the different bodies inhabiting the scene. He thus suggests that video methodologies may best be used as a complement to, rather than replacement for, "other corporeally invested research methodologies and other, more fleshy, recording machines," such as the ethnographic notes taken by their researcher on the thoughts and feelings that emerged immediately during the practice itself (Simpson, 2011: 350).

A second approach that has emerged in recent years relates to the analysis of existing images, exploring how specific images generate and mobilise affect and the various ends that are sought here. Work in this vein, as Jamie Lorimer (2010: 242) notes, has often been concerned with mapping the

> techniques employed by image makers to (dis)order their work and move their audiences, [seeking to] categorise images according to the logics of affect they evoke and to trace the micropolitical work done by different evocations couched in different affective logics.

Jamie Lorimer (2010) himself develops such an approach in his study of cinematic representations of elephants. His research outlines a range of affective logics through which elephant bodies are encountered through film, including affective logics of sentimentality in Disney's *Dumbo*, which reduces individual animals to an "anthropo-identity" with which the audience are encouraged to emotionally identify; affective logics of *awe*, like in David Attenborough's BBC series *The Life of Mammals*, which invest in imaginaries of the 'wild' that present non-human animals as the radical 'other' of the human subject; as well as affective logics of *shock*, such as in videos produced by People for the Ethical Treatment of Animals (PETA), which use violent imagery to raise awareness of the cruel treatment of elephants in captivity. These different affective logics are important, Lorimer argues, because they each implicate audiences in very different ways of thinking about and ethically relating to non-human animals, which can have very significant material consequences (such as the impacts that Disney films have had on inspiring audiences to support the conservation of large charismatic species, like elephants and lions).

Finally, geographers have recently become interested in thinking about some of the new spaces in which we encounter images in our everyday lives, including most notably social media. Social media platforms (like Instagram, Snapchat, and TikTok) are dominated by images, and these images have implications for how we imagine and experience specific places. For instance, take John Boy and Justus Uitermark's (2017) study of how users of Instagram in Amsterdam reassemble understandings of the city through their everyday visualisations of it. As part of their research, Boy and Uitermark (2017) accessed nearly 400,000 geotagged images created by more than 30,000 users in Amsterdam and also conducted interviews with Instagram users about their daily usage of the Instagram platform. Perhaps unsurprisingly, their research found that Instagram "constitutes a distinctive way of seeing that composes an image of the city is sanitised and nearly devoid of negativity" (Boy and Uitermark, 2017: 622). Our Instagram feeds are usually full of all kinds of desirable objects, attractive bodies and beautiful faces, trending foods, impressive landscapes, and witty observations. Rarely do we encounter "the messiness and occasional gloom and doom of the city" when we scroll these apps (Boy and Uitermark, 2017: 622).

Their research also highlighted the extremely segmented nature of Instagram and especially the power of local Instagram 'influencers' in shaping how the city is visualised and how their posts (and the attention they receive through comments and likes) contribute to the perpetuation of existing socio-spatial inequalities in the city. This highlights one of the main limitations of social media as a source for conducting visual research, which is about the biases of social media imagery that – on average – tends to be over-representative of wealthy people and privileged spaces. The 'vision' of the city encountered on social media, then, is nearly always a partial one, excluding many other diverse perspectives on and of the city (especially of marginalised groups) that rarely manage to make it on to the algorithmically curated 'Feeds' or 'For You Pages' of these platforms.

SENSING BEYOND THE HUMAN

In addition to opening research to sensory registers long neglected in the discipline (like sound, touch, and other modes of embodied feeling), another key emphasis of the experimental imperative in cultural geography research has been the attempt to expand the remit of what kinds of bodies count as legitimate research subjects. With the development of more-than-human, post-phenomenological, and non-representational approaches, cultural geographers have been at the very forefront of challenging the humanist emphases of traditional qualitative methodologies that continue to privilege human modes of understanding, communication, and meaning-making in research. While methodological innovations have sometimes lagged behind theoretical developments in cultural geography, recent years have seen a flurry of interest in developing new methods and techniques that can open research to a range of non-human beings, bodies, and objects traditionally ignored as active agents in the making of our worlds (Dowling et al., 2017; Williams et al., 2019).

One important area of methodological innovation in thinking and researching the non-human emerges from recent work developing post-phenomenological geographies that we introduced in Chapter 4. Post-phenomenological "styles of analysis," as Ash and Simpson (2019: 140) put it, are attentive to the nature of how beings interact with and sense the world, but unlike traditional phenomenology (and hence the 'post-'), they seek to extend this analysis beyond just a concern with the experience and awareness of human subjects but also that of non-human objects. This obviously raises a whole series of methodological questions about how exactly academics can cultivate a greater sensitivity to the agency of non-human objects in research.

To address this, Ash and Gallacher (2015: 70) experiment with a new set of methodological vocabularies that can assist researchers in "becoming attuned" to complex material forces and relations that structure situations beyond the realm of conscious human awareness. One of these terms is *vibration*. Vibration as a qualitative, barely-felt intensity is something "common to all bodies and objects and so cuts across distinctions between the human and nonhuman and the organic and inorganic" (Ash and Gallacher, 2015: 76). Vibrations are also forces that move between and through objects (like sound waves moving through water), and in this sense vibration is a concept that allows cultural geographers to attune to the novel relations created through encounters between (human and non-human) bodies. Ash and Gallacher (2015: 79) explore the implications of vibration as a methodological "unit of sense" through discussion of ethnographic research into children's water play. They note how vibration provides a different – more embodied and sensory – way of writing up the relationships that emerge through the physical interactions of all the objects involved in the play (the water, plastic cups, and water wheels, the child's hands and body):

> Here the vibrations produced by the water as it splashes around the play table may conjure feelings, colours, or other affects, both literally and figuratively in the child, and, thus, provide an enlarged set of descriptors to communicate what it feels like to play, or how one learns to sense the qualities and capacities of substances and materials.

Thinking through vibration, therefore, enables the generation of accounts of research that are more attentive to the material exchanges, sensory translations, and forceful differentiations of the human bodies and non-human objects that comprise our empirical field sites.

While supportive of such attempts to think of the conditions of experience beyond the terrain of the human subject, we argue that post-phenomenological approaches nonetheless continue to place constraints on cultural geographic thought and practice in relation to the non-human. These limitations relate to the fact that post-phenomenology continues to perceive the world as a collection of empirically discernible and individuated entities, merely replacing one individual (the subject) with another (the object) (Roberts, 2019). Despite its appeals to the contrary, post-phenomenology remains tied to a humanist lineage of thought that elevates the individual to a transcendent principle of experience and reduces relation to the status of an 'interaction' between individuated terms. What is lost is the capacity to think, the power of relations and encounters to rupture the already-given and give rise to novel modes of intensive transformation that cannot be inventoried in advance.

Our own work has thus sought to creatively explore how we might prioritise immanent relations over transcendent individuals in our research practices (see Williams et al., 2019; Lapworth, 2019). Part of this has been to emphasise that the development of a genuinely post-humanist methodology in cultural geography is about more than just engaging with a fuller range of the body's sensory engagements with the non-human world. It also demands that we dismantle "the humanist architecture on which theories of sensing continue to be built" (Lapworth, 2019: 657). This humanist architecture can be seen, for instance, in geographical discussions around the use of film in ethnographic research to capture the lived experience of embodied practices. Such approaches continue to assert the primacy of the subject-world relation in research, overlooking the capacity of film to produce consistencies of sense that no longer begin or end with the form of the human subject. An example of this more post-human kind of ethnography can be found in the experimental films of the Sensory Ethnography Lab. In their film *Leviathan*, for example, experimentation with the perceptual and sonic affordances of digital GoPro cameras (especially their 'jerky' vision and 'muffled' sound) to generate a more (dis)embodied and (non)human perception of the world. *Leviathan* thus explores what a post-humanist and non-phenomenological approach to research with film in cultural geography could look like. It would be an approach that pushes ethnographic attention beyond the exclusive domain of human meaning and sense to instead engage with various "nonhuman forces and durations that are a crucial part of our research ecologies, but which are so often obscured by our disciplinary habits of striving to uncover meanings and representations" (Lapworth, 2019: 659).

REDISTRIBUTING EXPERTISE

DISSEMINATION

In a recent review of qualitative research across human geography, Robyn Dowling, Kate Lloyd, and Sandie Suchet-Pearson (2017: 828) argue that the discipline's overwhelming reliance on dominant academic forms of textual communication represents "one of the major blockages stunting movement in methodological innovation." Running lockstep with the methodological experimentation discussed earlier, they argue, should be innovative thinking about how we communicate, present, and engage the wider public with the impacts of cultural geographic research.

Of course, the written word and the academic journal article remain the primary means through which cultural geographers disseminate their ideas. During your own university studies, your capacity to understand and communicate geographical knowledge will be principally evaluated through the different pieces of writing that you are asked to produce. Despite its centrality, the process and practice of writing in geography is something that has for a long time received very little attention. However, with the expansion of the interdisciplinary field of the geohumanities (see **Box 1.4**), recent years have seen a range of attempts to enliven a sense of what geographic writing can do beyond the merely functional and denotational emphases of conventional written discourse. For example, several cultural geographers have turned to literary and other forms of creative writing to experiment with new modes of expression that might "stretch words beyond the limitations defined by their ordinary usage" and thus unlock new perspectives on the world (Roberts, 2019: 645). Tim Cresswell, for instance, has written about both the possibilities and risks of merging his writings as a poet with his academic writings on the concepts of place and landscape. Importantly, he stresses that poetry and geography are very different practices and that being able to write well in either domain is the (not guaranteed) outcome of a lengthy and challenging apprenticeship. Despite the various personal and institutional challenges, Creswell (2013: 144) argues that the process of becoming a poet has subtly transformed the craft of his writing, noting that he is slowly "letting the attention to form, the use of the space of the page, and some elements of repetition and rhythm enter my academic prose."

In addition to experimenting with new modes of creative writing, cultural geographers have also sought to explore new ways of thinking about the role and potential of writing in the context of our research. Delyser and Hawkins (2013: 132–133) argue that much of this work seeks to reframe writing not simply as an "*a posteriori* representation, occurring after the fact of thinking and investigating" but rather as an "embodied process that shapes research itself." Other geographers, however, argue that such conceptions of writing as an 'embodied process and practice' tend to constrain writing to the humanist and phenomenological coordinates of our lived, subjective experience (Roberts, 2019). There is thus growing interest in the development of 'post-phenomenological' (Ash and Simpson, 2019) or 'post-humanist' (Roberts, 2019) styles of writing that experiment with the intensive powers of the writing to think and express forces beyond the realm of the human. Here, the aim of writing is no longer simply about narrating or storying the experience of a knowing subject, but rather about creating new and unexpected connections between words and things in the world (e.g., the objects or places that constitute the focus of our research) in ways that can profoundly change how we think and feel about these very things.

Beyond creative approaches to writing, the past few years have also witnessed an explosion of creative exploration of novel expressive modalities for practising and disseminating cultural geographic research, including things like the production of theatrical plays, songwriting, comic books, landscape painting, zines, and documentary films. Such innovative modes of presenting research don't just afford opportunities for disseminating cultural geographic work to new audiences and publics (who may be turned off by more stale, academic prose), but they also offer the potential to uncover different kinds of stories from fieldwork that are difficult to capture in words. This experimental ethos, for example, underpins Sage

Brice's (2024) explorations of drawing as a geographical methodology. While cognisant of the long and violent history of drawing in the geographic discipline – and especially field drawing as a tool of Indigenous dispossession that submits other people and places to colonial orders of knowledge, meaning, and value – Brice argues that observational drawing can be recast as an immersive process of seeing, recording, and critically questioning phenomena encountered in the field. Brice (2024: 207) argues that the art of observational drawing might be understood to cultivate a kind of vulnerability, "where 'vulnerability' names not only a passive condition of susceptibility but an ontological orientation in research." Drawing's highlighting of the fragility of positionality and perspective, she argues, can offer powerful means to interrogate and question the presumed stability and fixity of identities and concepts in ways that may open to new possibilities of social transformation.

COLLABORATION

It is well established that many of the most urgent problems facing humanity in the twenty-first century cannot be solved by the approaches or methods of any one discipline alone. Such 'wicked problems' (a term used to describe problems that are highly resistant to clear or single solutions) instead demand diverse epistemological and (trans)disciplinary perspectives. Cultural geography has a long and rich history of collaboration, not only with other disciplines across the natural and social sciences, but importantly also with the knowledge practices and vernaculars of communities beyond academia. In practising and producing collaborative knowledge, cultural geographers have been particularly sensitive to the need to challenge dominant forms of authority (often reinforced by conventions of academic publication) that presume sole academic authorship (Cook et al., 2005). Cultural geographers have sought to disrupt this illusion of sovereign and exclusionary authorship through a variety of techniques and tactics. An example here is the work of Ian Cook, who has used, since the late 90s, the *nom de plume* of 'Ian Cook et al.' in his published work and academic profile. The 'et al.' for Cook is thus a shorthand that acknowledges the vast array of human (friends and family, academic collaborators, research subjects) and non-human (tape recorders, passports, computer programmes) agents that collectively make research possible. As he/they (Cook et al., 2005: 22–23) explain(s):

> Don't write as if you're one of those Cartesian individuals. Those atomistic, presocial vessel(s) of abstract reason and will. Or the kind of individual who knows exactly who s/he is and how this makes a difference. Please! You're a collective. Like 'Ian Cook et al.' . . . Other people help you to know. Not just your research subjects. But those you mention in acknowledgements, bibliographies, film credits. And more besides. . . . This is where debates about positionality and situated knowledge usually diverge. In the latter, research is not done only by 'people', but by socio-technical hybrids, cyborgs and actor networks.

This understanding of academic research as inherently collective and more-than-human is also something taken up, and further politicised, in recent *decolonial* and *indigenous* geographies. Here, collaboration becomes much more than just a methodological choice. It is instead reframed as an ethical commitment to unsettling the colonial legacies of geographic research (which have included things like the perpetuation of inaccurate stereotypes and the adoption of a pathologising lens in the study of Indigenous communities) by foregrounding themes of co-production, reciprocity, and the authority of historically marginalised ways of knowing (Thambinathan and Kinsella, 2021). However, decolonial geographers also strike a note of caution given the growing interest in community-focused research amongst universities and finding institutions, noting that collaborative research methods are not, in and of themselves, decolonising. Coombes et al. (2014: 847), for instance, argue that collaborative research has the potential to do more harm than good when it is "impact agendas and not Indigenous needs driving [collaborations], possibly generating an inauthentic and counteractive zeal for collaboration." Instead, genuinely transformative forms of collaborative research are those that privilege long-term relationships, accountability, and community-defined goals over extractive, instrumental, or impact-driven agendas.

An interesting example here – and one that extends a sense of collaboration beyond just human participants – is the research of

Australian geographers Lloyd, Wright, and Suchet-Pearson with Bawaka Country. Bawaka Country is an Australian Aboriginal homeland in northeast Arnhem Land (Bawaka Country et al., 2016). Giving first author status to Bawaka Country attempts to de-centre both non-Indigenous and human authority, highlighting Country itself as that which "guided, inspired and enabled" the research (Bawaka Country et al., 2016: 468). Here, the authors are referring to Aboriginal Australian understandings of Country as that which incorporates "land, sea and rivers, as well as animals, tides, waters, wind, insects, rocks, plants, languages, emotions, songs and ancestors" (Dowling et al., 2017: 828). Bawaka Country is thus a more-than-human collective of which the human authors are only a small part, one enmeshed in kinship relationships that bring with them "a range of ethical obligations including the need to attend, share, and care" (Dowling et al., 2017: 828).

Another direction of collaborative opportunity and innovation relates to growing interest in 'art-geography' collaborations, where we see cultural geographers working together with artists and other creative practitioners to develop new research perspectives on cultural geographic concepts. John Wylie, for instance, reflects on the impacts of working on a practice-led project with the British visual artist, Catrin Webster, for his research on the concept of landscape (Wylie and Webster, 2019). As part of this year-long project, Wylie sat for extended periods with Webster, learning the techniques and skills of *en plein air* painting and drawing. Wylie and Webster note that while the phrase 'art-geography collaboration' might sometimes seem to imply the collision of two quite different worlds, their own practice uncovered much productive overlap of interest in the "phenomenologies and materialities of spatial practice and perception" (Wylie and Webster, 2019: 34). Wylie chose the term 'eye-opener' to describe the potentially transformative implications of encounters across disciplines. As he puts it:

> In the end, for me, there was revelation of a kind. Having experienced doubts about how geographers, using ideas of embodiment, materiality and performance, invoked the feeling of lived and affective spaces, the experience of drawing landscape, near and far, disclosed the possibility that you could attend to lived experience without succumbing to a form of phenomenological

> naturalism. Drawing is expressive and provisional. It does take form as a new and ongoing line amid a world of flowing lines, an 'ecstacy of spaces'.
>
> (Wylie and Webster, 2019: 44)

In addition to learning new skills for re-presenting spaces (like Wylie's acquisition of techniques of painterly observation), art-geography collaborations have also provided new spaces and processes for disseminating cultural geographic knowledge. In addition to collaborative journal articles, geographers have also worked with artists to produce exhibitions in galleries and museums on geographical themes (Enigbokan and Patchett, 2012). While not without their own ongoing legacies of exclusion (Tolia-Kelly and Raymond, 2020), the exhibition space affords geographers the opportunity to harness the potential of the arts to engage with broader audiences, enhance public awareness of social and ecological issues, and expand the reach of cultural geographic research.

While such interdisciplinary collaborative practices are increasingly in vogue across the social and natural sciences, some cultural geographers have argued that it is important to remain cautious about the more instrumental logics that sometimes underpin art-geography collaborations, in which it is a specific end product (e.g., a new 'innovative' product or technique) that is foregrounded over the open-ended process of research creation (Lapworth, 2015). In an important intervention, Nina Williams (2016) argues that arts-based methods, and art-geography collaboration, can do much more than simply provide new opportunities for disseminating geographic research to the public. She argues that such creative practices can also generate new perspectives on our research, enabling new ways of relating to the more relational, unconscious, and affective dimensions of encounters in the field that are so often glossed over by the standard suite of disciplinary methodologies.

CONCLUSION

If cultural geographers in the first decade of the new millennium expressed concern that conceptual developments in the subfield far outpaced methodological developments, then the second and third decades saw cultural geographers putting great effort into catching up. This chapter has explored this intensification of methodological experimentation in the subdiscipline, as cultural geographers increasingly recognise that addressing the non-human, affective, and non-representational dimensions of cultural life demands a move beyond traditional interpretative frameworks and default modes of presentation and dissemination. We highlighted two main directions of methodological innovation in contemporary cultural geography. The first relates to ongoing attempts to extend cultural geography's sensory palette beyond its traditional focus on the 'textual' and 'visual' domains through a suite of multi-sensory and post-humanist methodologies that emphasise a fuller range of the human body's sensory engagement with the world. The second area of experimentation relates to the growing interest in creative and arts-based methodologies in which we see cultural geographers engaging with the arts and other practices (including film, comic books, creative writing, and drawing) to explore new pathways for the production and dissemination of cultural geographic research. Such approaches carry great possibilities for connecting a more diverse range of audiences with the significant contributions of cultural geographic research to many of the most pressing challenges facing society today.

FURTHER READING

Boyd, C. "Postqualitative geographies." *Geography Compass* 16, no. 10 (2022): e1266. https://doi.org/10.1111/gec3.12661

Dewsbury, J-D. "Performative, non-representational and affect-based research methods." In D. Delyser, S. Herbert, S. Aitken, M. Crang and L. McDowell (eds.) *The Sage Handbook of Qualitative Geography* (pp. 321–334). London: Sage, 2010.

Dowling, R, K. Lloyd and S. Suchet-Pearson. "Qualitative methods III: Experimenting, picturing, sensing." *Progress in Human Geography* 42. no. 5 (2017): 779–788. https://doi.org/10.1177/0309132517730941

Vannini, P. (ed.). *Non-Representational and More-than-Human Research: Vitalist Methodologies for the End of Data*. London: Routledge, 2025.

Williams, N., M. Patchett, A. Lapworth, T. Roberts and T. Keating. "Practising posthumanism in geographical research." *Transactions of the Institute of British Geographers* 44, no. 4 (2019): 637–643. https://doi.org/10.1111/tran.12322

REFERENCES

Ash, J. and L. Gallacher. "Becoming attuned: Objects, affects, and embodied methodology." In N. Perry and C. L. Medina (eds.) *Methodologies of Embodiment Inscribing Bodies in Qualitative Research* (pp. 69–85). London: Routledge, 2015.

Ash, J. and P. Simpson. "Post-phenomenology and method: Styles for thinking the (non)human." *Geohumanities* 5, no. 1 (2019): 139–156. https://doi.org/10.1080/2373566X.2018.1543553

Bassett, K. "Walking as an aesthetic practice and a critical tool." *Journal of Geography in Higher Education* 28, no. 3 (2004): 397–410. https://doi.org/10.1080/0309826042000286965

Boy, J. and J. Uitermark. "Reassembling the city through Instagram." *Transactions of the Institute of British Geographers* 42, no. 4 (2017): 612–624. https://doi.org/10.1111/tran.12185

Bissell, D. "How environments speak: Everyday mobilities, impersonal speech and the geographies of commentary." *Social & Cultural Geography* 16, no. 2 (2015): 146–164. https://doi.org/10.1080/14649365.2014.958520

Bissell, D. "Questioning quotation: Writing about interview experiences without using quotes." *Area* 55, no. 2 (2023): 191–196. https://doi.org/10.1111/area.12854

Boyd, C. and M. Duffy. "Sound, geography, and non-representational theory." *Unlikely: Journal of the Creative Arts* 6 (2020). (np.). https://unlikely.net.au/issue-06/sound-geography-and-non-representational-theory

Brice, S. "Critical observational drawing in geography: Towards a methodology of 'vulnerable' research." *Progress in Human Geography* 48, no. 2 (2024): 206–223. https://doi.org/10.1177/03091325231208899

Burdon, G. "Sound art geographies: Listening at the limits of audibility." *Geography Compass* 19 (2025): e70022. https://doi.org/10.1111/gec3.70022

Butler, T. "Memoryscape: How audio walks can deepen our sense of place by integrating art, oral history and cultural geography." *Geography Compass* 1, no. 3 (2007): 360–372. https://doi.org/10.1111/j.1749-8198.2007.00017.x

Carter, S. and D. McCormack. "Film, geopolitics and the affective logics of intervention." *Political Geography* 25, no. 2 (2006): 228–245. https://doi.org/10.1016/j.polgeo.2005.11.004

Chion, M. *The Voice in Cinema*. New York: Columbia University Press, 1999.

Cook, I. et al. "Positionality/situated knowledge." In D. Atkinson, P. Jackson, D. Sibley and N. Washbourne (eds.) *Cultural Geography: A Critical Dictionary of Key Ideas* (pp. 14–24). London: IB Tauris, 2005.

Cook, S., J. Shaw and P. Simpson. "Jography: Exploring meanings, experiences and spatialities of recreational road-running." *Mobilities* 11, no. 5 (2016): 744–769. https://doi.org/10.1080/17450101.2015.1034455

Coombes, B., J. T. Johnson and R. Howitt. "Indigenous geographies III: Methodological innovation and the unsettling of participatory research." *Progress in Human Geography* 38, no. 6 (2014): 845–854. https://doi.org/10.1177/0309132513514723

Country, B., S. Wright, S. Suchet-Pearson, K. Lloyd, L. Burarrwanga, R. Ganambarr, M. Ganambarr-Stubbs, B. Ganambarr, D. Maymuru and J. Sweeney. "Co-becoming Bawaka: Towards a relational understanding of place/space." *Progress in Human Geography* 40, no. 4 (2016): 455–475. https://doi.org/10.1177/0309132515589437

Crang, M. "Qualitative methods: Touchy, feely, look-see?" *Progress in Human Geography* 27, no. 4 (2003): 494–504. https://doi.org/10.1191/0309132503ph445pr

Creswell, T. "Geographies of poetry/poetry of geography." *Cultural Geographies* 21, no. 1 (2013): 141–146. https://doi.org/10.1177/1474474012466117

Deleuze, G. *Cinema II: The Time-Image*. London: Continuum, 2005.

Delyser, D. and H. Hawkins. "Introduction: Writing creatively – process, practice and product." *Cultural Geographies* 21, no. 1 (2013): 131–134. https://doi.org/10.1177/1474474012469006

DeSilvey, C. "Art and archive: Memory-work on a Montana homestead." *Journal of Historical Geography* 33, no. 4 (2007): 878–900. https://doi.org/10.1016/j.jhg.2006.10.020

Dewsbury, J-D. "Performative, non-representational and affect-based research methods." In D. Delyser, S. Herbert, S. Aitken, M. Crang and L. McDowell (eds.) *The Sage Handbook of Qualitative Geography* (pp. 321–334). London: Sage, 2009.

Dewsbury, J-D. and S. Naylor. "Practising geographical knowledge: Fields, bodies, dissemination." *Area* 34, no. 3 (2002): 253–260. https://doi.org/10.1111/1475-4762.00079

Dowling, R, K. Lloyd and S. Suchet-Pearson. "Qualitative methods I: Enriching the interview." *Progress in Human Geography* 40, no. 5 (2016): 679–686. https://doi.org/10.1177/030913251559688

Dowling, R, K. Lloyd and S. Suchet-Pearson. "Qualitative methods III: Experimenting, picturing, sensing." *Progress in Human Geography* 42, no. 5 (2017): 779–788. https://doi.org/10.1177/0309132517730941

Duffy, M., G. Waitt and T. Harada. "Making sense of sound: Visceral sonic mapping as a research tool." *Emotion, Space & Society* 20, (2016): 49–57. https://doi.org/10.1016/j.emospa.2016.06.006

Edensor, T. "The ghosts of industrial ruins: Ordering and disordering memory in excessive space." *Environment and Planning D: Society and Space* 23, no. 6 (2005): 829–849. https://doi.org/10.1068/d58j

Engelmann, S. "Weathering three storms: Experiments in an elemental geohumanities." *Geohumanities* 9, no. 2 (2023): 524–540. https://doi.org/10.1080/2373566X.2023.2232434

Enigbokan, A. and M. Patchett. "Speaking with specters: Experimental geographies in practice." *Cultural Geographies* 19, no. 4 (2012): 535–545. https://doi.org/10.1177/1474474011422030

Gallagher, M. and J. Prior. "Sonic geographies: Exploring phonographic methods." *Progress in Human Geography* 38, no. 2 (2014): 267–284. https://doi.org/10.1177/0309132513481014

Kinkaid, E. "Positionality, post-phenomenology, and the politics of theory." *Gender, Place & Culture* 29, no. 7 (2022): 923–945. https://doi.org/10.1080/0966369X.2021.1891867

Koh, L. and A. Lapworth. "Refiguring habits of subjectivity, communication, and space in online video calls." *Area* 56, no. 2 (2024): e12903. http://dx.doi.org/10.1111/area.12903

Lapworth, A. "Beyond bifurcation: Thinking the abstractions of art-science after A. N. Whitehead." *Transformations: Journal of Media and Culture* 26, (2015): 1–12. https://www.transformationsjournal.org/wp-content/uploads/2016/12/Lapworth_Transformations26.pdf

Lapworth, A. "Sensing." *Transactions of the Institute of British Geographers* 44, no. 4 (2019): 657–660. https://doi.org/10.1111/tran.12327

Latham, A. "Research, performance, and doing human geography: Some reflections on the diary-photography, diary-interview method." *Environment and Planning A: Economy and Space* 35, no. 11 (2003): 1993–2017. https://doi.org/10.1068/a3587

Longhurst, R., E. Ho and L. Johnston. "Using 'the body' as an 'instrument of research': Kimch'i and Pavlova." *Area* 40, no. 2 (2008): 208–217. https://www.jstor.org/stable/40346115

Lorimer, H. "Caught in the nick of time: Archives and fieldwork." In D. Delyser, S. Herbert, S. Aitken, M. Crang and L. McDowell (eds.) *The Sage Handbook of Qualitative Geography* (pp. 248–273). London: Sage, 2010.

Lorimer, J. "Moving-image methodologies for more-than-human geographies." *Cultural Geographies* 17, no. 2 (2010): 237–258. https://doi.org/10.1177/1474474010363853

Lorimer, J. and S. Whatmore. "After the 'king of beasts': Samuel Baker and the embodied historical geographies of elephant hunting in mid-nineteenth-century Ceylon." *Journal of Historical Geography* 35, no. 4 (2009): 668–689. https://doi.org/10.1016/j.jhg.2008.11.002

McCormack, D. "A paper with an interest in rhythm." *Geoforum* 33, no. 4 (2002): 469–485. https://doi.org/10.1016/S0016-7185(02)00031-3

Merriman, P. "Automobility and the geographies of the car." *Geography Compass* 3, no. 2 (2009): 586–599. https://doi.org/10.1111/j.1749-8198.2009.00219.x

Mills, S. "Cultural–historical geographies of the archive: Fragments, objects and ghosts." *Geography Compass* 7, no. 10 (2013): 701–713. https://doi.org/10.1111/gec3.12071

Mol, A. *The Body Multiple: Ontology in Medical Practice*. Durham, NC: Duke University Press, 2002.

Patchett, M. "Archiving." *Transactions of the Institute of British Geographers* 44, no. 4 (2019): 650–653. https://doi.org/10.1111/tran.12325

Rancière, J. "A few remarks on the method of Jacques Ranciere." *Parallax* 15, no. 3 (2009): 114–123. https://doi.org/10.1080/13534640902982983

Roberts, T. "Writing." *Transactions of the Institute of British Geographers* 44, no. 4 (2019): 644–646. https://doi.org/10.1111/tran.12323

Rose, G. *Visual Methodologies: An Introduction to Researching with Visual Materials*. London: Sage, 2023.

Schafer, R. M. *The Soundscape: Our Sonic Environment and the Tuning of the World*. Rochester, NY: Destiny Books, 1977.

Simpson, P. "A sense of the cycling environment: Felt experiences of infrastructure and atmospheres." *Environment and Planning A: Economy and Space* 49, no. 2 (2017): 426–447. https://doi.org/10.1177/0308518X16669510

Simpson, P. "So, as you can see . . .': Some reflections on the utility of video methodologies in the study of embodied practices." *Area* 43, no. 3 (2011): 343–352. https://doi.org/10.1111/j.1475-4762.2011.00998.x

Smith, S. J. "Beyond geography's visible worlds: A cultural politics of music." *Progress in Human Geography* 21, no. 4 (1997): 502–529. https://doi.org/10.1191/030913297675594415

Stratford, E. "Mobilising a spatial politics of skateboarding." *Annals of the American Association of Geographers* 106, no. 2 (2016): 350–357. https://doi.org/10.1080/00045608.2015.1100062

Thambinathan, V. and E. A. Kinsella. "Decolonising methodologies in qualitative research: Creating spaces for transformative praxis." *International Journal of Qualitative Methods* 20, (2021): 1–9. https://doi.org/10.1177/16094069211014766

Tolia-Kelly, D. and R. Raymond. "Decolonising museum cultures: An artist and a geographer in collaboration." *Transactions of the Institute of British Geographers* 45, no. 1 (2020): 2–17. https://doi.org/10.1111/tran.12339

Urry, G. "Neither presencing nor absencing: The stagnation of sensing-towards-presence in the call centre." *Transactions of the Institute of British Geographers* 39, no. 1 (2014): 26–37. https://doi.org/10.1111/tran.12005

Whatmore, S. "Materialist returns: Practising cultural geography in a more-than-human world." *Cultural Geographies* 13, no. 4 (2006): 600–609. https://doi.org/10.1191/1474474006cgj377oa

Williams, N. "Creative processes: From interventions in art to interallic experiments through Bergson." *Environment and Planning A: Economy and Space* 48, no. 8 (2016): 1549–1564. https://doi.org/10.1177/0308518X16642769

Williams, N. "Listening." *Transactions of the Institute of British Geographers* 44, no. 4 (2019): 647–649. https://doi.org/10.1111/tran.12324

Williams, N., M. Patchett, A. Lapworth, T. Roberts and T. Keating. "Practising posthumanism in geographical research." *Transactions of the Institute of British Geographers* 44, no. 4 (2019): 637–643. https://doi.org/10.1111/tran.12322

Wylie, J. and C. Webster. "Eye-opener: Drawing landscape near and far." *Transactions of the Institute of British Geographers* 44, no. 1 (2019): 32–47. https://doi.org/10.1111/tran.12267

Yusoff, K. "Antarctic exposures: Archives of the feeling body." *Cultural Geographies* 14, no. 2 (2007): 211–233. https://doi.org/10.1177/1474474007075355

8

EPILOGUE

> A project is the humble, yet resilient mode of address that is not only 'against' but also in favour of something. It is a constitutive, generative force, which relies on forms of affective encounter across our multiple differences.
>
> (R. Braidotti, 2025: 536)

We have now arrived at the end of our introduction to cultural geography. Whether you have read it cover to cover, or dipped in and out of specific chapters, we hope this book has translated some of the excitement, energy, and inspiration that we ourselves have been fortunate to have experienced as readers (and, more recently, writers) of cultural geography during our academic careers. Cultural geography has certainly transformed our lives. We don't just mean in the sense of providing us with a career and income, as important as those things are, and as grateful as we are for them. What we mean is that it has literally changed how we think and live. Writing this introductory book has been a veritable adventure, allowing us to revisit our own first transformative encounters with cultural geography and to reflect on what it was that captivated us about this unique corner of the academic landscape. And we've realised that what hooked us in wasn't any one specific text, thinker, problematic, or approach. It is instead what we call the *ethos* or ethical project of cultural geography.

The purpose of this final chapter is to provide a tentative, somewhat speculative sketch of what we think this ethos entails. Doing so comes with some risks – in particular, the risk of over-determining the multiplicity of voices and the diversity of

DOI: 10.4324/9781003542667-8

conceptual frameworks that make cultural geography such an exciting intellectual community to participate in. We also want to acknowledge that you, our readers, may have arrived at your own understanding of cultural geography's ethos through the course of reading this book. All the better! It is for these reasons that we have opted to finish the book with a short epilogue rather than a longer, more developed conclusion. Those readers who were expecting a tidy synthesis of the key problematics covered in this book might be disappointed; however, we believe this approach is more in keeping with the outward-looking restlessness that characterises cultural geographic thought and practice. In an ever-changing world, what are needed are forms of thinking that disrupt traditional desires for easy solutions. Cultural geography, we believe, provides such an approach, and it is in this spirit that we have approached the writing of this epilogue.

What, then, do we have to say about the ethos of cultural geography? Two things. First, we think that one of cultural geography's key strengths lies in the way it *ties the politics of critique to an ethics (or ethos) of creativity*. We, like many other cultural geographers, believe that critique – that is, refusing to accept the status quo and asking what other possibilities of thought and life could emerge – is a vital component of what it means to do cultural geography today. We write this book during dangerous times. Authoritarian leaders around the globe are targeting critical thinking, which they caricature as an expression of 'woke' ideology. In the United States, leading universities are passing on lists of critical thinkers to the Trump administration (including the philosopher and gender theorist Judith Butler, whom we have written about in this book). The reason for this? Authoritarian rule is fundamentally threatened by critical thinking. It doesn't want you to question the status quo, to reassess the ideas you have inherited from previous generations, or to consider who stands to gain from (and who is harmed by) existing habits of thought. All it wants is for you to feel threatened, a feeling which can then be weaponised in the service of its own thinly veiled self-interests.

Cultural geography provides a powerful tool for thinking critically in these dangerous times. We hope that, by reading this book, you have obtained a deeper grasp of the need for critical thinking in relation to key concepts and ideas that shape cultural life. Cultural geography's critical ethos is reflected in its attempts to question 'nature' as a universal concept, as well as its sensitivity to the very real social harms associated with Eurocentric 'wilderness' narratives. But there are many other examples that we have discussed, including critiques of representation, sex, politics, etc. The point we want to make here is that cultural geography's desire to critically interrogate the familiar habits of thought that shape contemporary culture stems from an awareness that these habits are entangled with power, oppression, exclusion, and violence. In other words, they are no longer fit for purpose because we understand their potential to marginalise and cause harm. Like all habits, our ways of thinking can become deeply ingrained, but precisely because they are habits and not unchanging rules, they can also be changed!

This leads us on to creativity. Cultural geography, we argue, places critical thinking and the politics of critique in the service of creative experiment and innovation (Williams, 2022). Indeed, we believe that cultural geography reaches its most politically impactful critiques when it creates something new, when it develops new practices, or when it engenders new ways of thinking. Without an ethos of creativity, critique has a tendency to turn inward on itself and can lead to the kind of despair, resignation, or resentment associated with what existentialist philosophers like Friedrich Nietzsche called *nihilism*. Anchoring critique in an ethos of creativity makes it stick; it gives our collective desire (the desire to resist the status quo) something to work with – or, to paraphrase Deleuzian philosopher Rosi Braidotti, a *project* in favour of new realities that escape oppositions. Some (including Braidotti herself) might describe this as an 'affirmative' ethos. What we want to emphasise, however, is the sense in which cultural geography is a place where political critique is fostered in and through creative experiments with the new, whether this be by using new concepts like affect and assemblage, or developing innovative research methodologies.

Cultural geography folds the political force of critique into an ethos of creativity. This statement summarises our first point. But we also have a second, which is about the way this folding of the political and the ethical relates in turn to the question of the human – and here, what we are referring to is the simultaneously philosophical *and* geographical question of what it means to be a human being in relation to a more-than-human universe. For many people, when they hear or read the word 'culture,' what comes to mind is an idea of a human realm that is fundamentally different in kind from the rest of the so-called 'natural' world. Culture, from this perspective, is what separates human beings from everything else that exists; it is what makes us exceptional beings and legitimises anthropocentric ways of thinking. Cultural geographers are critical of such human exceptionalism because their fundamental starting point is not the human in isolation but rather the human-in-relation. For many cultural geographers today – including ourselves – this critique of humanist habits of thought and the associated model of culture has become one of the most important political interventions to have been developed within the field in recent years.

But what saves cultural geography's political critique of the human from a future characterised by self-loathing and nihilism is, we believe, its creative commitment to thinking of the human (and, with it, culture) anew. With regard to the question of what it means to be human, then, we would argue that what cultural geography offers is an exciting opportunity to create a radically new concept of culture itself. Cultural geography's creative ethos lies, then, in its ability to pose new questions in light of its political critique of human exceptionalism. What if culture was no longer thought of as a barrier or container that demarcates a fundamental separation between humanity and everything else that exists? Could we experiment with new ways of thinking where culture is more like a lens that refracts the interconnectivity of all things and focuses them on the plane of human experience? What would it mean to study 'the human' from this more-than-human perspective? These are the kinds of questions that populate the cutting-edge of cultural geography's creative ethos. If they are the kinds of questions that interest you, then, we assure you, cultural geography is a great place to be.

REFERENCES

Braidotti, R. "Intelligence, affirmative ethics and the anti-fascist life." *Deleuze and Guattari Studies* 19, no. 4 (2025): 524–537. https://doi.org/10.3366/dlgs.2025.0616

Williams, N. "The problem of critique in art-geography: Five propositions for immanent evaluation after Deleuze." *Cultural Geographies* 29, no. 3 (2022): 335–352. https://doi.org/10.1177/14744740211029281

INDEX

Note: page numbers in **bold** indicate boxes and page numbers in *italics* indicate figures on the corresponding page.

For Product Safety Concerns and Information please contact our EU representative GPSR@taylorandfrancis.com
Taylor & Francis Verlag GmbH, Kaufingerstraße 24, 80331 München, Germany

www.ingramcontent.com/pod-product-compliance
Lightning Source LLC
LaVergne TN
LVHW011934090926
847529LV00029B/212
* 9 7 8 1 0 3 2 8 9 0 7 7 7 *